MASACCIO

LUCIANO BERTI

MASACCIO

1967

THE PENNSYLVANIA STATE UNIVERSITY PRESS

UNIVERSITY PARK and LONDON

to Anna

CONTENTS

LIST OF PLATES

LIST OF FIGURES

PROBLEMS AND VIEWPOINTS

There is a singular modernity, something transcending dates and even time itself, which constitutes the quite special glory of Masaccio. Fantastic as the notion may seem, certain details of his paintings would not appear out of place in an exhibition of art of our own time, such as the Biennale of Venice, and some ancient Greek or Roman, miraculously transplanted to the year 1428, might very well feel quite at home with Masaccio's frescoes.[1]

Throughout a century or more the frescoes in the Brancacci Chapel in the church of the Carmine were the fountainhead and inspiration for Florentine painting of the Renaissance. A great diversity of styles, in a development which to us now seems long and devious, all took their common origin from those frescoes. Vasari's list of those influenced by these frescoes—and he must have had his reasons for making it—runs from Fra Angelico and Filippo Lippi, Castagno and Baldovinetti through Verrocchio, Botticelli, Filippino Lippi, Ghirlandaio and includes even Leonardo, Perugino, Fra Bartolomeo, Michelangelo and Raphael. To these he adds Andrea del Sarto, Franciabigio, Rosso, Pontormo, Alonso Berruguete, Perin del Vaga and Baccio Bandinelli: thus even the troubled, anti-classical spirit of the first Mannerists found something meaningful in the Brancacci Chapel—as proof, look at the Bachiacca painting in Amsterdam [Figure 6] with its city crossroads conceived no differently than Masaccio himself depicted the urban scenes of a popular quarter, and its decked-out youths, brothers to those of Masaccio, city-boys with a city surliness (true, *their* curbstone gossip is not about the war against the Duke of Milan but, instead, about the threat or aftermath of the siege of Florence by Charles V).[2] So lively was the memory and challenge of Masaccio that Perin del Vaga, Florentine in origin but a partisan of the new Roman "Grand Manner" of Raphael, went so far as to attempt to prove by one of his own drawings, to his colleagues who had remained at home in Florence, that thenceforth even their great Masaccio had rivals.[3]

These slight, ephemeral examples have been chosen deliberately. It would require a full-length book in itself to show in detail how the heritage of Masaccio was exploited first by one then by another, re-worked in new fashions, and enriched in diverse ways in the course of the Florentine Renaissance which culminated finally in the classicism of the early sixteenth century. The whole question of Masaccio and the Renaissance, rich in possibilities as it is, remains to be written or, at least, to be re-written and brought up to date.[4] It is clear, however, that the achievement of Masaccio was an active and indeed dominant factor in the development of the figurative arts, in Florence at least, and this even before the writers of the time got around to finding a place for the young genius in their chronicles and accounts. One artist passed on the word to another to go look at the new paintings in the Carmine at a time when literary men were perhaps still singing the praises of Giotto, misled no doubt by the deliberate silence of Ghiberti about his most dangerous rivals.[5]

But fame came soon. The early death of Masaccio was, we know, bitterly mourned by Brunelleschi. Soon after, in 1436, Alberti cited Masaccio among the five artists (the only one of them no longer living, so the citation was not made out of self-interest) who at his arrival in Florence had revealed to him the marvelous re-flowering of a new art, peer to that of Antiquity.[6] And while from at least 1430 on Florentine painters were generally described as disciples of Masaccio, more specific references were made by Filarete sometime between 1460 and about 1464, by Manetti around 1472, and by Giovanni Santi after 1482. Finally the fame of Masaccio spread even to the wider sphere of historical annals with Landino in 1481 to whom we owe the celebrated, and highly accurate, description of Masaccio as "that most excellent imitator of nature, of great renown and universal talent, skilled in composition and with a style sober and unadorned." This was the summing-up of everything implied in previous critical evaluations. It was the more significant for having been made at a moment when the taste of Landino had progressed so far as to fall into line with that of the Medici, of Lorenzo himself perhaps.[7]

Masaccio moreover emerged unscathed from the judgment of three great intellects, and these were judgments of vastly greater significance than those of any historian or chronicler. First, Brunelleschi, whose opinion was rendered during the painter's own lifetime. Then Leonardo who established the historical line or, better, the graph of history's rise and fall: Antiquity—Medieval Mannerism—Giotto—Fourteenth-century Mannerism—Masaccio; in this scheme, Masaccio constituted the highest point ("with perfect works"), attaining the level of Nature herself, the "mistress of masters," that is to say, then, the plane on which for Leonardo modern art was to operate. As for Michelangelo, it is significant that among his earliest surviving drawings (or at least those attributed to him)[8] there should be two copies, one from Giotto and the other from the lost fresco of the *Consecration* by Masaccio.[9]

Without much apparent effort, the young Buonarotti was able to rework Masaccio's figures into his own idiom where they became grim prophets of titanic bulk [Figure 44]. And although we have no first-hand evidence of anything specific Buonarotti may have said about Masaccio (he was always chary of words), there is the story of his visit along with Vasari to Santa Maria Maggiore in Rome where there was the Colonna triptych by Masolino and Masaccio when "he praised it greatly, adding that those men were living in the time of Masaccio."[10] Likewise, the epitaph for Masaccio by Annibale Caro, which appeared already in the 1550 edition of Vasari's biographies, is most suggestive and certainly must not have been dashed off thoughtlessly, however high-flown its rhetoric may seem: "Buonarotti taught all the others, from me alone he learned."

This is not, however, the place to explore the critical history of Masaccio. Here we can only recount some pertinent details to show what we mean by his "modernism." Therefore, from the fundamental text of Vasari—from which we shall have to quote many times in the course of this study—we shall limit ourselves for the present to recalling what he said of the figures in the polyptych of Pisa almost a century and a half after it was painted, that there are some which appear most modern.[11] Briganti[12] has found—in of all places—the esoteric mannerist setting of the Studiolo of Francis I de Medici in the Palazzo Vecchio of Florence (contemporary with Vasari) a nude figure borrowed by Macchietti for his *Baths of Pozzuoli* from the "Shivering Man" in the Carmine frescoes.

As for Masaccio's fortune after the Renaissance, certainly those times were not likely to appreciate his modernity as a still inexhaustible source for their art; eclecticism virtually forgot the remote past of the fifteenth century to nourish itself on the great names of the sixteenth century, on Raphael, Correggio, Titian, Veronese and the others, with a special preference for the Venetian school. Masaccio's modernity and fame were thenceforth entrusted to history, or at least to that history which was something more than the repetition of dull shibboleths, and each age sought out in him those values which best corresponded to its own ideals. Thus, for one, we are struck by the sensitivity of Lomazzo who, in 1584, remarked on the pictorial fluency chiaroscuro lent to Masaccio's forms ("he achieved all this by no more than lighting and shading his figures without drawing outlines") although it is obvious that this coincided with one of the ideals of Italian painting in the seventeenth century. Nor can one be sure that Sandrart, borrowing from Vasari for his book of 1683, the *Academia*, did not choose to stress precisely those aspects most attractive to Baroque taste, especially Masaccio's virtuoso skill in perspective, particularly in foreshortening from below. But let us skip a century to 1782, the year when the Brancacci Chapel, newly restored, was re-inaugurated after the disastrous fire which swept the Carmine in 1771. This was the same year in which the tribunal of the Inquisition was abolished in Tuscany with a public burning of its instruments of torture. A fresh and ever more impetuous wind was blowing, bringing change and modernism and renewal. If we re-read the opinions pronounced in those last years of the eighteenth century by the English landscape painter Patch in 1770, by Reynolds in 1784 who had studied the Carmine for himself, by Mengs in 1783 and by the Abbot Lanzi in 1795, we find that even in those changing times the high opinion of Masaccio persisted unchecked (although, to be truthful, his frescoes were not well distinguished from the later additions of Filippino Lippi). For Patch, Masaccio was a third "philosopher" alongside Brunelleschi and Donatello, and it is known what value the Enlightenment placed on that term. For the neoclassicist Mengs, Masaccio and Leonardo taught Raphael to take into account "Nature in all her essence and, above all, the passions of the soul and how they move the body." According to Lanzi's schema of great stages in history, Masaccio is "the genius who created an epoch in painting."

Nor was nineteenth-century criticism less perceptive. Stendhal (in 1811-17), in true Romantic fashion, seized upon the "expression" in Masaccio, something for him over and beyond accuracy in drawing and virtuosity in color; though he did find Masaccio inclined to be somewhat sober... but then, "I have witnessed in my life five or six great deeds, and I was struck by the simple air of the heroes." And Masaccio's continued significance for modern times is amply admitted when Stendhal says, "Although our eyes, surfeited by the master-pieces of the later age, experience some difficulty in deciphering Masaccio... it must be re-cognized that he was the first painter whose merit was not merely historical but, indeed, real." D'Agincourt, in his book published in 1823, although he mistakenly bases his judg-ment on a *Miracle of Saint Zenobius* by Gozzoli, now in Berlin, has the significant impression that "each figure seems to be... a portrait." Rumohr, as early as 1827, succeeded very well in distinguishing the various hands that worked in the Brancacci Chapel. True, he follow-ed in the tracks of Vasari but not without setting up his own stylistic criteria. Thus, he found Masolino approaching a Renaissance style but still with something of Giotto in him, Masaccio with a soft and modeled plasticity and with the imprint of "a stern soul concern-ed with grave matters and moral dignity," and Filippino with a refined and fluid manner and an elegant talent which is however somewhat lightweight and undefined. Moreover, Rumohr believed he could distinguish two stylistic phases in Masaccio: the upper frescoes more daring and with greater contrasts in chiaroscuro but also with excessive marginal luminosity, as we would say today,[13] so that the forms "take on everywhere a certain dark and somber aspect"; the lower tier, on the other hand, better balanced.

Rumohr remarked also that subsequent art deviated from the heritage of Masaccio to concern itself with details and analysis; only in the classicism of the early sixteenth century was there a return to such grandiose essentiality. Moreover, he sensed intuitively that the deviation was due in part at least to Fra Angelico, a supposition that has been taken up again in our times.[14] Moreover, Rumohr's notion of a virtually dialectical antithesis between Masaccio and Fra Angelico was adopted and developed further by no less a figure than Georg Hegel in 1835: the chiaroscuro modeling and the co-ordination of forms in Masaccio synthesize with the psychological attitude and the "inner co-ordination" of Fra Angelico to lead the early Renaissance to a lively and naturalistic art which had both fresh ingenuity and intense religious feeling.

Further, the link between Masaccio and Raphael proclaimed by Delacroix in 1830, Passavant in 1839,[15] and even Ruskin in 1845, was of course inspired by a neoclassicist point of view, but it also singles out the fundamental, classical role of Masaccio. Delacroix asserts that "the merits and shortcomings of the Italian painters who preceded him [Masaccio] are inextricably mixed with those of the German school" [German here means Gothic]. And for Delacroix, Masaccio alone brought into being the "splendour of the Italian school, ... that enchantment, characteristic of it, of true expressions joined with a great beauty and a great purity." As for Ruskin, he maintained that all subsequent art derived from Masaccio, including that of Raphael and the others, with the exception of the art of the colorists for whom the case is different.

If more evidence is needed, there was Milanesi, in 1848, who repeated the ideas of Rumohr and Hegel but was nevertheless equipped with concrete knowledge of the gradual development of history and so warned against considering Masaccio as the mythical one-and-only founding father. And Cavalcaselle in 1864 expressed satisfaction that the dangers of direct influence from Masaccio had been avoided, an influence which, he felt, would have led art into a strange and excessive path (indeed, if we think of the first partisans of Masaccio, Francesco d'Antonio or the young Vecchietta, we must admit that he was not wrong). Moreover, in opposition to Muntz, he maintained that Masaccio's style was not one of mere realistic virtuosity, like those of Uccello and Castagno, but instead possessed a powerful simplicity. In 1896 Schmarsow claimed that the *Trinity* applied the architectural principles of Brunelleschi in a work of art before they had been tested in reality, anticipating the recent theories of Francastel. He spoke also of "the last fragments of Masaccio's activity which indicate the beginning of a new quest rather than the last word of the master," a pronounce-ment which, whatever its motivation, is reassuring when one thinks of Masaccio's work in Rome in 1428.

It may seem strange that, as Pittaluga has remarked,[16] in the final analysis the nineteenth cen-tury, for all its Romanticism, did not make something of the "Romantic" side of Masaccio's art (which would have meant contrasting him with Fra Angelico in a further extension of the original notion of Rumohr and Hegel); instead, it chose to stress his naturalistic, progres-sive, classicist side. Stranger even, our century, absorbed as it is with pure vision, has unexpectedly made much of those "Romantic" values which, for it, constitute Masaccio's "modernity." This is true not only of critics but of artists also, as is attested by the inspiration modern Italian painters like Soffici, Rosai and even Carrà and Cagli have found in Masaccio.[17] But perhaps this is merely a matter of critical thought lagging behind artistic vision. Eyes educated to the neoclassicism and academicism of nineteenth-century art gathered what they could from Masaccio, despite and because of this handicap—and this precisely at the time when Romantic critical theory was contrasting Masaccio with Fra Angelico. Twentieth-century eyes, on the other hand, which in a certain sense have become extremely "Romantic," have seen by preference a Masaccio who is melancholy, dark-humored, revolutionary, "communist" even and, what is more, "religious," stoical and the like (coming after those of Pittaluga and Salmi, Longhi's study of 1940 is a good example of this)—and this in a situation where, a few years ago, no one dared talk of "naturalism" except as something to be transfigured, of perspective except as a lyrical device, of humanism except in its Christianized guise! For such reasons the birth salver with the *Nativity of the Virgin*, now in Berlin, was dropped out of the list of Masaccio's works—except by those who found in it "a tragic anti-bourgeois irony" and "the grim mood of the hired musicians" [18]—and the *Trinity* of Santa Maria Novella was accused of "diminished creative spontaneity."[19] Today, however, perhaps we can look at Masaccio with a different and greater objectivity, precisely because a painter like Rosai belongs already to the past, and because Western painting in general, with minor exceptions, is experimenting a new path whose essence is entirely different from that of Masaccio and has launched out into a new epoch in which probably everything will be different. Now we look at Masaccio from another angle. The "modernism" of Masaccio is amply confirmed by the keen interest aroused today by attempts at greater historical objectivity which have nothing to do with any passing fads, least of all with the art collectors' market.

For decades now, in Italian schools there has been a standard, classical, elementary exercise familiar to everyone: distinguish between Masaccio and Masolino on the basis, preferably, of their similar frescoes with Adam and Eve in the Carmine or of the so-called *Metterza Saint Anna* on which they collaborated. Even the least gifted student has no difficulty with this, however naive the results may be, for the evidence is plain to see. The two painters who worked on the same scaffolding—"though they were a world apart" as has been said— have become a standard example for teaching purposes. True, recently a well-known literary personality made the gaffe of locating that scaffolding in "the Chapel of the Arena at Padua" and an art historian rushed in to correct him, saying that the famous collaboration of the two artists did not take place in that chapel (actually painted by Giotto) but rather in... San Clemente in Rome (this is an example of criticism *à la* Longhi which relies on "recollections" rather than on the more simple and certain facts of history).[20] And yet, not even this seemingly unshakeable rock, the distinction between Masaccio and Masolino which is always considered the classic example of the Italian strictly aesthetic approach, is beyond attack. Two noted French critics and scholars have declared themselves somewhat skeptical about the sharp distinction Italians make between these two artists, basing their arguments on the shallow perspective of the donors in the Sant'Ambrogio painting and of the Brancacci Chapel. For Pierre Francastel, Masaccio is a hero invented by Vasari whose superiority to Masolino remains to be proved as does, moreover, the possibility of any clear distinction between the two artists; in short, according to Francastel, there is no extraordinary progress over the past in Masaccio's work, certainly nothing equivalent to the revolution brought about by Brunelleschi.[21] Much more prudent and better informed, André Chastel nevertheless has obviously been influenced by Francastel and questions the distinction between Masaccio and Masolino ("it is not always easy to tell Masaccio from his master"), is somewhat moderate in his admiration for the former, and to the latter assigns the entire fresco in the Carmine of the story of Tabitha: "What is owing to him is, in essence, the presentation of figures in a more coherent space." [22]

Merely to be scandalized by these notions cannot disprove them. Nor is it enough to remind Francastel that the "hero" Masaccio was not invented by Vasari but by Masaccio's own contemporaries Brunelleschi and Alberti, even if he cannot see for himself how right they were. The distinction on stylistic grounds does not seem to impress these scholars overmuch; brushing it aside, they point out or could point out that Masolino also was capable of natura- listic treatment beginning with the *Madonna* of Bremen in 1423, that he was an effective reporter of the life about him, exploited perspective, depicted porticoes with semicircular arches and Ionian orders, employed the humanist alphabet in inscriptions,[23] and at Castiglione Olona painted his "Mirabilia Romae" fresco evoking antiquity... Are these not all Renaissance traits? As for the stylistic traits, we must concede that for non-Italians the more cosmopolitan elegant grace of Masolino may be more pleasing than is the stern severity of the local Florentine tradition which is so typical of Masaccio's sober, unadorned manner.

Here we find ouselves caught in a most intricate labyrinth. Such an approach opens the door to still other conclusions more widespread in their effects and causes. Among these are the well-known attempts of German philologically-minded critics, from Schmarsow to Oertel and even Van Marle, to identify as Masaccio's the major part of the works generally given to Masolino, from the *Madonna* of Bremen and the frescoes in San Clemente all the way to the Carmine itself. To call these all early works— *Frühwerke*— of Masaccio is admittedly a not entirely unreasonable hypothesis of a gradual development in the stylistic evolution of Masaccio. If we concede that it is merely a matter of greater familiarity with the science of perspective, of increased mastery of psychological expression, of tighter formal condensation, then the earliest works by Masaccio could just as well be given to Masolino. Is there really such an abyss between the angel attributed to Masaccio in the Metterza painting and the *Madonna* in Bremen, between the Mellon Collection portrait attributed to Masaccio and the young dandy in profile in the fresco of the story of Tabitha?

Moreover, this de-emphasizing of the split between Masolino and Masaccio is itself no more than one of many specific applications of another, more general de-emphasizing process now current outside of Italy and proposed, undoubtedly, with the best of faith. This concerns the entire Italian Renaissance itself. To sum up the argument in, admittedly, the broadest possible terms: just as Masolino and Masaccio do not differ overmuch, was there really a great difference between the Flemish towns and Florence in the early fifteenth century as regards their social and political structures, or between the French and Burgundian feeling for the *décor de la vie* (as expounded by Huizinga) and that of the Italians? Within the northern Renaissance one finds couplings analogous to that of Masolino and Masaccio: the brothers Hubert and Jan van Eyck, for instance, or the three Limburg brothers, or Campin and Van der Weyden coming soon after; Claus Sluter's powerful sculpture preceded Donatello's; even the art of the late fifteenth century in Florence, that of Filippino Lippi for one, took a "neo-Gothic" turning and came under the Flemish or Northern influence prevalent elsewhere throughout Europe. It is true, of course, these thinkers argue, that the Italians profited in the earliest phases from the abundant remains of Antiquity all about them and from their more direct and clear-cut Latin tradition, both of which were to bring about a preponderantly archaeological and classicizing tendency in the arts of Italy which did not affect European taste in general until the following century.

In essence, because every standpoint taken leads to further consequences, besides blurring out the contemporary differences and stressing the similarities these writers have had to apply an equally broad and unconventional vision to tracing out the ancient precedents and continuity, to pinning down the many steps in each transition, to exploring the substratum. We are shown the Renaissance as a product, if not a distortion, of the new fresh medieval spiritual awakening initiated by the Franciscan movement, as it is for Thode, Burdach and Neumann; or we are given the genealogical tree of Pre-Humanism; or, more recently, we have had the Renaissance exposed by Hauser and Antal as a sociological phenomenon, the logical culmination of the great capitalistic structures and forces set into motion in the late Middle Ages (Hauser recognizes the priority of Italy in this). Burckhardt is still admired but left behind.[24] Thus, to ascertain if Masaccio is truly separable from Masolino, and how, involves over and beyond a simple aesthetic distinction an immense and difficult problem in historical analysis.

Far from presuming to resolve such a question in these few pages, there may nevertheless be some point in considering it, however briefly, if for no other reason than to provide an ample base for our discussion of Masaccio.

Among Italians today there is a widespread impression (pinned down with characteristic precision by Luisa Becherucci) that at this particular moment in Italy figurative "form" takes precedence over all other historical elements and is at the core of all our problems. If true, it may be that purely figurative, formal solutions were decisive in the Italian Renaissance, and that they were more advanced and more significant than those of any other aspects of spiritual and social life.

But how could such an attitude come about? It will be recalled that Italian society was primarily made up of artisans, of handicraftsmen, and that of Florence particularly so, for in that city handicrafts were the principal resource on the international market. City life was centered around them, in much the same way as today industry dominates in the large automobile manufacturing cities such as Detroit and Turin. Every family or group of families counted among its members a stone-carver or a furniture-maker or a weaver, that is, an artist of some sort.[25] With this in mind, it takes no stretch of the imagination to see how immediate was the circulation of ideas between the other cultural and social groups and those concerned with the arts and crafts. It is not too daring, then, to suppose that figurative form must have been appreciated more keenly and by more people than today, and that it may well have served, in the final analysis, as a sort of common language between social groups through which new ideas were revealed and debated, even—by implication at least—ideas of a broader, more general import. Revelation, debate, and resolution: these remind us, as Cassirer puts it, of the profound truth which Humboldt sensed intuitively: that language is not merely a consequence of thought but is itself one of the essential phases in the formation of thought.[26]

A few examples will clarify and prove this point. It is obvious that the cultural and political myths of the humanists—the wisdom to be found in Antiquity, the choice of Rome as model—which were already dominant and influential in the Florence to which Masaccio came, must soon have come to affect the figurative arts, even the minor arts and crafts, and must have determined the new direction they took. But when, in Florentine dwellings first and then throughout the Peninsula, the marriage-chest indispensable to every household came to take on a Renaissance rather than Gothic form, even within the intimacy of private homes there was felt to be a new and typically Italian style instead of the older Gothic style which belonged to all of Europe. Through this, the new style was revealed and spread, as if by osmosis, and also the new figurative language. As for the debate and the final resolution, it suffices to think of the immeasurable historical significance of what occurred in Brunelleschi's thinking. He it was who associated the return to the antique, which might have remained mere imitation, with an entire new way of thinking, a *novus ordo*, that of perspective, and this was a product of individual creativity by means of which art succeeded in prying loose all the rest of culture from its traditional bases.

On the other hand, the most profound and coherent implications of Brunelleschi's approach to perspective—conceived not as one more means among many to achieve illusion in imitation, as it was for the Flemish, but rather as a fundamental discipline of measure and scientific rigor—set Italian art off on a dual track: either geometric and idealistic metaphysics as in Piero della Francesca and others or, instead, relentless realistic investigation by means of anatomy, a science which really is nothing less than an "organic perspective" of the human body, and this was the way of Castagno and Pollaiuolo. The ultimate consequences of this dichotomy extend not only to the special character of the art of the Italian Renaissance but even further: we can perhaps place on these same two tracks a Galileo and a Machiavelli, and it is not irrelevant that both belonged to that same city, Florence. Moreover, there is another aspect, this one in part negative: the principles to which Brunelleschi gave rise, and which as we know were rigidly intellectual and individualistic, must have reinforced the strict Humanism then typical of Italian culture and accessible only to an elite, without sentimental appeal to the masses, without indulgence in cosmic or romantic flights of feeling. Look at a Florentine painting and a Flemish painting of the early Renaissance: it is easy to guess from which side would spring the Reformation. Finally, a third example, another analogy with the figurative arts: looking at Paolo Uccello being driven half-mad by his drawings of many-sided hat frames, his *mazzocchi*, "spheres with seventy-two facettes like diamonds, and on each facette shavings twisted around sticks" (Vasari), or other desperate but significantly forward-looking problems in perspective, his contemporaries could well have drawn from these mad efforts a lesson in moderation and skeptical limit much like what they were reading in the pages written at the same time by Nicholas of Cusa, who warned that thought can only approximate reality, just as a polygon, no matter how the number of its sides is increased, can never become a circle.

If these basic observations have some validity, then certain notions expressed in the past perhaps take on new significance.[27] Burckhardt, as is known, had singled out as the minimum possible common denominator of the Italian Renaissance nothing less than an aesthetic attitude which made of politics, of social behavior, of culture so many manifestations of art, whatever may have been their specific ideological and ethical factors. But on the basis of what has been said here, Burckhardt's *homo faber* turns out to correspond in the final analysis to the artisan-artist who transforms the available material into a personal object. We can see him then as the ideal exponent of the celebrated elegant science of life of the Renaissance, neither too idealistic nor too cynical, always an individualist but with all his faculties in harmony. All the old absolute ideals fade away except for that of form itself, which ennobled all realizations in some way or other. What at that time dominated among the Italians was, above all, the visual sense. The fact is, Humanism brought about a decline in the exact sciences. As a scientist, Leonardo depended on visual intuitions, and his ideal was not the discovery of measurable relationships between objects outside of himself but, rather, "the transmutation of himself within the mind of nature," the identification of himself with nature as a kindred artistically creative spirit. Stubborn in their insistence that there was no breach between the Renaissance and the Middle Ages, nor between Italy and Europe in the fifteenth century, foreign scholars nevertheless concede that Italy "did indeed find for the aspirations which were common to the entire Western world new forms and richer forms which its neighbors later took from it, and this holds true not only for art but also for many other aspects of civilisation." Further, all the defects—and they are serious—of Italy in the Renaissance, its political anarchy, its unbridled economic license, the particularism of its states and individuals, these do not so much give rise to a dramatic situation of Darwinian struggle for survival and the triumph of the most gifted (something like the frontier struggles in pioneer America) as to a general flowering of cultural refinement. Burckhardt's vision of the Renaissance may well have been influenced by the liberalism of his times, and may err or be excessively optimistic in many of its particulars. Nevertheless, despite all the modifications brought to his notions since, and despite our different social outlook, it is a fact that today we tend to see the Renaissance as he did, as an essentially artistic phenomenon. This overall tendency to conceive everything as art (as today we see everything in terms of politics) is, to say the least, astonishing. Nothing similar can be found except in ancient Greece. It was perhaps neither an accident nor special pleading that led Alberti, writing at the dawn of the Renaissance, in 1436, to consider the chief trait of Antiquity to be that superabundance of "painters, sculptors, architects, musicians, geometers, rhetoricians, astrologers and suchlike most noble and most marvelous intellects such as in our time are both rare and seldom worthy of great praise."[28] Not that for Alberti modern times lacked outstanding politicians or warriors or merchants or religious leaders, but that this plethora of great figures connected with the arts and sciences seemed to him the supreme merit of Antiquity. This, coming from Alberti, is of great significance, since he himself began in the arts and went on to mathematics and literature.

But why did this particular moment in Italy, and first of all in Florence, mark the apogee of "form"? This phenomenon—the concentration and condensation of so much vitality towards formal, and above all artistic, ends—is not satisfactorily explained by the so-called "origins" of the Renaissance. Not by the development of Franciscan and late-Medieval spirituality which certainly would not culminate in such an essentially aesthetic and even, in some ways, irreligious attitude. Nor as the peak of capitalistic rationalism, from which one might expect an emphasis on science and economics rather than on the figurative arts. Nor even by the abundance in Italy of vestiges of Antiquity, since it was precisely Florence which was poorest in archaeological resources.[29] In any event the process of re-birth did not start simply as a respectful imitation of these but instead as a profound reinterpretation of them.

Unless we are to attribute the triumph of the formal element to something innate in the Italian spirit, we should seek for an explanation less far afield than those proposed above. That means the outstanding cultural phenomenon of the epoch, Humanism, which had

1 - TRIPTYCH OF SAN GIOVENALE (*detail:* Saint Juvenal) - *Church of San Giovenale in Cascia* - REGGELLO

2 - TRIPTYCH OF SAN GIOVENALE - *Church of San Giovenale in Cascia* - REGGELLO

3 - TRIPTYCH OF SAN GIOVENALE (*detail:* Saint Bartholomew) - *Church of San Giovenale in Cascia* - REGGELLO

4 - TRIPTYCH OF SAN GIOVENALE (*detail:* Saint Anthony Abbot) - *Church of San Giovenale in Cascia* - REGGELLO

5 - TRIPTYCH OF SAN GIOVENALE (*detail:* an angel) - *Church of San Giovenale in Cascia* - REGGELLO

6 - TRIPTYCH OF SAN GIOVENALE (*detail*: Madonna and Child)
Church of San Giovenale in Cascia - REGGELLO

emerged suddenly at the end of the preceding century and whose major center was in Florence. Humanism is, in fact, a typically and singularly formal culture which proposes to the entire spiritual life of man a formalistic model, and finds in that model its greatest intellectual potentiality. It suffices to recall that the surviving texts of Antiquity were above all literary works in which ancient wisdom was presented in highly stylized form, and that the Latin to which Humanism had recourse from the outset as the most direct means of assimilating and emulating Antiquity was itself a kind of language-form and quite artificial. However, the culture of Humanism was not, in fact, either excessively artificial or sclerotic but, like the formal element itself, appeared to possess and to demonstrate an instinct for selection, to seek for equilibrium, flexibility and the best possible solution. The fact is, Humanism brought about a rapid enriching of ideas and provided the myths needed to encourage not only the break with tradition and to justify it but also to permit men to adjust to the new thought, to live with it in harmony, to sublimate their feelings about past and present. Literary historians tell us that the Latin of the first Humanists, until around the middle of the fifteenth century, regained by its improved methods the elasticity lacking in medieval Latin and that it was used with a certain dexterity, without allowing grammatical and stylistic rules to become stumbling-blocks and without hesitating to enrich itself with the more spontaneous idiom of vernacular Italian; in this, there are certain striking analogies to the figurative arts. On the other hand, the vernacular itself was perhaps burdened with outworn historical and spiritual elements inherited from the great fourteenth-century writers who had built it up. From this arose two separate linguistic practices. The vernacular retained its traditional functions, and in the accounts of the chroniclers served to mirror the insignificant incidents of everyday life. Latin, however, was the language of oratory and history and, as such, could affect the shape of things to come, could give them a certain style as well as a scheme of general values, since it itself moved on a plane universal in both space and time, reaching back to the most ancient wisdom. The linguistic formalism of Humanism was therefore neither narrow nor stultifying, nor was the ancient wisdom it propounded locked and fixed within the rigid limits of a *Summa* (as medieval learning had been). On the contrary, it was dynamic and open to change: each new manuscript discovered— and even those which it was known remained to be discovered—brought in new doctrines and new stylistic models. No other epoch ever enjoyed the same extraordinary good fortune of being stimulated by sensational rediscoveries of the remote past. Nor was this a matter of literature only: the same thing was occurring in the world of art, through archaeological finds.

There is more to this. We have spoken of the adaptability and of the efficacy of this culture of forms. The political functions assumed by the earliest Humanists who gained political positions as advisers were such as to astound us today. Though some ideological compromising might be involved, the Humanists nevertheless proved that it was possible to give an artistic, aesthetic orientation to all aspects of life. The enemies of Florence claimed to have received more blows from the letters of Coluccio Salutati than from the city's men-at-arms. Leonardo Bruni, successor to Salutati and contemporary of Masaccio, always applied humanistic principles to the modifications in political theory called for by the changing times: after Dante's support of the Imperial cause and after Petrarch's nationalism, with Bruni there came the conception of the city-state and, above all, of Florence which set itself up to be the Athens of Italy. The political structure of Florence was acclaimed by Bruni as a "musical" harmony of its various institutions, and its theoretical ideology became stylized into democratic republican form. As a historian, Bruni rises from the realistic plane concerned with particulars to a higher level of idealistic and logical thought where there prevails "beyond question the principle of synthesis and typology." [30]

Thus, it was perhaps above all Humanism with its diverse and even specious argumentation which reassured the fifteenth-century Italians that their nation was not crumbling in chaos, and which quite calmly proceeded to justify even such opposed systems as the *signoria* and the republic and to show how to sidestep a head-on collision between the Church and Humanistic modernism based on pagan Antiquity. The Church, in fact, after some initial resistance, came around to favoring Humanism, regarding it correctly as something like a new expression of its own universality. [31] As for antique learning, it could always be explained allegorically, and in Florence there was Marsilio Ficino who was attempting to reconcile Christ and Plato, to safeguard faith while at the same time guaranteeing the freedom and prestige of science. But it was also true that pagan Antiquity also constituted, however tacitly, an anti-religion to be called on if needed.

Nor should all this be thought of in terms of the old stereotyped caricature of the greedy, servile Humanist. Whatever the Italian shortcomings in the Renaissance, form as such was an active and often positive principle. Humanist culture was in no way alien to its times, but was one of the most authoritative and respected intellectual doctrines ever known. The statesman or great merchant who favored it was not only a demanding patron but also, as we well know, among its fervid disciples. It reached the ordinary citizen, content to lead the modest life of his class, by means of the various channels of social life. This was not merely a question of new public buildings going up, of public festivals and ceremonies, of jobs being done and ideas being bruited about, but also of a more general current which must have brought a feeling for higher values to the most humble cogs in the social mechanism. The emphatic stylization with which fifteenth-century art depicts the daily life of the time cannot be a complete falsification: the treatises on the art of living, such as those of Alberti, expressed satisfaction with the middle-class way of life, and it is a fact that there were no violent social upheavals such as had taken place in the preceding century. These are certainly proof of a genuine appreciation of both ideal and practical values in all social strata.

If then Humanism itself was based on a specific culture which had the configuration and the vital dynamism of a "form," there remains the question of how a more all-embracing and definite solution came about elsewhere, in the figurative arts. Notwithstanding the many out-of-date aspects of artistic activity which survived due to the rigid hierarchy of social organisms, the prestige of art had been steadily rising ever since the Romanesque revival of culture. Expressive vehicle for high ideals and powerful social needs, art inevitably was driven to cast off whatever yokes still bound it. It was only natural that Florence should have grasped immediately the importance not only of a Dante but also of an Arnolfo who designed its principal monuments, of a Giotto whose painting had proved a revelation throughout Italy. As we shall see, prestige in the realm of art thus became increasingly one of the cornerstones of Florentine politics. Florence's challenge to Milan and its own rapid expansion are reflected, in a certain sense, at the end of the thirteenth and the beginning of the fourteenth century in the busy workshops of the great new cathedral where the first decisively classical, archaeological notions of the Renaissance were being developed by artists like Ghiberti, Nanni, Niccolò Lamberti and the young Donatello.

The cupola of the Cathedral gave Brunelleschi his great opportunity for a new and decisive step towards a renaissance of art. It must be understood that Brunelleschi possessed the genius to make himself the interpreter of a widespread, if as yet unconscious, state of expectation of something new when he proposed himself, in the years between 1418 and 1420, as "humanist architect" to be charged with the restoration of the ancient walls.[32] When after a fierce struggle he won first the competition and then the direction of the construction of the cupola, the rebirth in art was definitely launched. Along with the new chief-of-works of the Cathedral there triumphed his party of confirmed enthusiasts for the Renaissance, a party whose left wing included, from the outset, Masaccio. But in a great leap forward, Humanism in the visual arts soon outdistanced literary and cultural Humanism. To understand this, we must remember that Brunelleschi was not concerned only with a classicizing revival but also, and directly, with the "flesh and bones" of Antiquity: its essential theoretical and technical foundations. The exceedingly difficult technical problems he had to face in building the cupola provided the stimulus for this exploration of basic principles.[33]

Having carried speculation so far, only a short step separated the thought from the deed, from invention itself. That step involved a radical re-orientation. Considered from such a point of view, which seeks to dig below surface appearances, the claim that the design of the cupola of the Cathedral is an equivocal compromise between Gothic and Renaissance because of the acuteness of angle in its arch proves quite simply unfounded. The truth is, the cupola is the first grandiose and basic manifestation of the Renaissance. It is the product of one man's mind, thought out, worked out down to the finest detail by a man who considered nothing too trifling for his concern, whether it be the mixing of the mortar or the manufacture of the bricks. Hence, the cupola demonstrates not only the vitality of a culture inspired by the Antique but also that of a single great individual. It would have been inconceivable without Brunelleschi himself, though to realize a project so theoretical and abstract, the full cooperation of the artisans was needed. Fortunately, as a personality, Brunelleschi was strong enough to bend the hidebound craft practices of the workers to his own will and to arbitrate their disputes. Without him, as is proved by the well-known story of the illness he feigned to show up his rival Ghiberti, work on the cupola simply could not go on. The cupola itself soon became a symbol of the power of Florence and of its extraordinary culture: "a great structure, a ladder to the skies, that casts a shade so great as to cover all the folk of Tuscany," said Alberti, who added—and this too tells us much about Humanism— "an enterprise such as, if I am any judge, would seem almost impossible to conceive in our own times and which perhaps was beyond the knowledge and the abilities of the Ancients."[34] In the meantime, radical to the hilt, Brunelleschi was working out his theory of perspective which can be described as a hand that grasps and closes down on the appearances of the world, at one and the same time objective and subjective, as Panofsky has rightly seen.[35] Donatello and Masaccio backed him up with equally radical solutions. The protean character of Donatello's thought as regards both feeling and sense, his synthesis of archaeology, naturalism and expressionism, were such as to provide a source for the most diverse interpretations throughout the Quattrocento. As for Masaccio, his was an ethical and deeply penetrating way of looking at human events. It is not difficult to imagine what such a society of learned Humanists and skilled workers who were both artisans and artists could glean from such a spiritual lesson, from such a process which slowly, quietly, confidently spread after its essential achievement in the decade between 1400 and 1430. The revival of the formal vocabulary of Antiquity was no more than one aspect among many. Art became one of the most authoritative and meaningful spokesmen for the new age in contrast to literary Humanism which, sooner or later, would have been caught fatally in its own inner contradictions, unable to go beyond the purely external goal it had set itself.

For better or worse, we have attempted to show the broad lines of this development. One important factor remains: if what we have maintained is true, that the problems of the Italian Renaissance centered upon and were resolved in figurative form above all, then every departure from these principles would inevitably have weighty consequences, like an angle which shoots its two trajectories off to infinity while opening wider and wider. And this is the case of Masolino and Masaccio. Theirs are separate trajectories. And while Masolino —despite all the re-evaluation that has seemed necessary—finally drops by the wayside and is lost, Masaccio steers straight and sure for a world entirely new.

If, in Florence and elsewhere in Italy, architecture had continued to exploit the pointed arch and spire, if sculpture had continued to be rough-hewn, and if painting, however great, had merely paralleled the Flemish art of the fifteenth century, all the Humanist texts in Latin would not suffice to demonstrate the originality of the Renaissance nor its decisive progressiveness. At various places in this book we shall have to talk of a parallel between Masaccio and Van Eyck, but it would be wise to insist from the outset on what we mean by this. Italian scholars have often discussed this question, speaking of Flemish use of light as against Florentine linear perspective, or of "Italian space, Flemish atmosphere,"[36] or of Masaccio's ethically and "historically" positive spiritual attitude[37] versus Van Eyck's serene contemplation of man and nature in "a most civilized and cultured fraternity of all their aspects."[38] It is possible moreover to emphasize Masaccio's radical position and his strict focus on the human element[39] in contrast to Van Eyck's profound respect for all objective values as well as his all-embracing range, a range so wide, at times, as to be highly impressive for all that it is still anchored to a medieval approach.

There is no doubt, for example, that Van Eyck's drawing of Saint Barbara in Antwerp is an anticipation of Brueghel in its terrible vision, at one and the same time microscopic and microcosmic, and in its suggestion of Babel-like folly. Nor can it be doubted that Flemish perspective, with its placing of objects in a spatial additive infinity unified by ethereal light, is a continuation, in a certain sense, of the Gothic spirit with its striving for infinity, though now it is trapped between heaven and a firm hold on earth. Nor can it be doubted that such microscopic analysis tended to divert Gothic sentiment into a backwater of unlimited analysis in which, with tragic consequences, the human focus might be lost. From the comparison of these two, Masaccio and Van Eyck, we can understand what role Masaccio's sobriety and measure, his extreme unification of all factors, his inflexibly willful force might play in establishing values of true stability, and not only in the realm of expression. The artist of "sober style" thereby shows himself to be also "skilled in composition" and "chaste" in conception. Even taking into account lost or ruined or misattributed works—possible evidence of a personality which might have had a wider range than is generally suspected—Masaccio would never have painted such limitless landscapes as those of Van Eyck. Masaccio's are held in by an unwillingness to scatter his figures and to subordinate them to a merely physical cosmic space. Masaccio can be described as a "walled" painter, just as Florence in his time was a "walled" city, even in its private dwellings; indeed, even Humanistic Latin had as its ideal a closed, synthetic language. Van Eyck's painting pulls the eye, as in a whirlpool, towards the background: one need only eliminate the convex mirror which reflects and inverts the spatial relationships in the room of the Arnolfini double-portrait to reduce Van Eyck to the stature of some seventeenth-century Dutch painter of interiors. Unlike Van Eyck's, Masaccio's treatment of space concentrates on the foreground in which the human drama is being enacted, so much so that one wonders if this is not his personal version of what he must have seen in theatrical performances. In the same way as he eschews immensity, so also does he eliminate what is superfluous. Working in the city famous throughout Europe for its sumptuous brocades, Masaccio—unlike Van Eyck—dresses his figures in the simplest of garments without indulging in any play with draperies and without concern with the over-elaborate fashions of his day. What after all are such ample draperies but a calligraphic disguise cast over the essential naked physical fact of the man they conceal, a vestige of the gratuitous elaborations typical of the Gothic?

Let us return to the subject of the rupture with the immediate past which Humanism proposed. The decisive choice of Latin pointed the way for the visual arts to an analogous drastic renewal. There came about a deep-rooted change, a stripping away of flesh down to the fact of bone, which was encouraged by a political moment of heroic austerity in the life of Florence. This revealed itself in the theoretical speculations of Brunelleschi, in Donatello's ardent impetuosity, in Masaccio's moral view. Michelangelo, we know, looked down on Flemish painting which seemed to him sentimental and fit only to please women and monks (the most conservative and unsophisticated members of society) or, at best, men of the

7 - SAINT ANNA, MADONNA AND CHILD WITH ANGELS - *Uffizi Galleries* - FLORENCE

8 - SAINT ANNA, MADONNA AND CHILD WITH ANGELS (*detail:* the Madonna) - *Uffizi Galleries* - FLORENCE

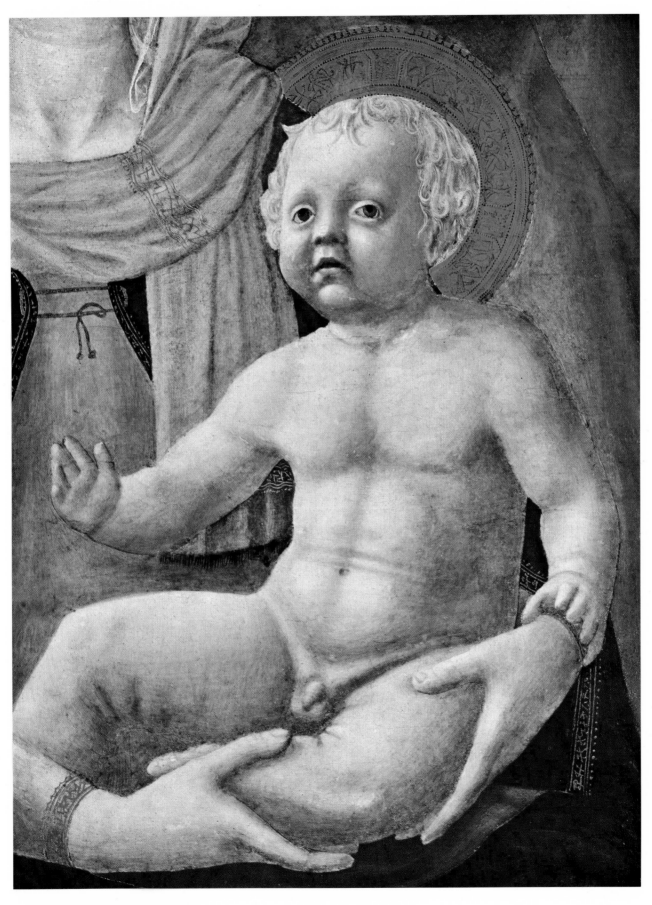

9 - SAINT ANNA, MADONNA AND CHILD WITH ANGELS (*detail:* the Child) - *Uffizi Galleries* - FLORENCE

10 - SAINT ANNA, MADONNA AND CHILD WITH ANGELS (*detail*: an angel) - *Uffizi Galleries* - FLORENCE

11 - SAINT AUGUSTINE, SAINT JEROME, A CARMELITE SAINT (from the Pisa polyptych) - *Museum* - BERLIN

better classes who might nevertheless lack any true sense of harmony. Michelangelo's attitude was based on a long-standing Italian tradition of which Masaccio represents a fundamental point and Giotto an antecedent.

Even without the lost painting Masaccio did for the Rucellai family which Vasari described as "a life-size representation of a nude man and woman," we can nevertheless compare the Adam and Eve of the Carmine with their counterparts by Van Eyck in Ghent. The Fleming has a deeper grasp of the science of anatomy, absolute fidelity to truth. His perspective is impeccable, for all that one has the impression of a stylistic rhythm which is still somewhat Gothic. The Eve with her prominent belly has much in common with the feminine types in the Book of Hours of the Duke of Berry, and the two figures are imprisoned like statues in narrow, high medieval niches. The figures are worked out to the finest details, and perhaps because of this they seem too material, as if, though carved with utmost care from marble or ivory, they were fundamentally alien to us, a little un-human. For his part, Masaccio works with greater spontaneity, almost roughly. But the result is far more dramatic, and in his form he unriddles the secret of uniting the vigor of the primitive with the superior idealization and harmony of the classic.

The Flemish mirror is too highly polished, reflects more than it should. Perhaps among the many reasons for which Michelangelo valued the unfinished art work, the *non finito*, there was also his repugnance for the brilliant Flemish manner and for the barrier it placed between reality and appearance. It was Masaccio's technique which had already shown Michelangelo how art need go only as far as necessary, how it can express a spirit which is not imprisoned in the finished object but alive and active and full of suggestion, free and creative still.

Perhaps the explanation of the great contrast between the naturalism of Van Eyck and that of Masaccio is a matter of national differences: on the one hand, the more dramatic and antagonistic relationship with nature of the man of the North which impels him to constant watchful attentiveness; on the other, the easy relationship with nature of the Southerner who can treat it with high-handed nonchalance while concentrating on the human element, an attitude typical moreover of the more individualistic character of the man of the South. Perhaps it was precisely in Masaccio that Italian painting of the Quattrocento found its single effective point of resistance to the powerful influence of Flemish art. One wonders if the Italy of Michelino da Besozzo, of Gentile da Fabriano, of Pisanello could have put up any comparable resistance.

Not that the wave of influence of Van Eyck did not reach Florence. It made itself felt already in the circular panel of Domenico Veneziano. The Madonna of Filippo Lippi in Tarquinia, dating from 1437, has an undeniable relationship to the Salting Madonna of the Master of Flémalle. Indeed, one wonders if the famous functional line of late Castagno and Pollaiuolo may not somewhat reflect the now well-established visit to Florence in 1450 of Van der Weyden with his expressionist power. It would be superfluous to recall all the Flemish influences affecting fifteenth-century painting in Italy, and how even Florentine attitudes were shaken when the great Portinari triptych of Van der Goes arrived there. Italy itself cannot boast of any comparable reciprocal influence. But it was Italian classicism which the painting of the Renaissance founded by Masaccio took as its guide, however much in the next century the tables were turned. Rome ignored the lesson to be learned, but Rome's great prestige during at least two centuries depended much on Masaccio whose death there Rome perhaps scarcely noticed.[40]

These general considerations must be supplemented by others more precise. Masaccio was a citizen of Florence. With this in mind there is no need to dwell at length on the well-known relationships of his art with the ethics of Humanism and with the contemporary neo-stoic philosophy of Salutati and, especially, of Bruni,[41] nor on the sociological aspects of the "regime" of the Albizzi so well explained by Antal.[42] Antal's work is based on a rigorous Marxist approach which, however, runs into difficulties when the author, in his final conclusions, is forced into a contradiction of his own thesis, considering Giotto and Masaccio products of those moments when the upper bourgeoisie exercised the greatest oligarchic power. For him, then, these two painters with their "concentrated, exact, scientific and classical styles," constitute "the expressive highpoint" of bourgeois rationalism. (One cannot help having a fleeting, reassuring idealistic impression that there must have been some sort of "liberal equity" in Florence which also encouraged a "free expansion" of artistic activity.) On the other hand, not enough attention has been paid to the very fine study of 1961 by Peter Meller with its complex and subtle interpretation of the Brancacci Chapel frescoes as a political allegory. These are said to refer to the contemporary war with Milan (there is a striking resemblance between Theophilus and Gian Galeazzo Visconti, the great *Conte di Virtù*), a war provoked by Maglino (note the allusion to the serpent in the Visconti coat-of-arms which would explain the inclusion of Adam and Eve in the cycle, otherwise difficult to account for). To this are opposed the peacemaking efforts of the Church, symbolized by Saint Peter.[43] The objective value of this study has been conceded even by a critic so alien to and unconcerned with such iconographical analysis as Cesare Brandi. It is stimulating in two ways, as a demonstration of the method of deciphering allegory and as an attempt to place Masaccio's art into a strictly political context.

As a matter of fact, the "Florentine empire," as has been shown however haphazardly by W. Welliver,[44] was a most active myth in the culture of Quattrocento Florence and is revealed in a complex of interrelationships and cross-influences with other, non-political activities that are none too obvious. For one, the "Beloved Woman" of the proponents of the new style may be considered a symbol of the beloved city. André Chastel[45] has pointed out a number of examples of the effects of this political creed: the feverish activity in the workshops of the Cathedral at the beginning of the fifteenth century and the achievement of the Brunelleschi cupola both were the result of fierce rivalry with Milan which at the same time was busily building its vast but still Gothic cathedral; the neglected art of mosaic was taken up again as a challenge to Venice; the spectacular Florentine public festivals in which, for these occasions only, the populace laid aside its usual sober attire, were aimed at impressing foreigners; Lorenzo the Magnificent went so far as to sacrifice domestic advantages in the visual arts in favor of his foreign policy, lending to other cities the finest talents of Florence: Verrocchio to Venice; Leonardo to Milan; Botticelli, Ghirlandaio and Signorelli to the Sistine Chapel; Filippino Lippi to Cardinal Caraffa.

There is no reason to be distressed by political symbolism in art, since art works generally lend themselves to allegorical interpretations on several different levels. The medieval taste for allegory lingered on throughout the sixteenth century and was the guiding principle in Landino's commentary on Dante, in Ficino's neo-Platonic synthesis, and finally in the work of Michelangelo. Even the folk of Florence in those days, as we are told by a Jewish observer of the time, had the habit of communicating by meaningful gestures and enigmatic and ambiguous allusions.[46] If Panofsky is correct in noting all the various symbols of marriage in Van Eyck's double portrait of the Arnolfinis, then it is just as legitimate to attempt to decipher the Carmine frescoes as Meller has done. But even in a broader context, it is possible and advisable to explore the relations between Masaccio and the history of Florence in his time. If history plays such an important role in Humanist philosophy, as Argan has seen with penetrating intuition,[47] we need not hesitate to examine it for what it may have to offer to our study. H. Baron has insisted on the importance that the conflict with Milan at the beginning of the fifteenth century had for Florentine "nationalism" (which included cultural manifestations as we have seen).[48] We have already pointed out that the splendid portrait of the tyrant Theophilus in the Carmine frescoes has a striking and undeniable resemblance to Gian Galeazzo Visconti. A new period of happier fortune,

21

which produced among others Masaccio, opened for Florence in 1402 with the death of Gian Galeazzo who had made himself master of Pisa, Siena, Arezzo and Bologna and striven to annihilate Florence in the deadly circle he had woven about it. Perhaps we have to thank the plague that killed the Duke for having saved the early Florentine Renaissance from stillbirth. The *Historia Florentia* of Leonardo Bruni comes to an end with that death which freed Florence for other efforts:

Ex illius confestim morte tamta rerum conversio secuta est, ut qui prius vi ullam salutis spem reliquam habebant, hi maxime confiderent: qui autem se vicisse putabant, omnem spem amitterent resistendi.

Over and beyond that point where the neo-Stoic impassible prose of the Humanist leaves off in a somewhat oracular tone in which chance and will seem to play a role, there is the unquestionable fact that Florence did indeed make a new start. Pisa, something of a Carthage in respect to the new Rome, Florence, was won over by gold and arms in 1406 and provided finally a close and safe naval base to replace that of friendly Genoa. Cortona was acquired in 1411 after having checked the King of Naples, Ladislaus. In 1413 Florence obtained free commercial access to the port of Leghorn which later, in 1421, it finally acquired by purchase from Genoa. In this way there came about the possibility of a great maritime policy oriented towards the East, for which reason in 1421 there was created the magistracy of the six Consuls of the Sea.

Felice Brancacci, who commissioned the chapel, belonged to that group of magistrates. In 1422-23 he went as Florentine ambassador to the Sultan of Egypt in Cairo to discuss trade increases which were channelled through the port of Pisa. It is interesting to note that both Brockhaus and Antal had vaguely supposed some sort of commercial-maritime significance in the Brancacci frescoes.[49] Meller does not agree. However, if we recognize the many possible levels of interpretation of an art work and if we keep in mind that the program of the cycle must have been formulated over a certain period of time and with possible deletions and variants, certain indications become, to say the least, suggestive. In the *Tribute Money*, the coin with which to pay the tax is found by Peter in the mouth of a fish near the shore, almost as if to say, as Antal puts it, "that the wealth of the State should be sought in the sea." The sea, in fact, figured conspicuously in the two upper lunettes, now lost, painted by Masolino: the Calling of the Apostles Andrew and Peter (which we know from the Giovanelli copy) and the Bark of the Apostles. It is rather unlikely that the second lunette showed the Shipwreck of Saint Paul on his voyage to Italy as told in *Acts*, 27, so it may been an allusion to the return voyage of Brancacci which was full of perils. Finally, Antioch, where

Theophilus was converted and the first church of St. Paul was set up, may represent the opportunities offered by the Orient.

Admittedly, allegorical interpretation is liable to go astray with subjective phantasies. However, the closely reasoned and penetrating argument of a specialist like Meller stands up under closer study of what was happening around Masaccio up to 1427. After the period which contemporary sources as reliable as diaries declare to have been prosperous,[50] events again took a stormy turn for Florence, as has been recently shown in exceptional fashion by Procacci.[51] Once the Milanese state was reconstituted, Filippo Maria Visconti resumed the old expansionist policy, subduing Genoa in 1421 and Forlì in 1423. The Florentines felt themselves threatened, and while Pope Martin V was still deliberating whether or not to speak out in their favor, the Florentine troops suffered overwhelming defeat at Zagonara on July 28th, 1424. The Duke boasted that he would soon bring the enemy city to its knees. Fortified by Humanist exhortations to behave like ancient Romans, Florentine courage held fast. In the dramatic council meeting of August 3rd, proud phrases were spoken, and one Niccolò del Bellaccio, in true Renaissance fashion, employed the experience of history to remind the citizens that the father of the present Duke of Milan once had seemed all-triumphant and that then the entire Milanese state crumbled beneath him, so *animus riassumendus est et viriliter incedere; et nos a Romanis origine, habemus* (Milan had the temerity to proclaim itself the "Secunda Roma"). The following year, among the recommendations given by the Signoria of Florence to the ambassadors sent by the Pope who hoped to act as mediator, was the declaration that in order to preserve their liberty (that is, the autonomy and power of Florence) the Florentines were prepared to spare nothing of their "goods, sons and brothers, and life itself and even to put into peril, without reserve, their very souls."

The year 1425 ended with a great victory for Florentine diplomacy. That same Lorenzo Ridolfi "who was ambassador from the Florentine Republic to Venice," as Vasari identifies him among those portrayed in Masaccio's *Consecration* in the Carmine, succeeded in obtaining from Venice a defensive and offensive pact against Milan. The fortunes of war were then reversed. Brescia was occupied, and the Florentine commissioner with the allied troops who besieged and took the city was no less than Felice Brancacci himself. On December 30th, 1426, through the good offices of the Pope, a peace treaty was signed. Visconti returned to the attack in the spring of 1427, but after the Milanese were defeated at Maclodio a more durable peace was achieved by the treaty of April 18th, 1428. Unlike Venice which won Bergamo, it cannot be said that the treaty gave much to Florence except that it guaranteed her integrity and liberty. Moreover, the financial burden was immense, leading to the setting-up of the *Catasto*, the special tax levy first planned in 1424-25 and finally launched in 1427[52] (there may well be a reference to this tax in the Carmine frescoes, in the scene of the Tribute Money which is rarely depicted elsewhere.) But the policy of check and balance in Italy now had the weight of authority behind it, and the alliance between Florence and Venice proved durable (indeed, it even induced Paolo Uccello, Filippo Lippi, Castagno and Dona-tello to move north) until the fatal turn of events in 1450. Meanwhile, war with Milan flared up again and did not cease until the victory at Anghiari in 1440. The optimistic popular ditty, "Ave Maria, grazia piena: when we've got Lucca, we'll take Siena," turned out to be contradicted by the unfortunate and unpopular war against Lucca in 1430-33. The following year, 1434, the oligarchic regime headed by the impetuous Rinaldo degli Albizi and which had prevailed in Masaccio's time fell, and the more discreet rule of Cosimo Medici began. This, however, takes us beyond the period which interests us.

In any event, Masaccio's connection with politics must be understood as something less external, more personal, than mere allegorical implications or vague influences from historical events. It led to a strengthening of still another aspect of Masaccio's ethical position, leading him, as it were, to speak with a proud Roman voice, to intensify his expression like those Florentine orators who were said to speak with just moderation but stentorian delivery:[53] a spirit typical of the times, proposed in theory and applied in practice, of egalitarian republi-canism, of militant virtue, of invincible pride.[54] The austerity of Masaccio's art is not unrelated to that of the city burdened with special taxes. The Saint Paul of the lost Carmine fresco was a portrait of Bartolo de Angiolino Angiolini who held various magistracies in the Republic, and, as Vasari put it, this likeness of a contemporary expressed Roman civic virtue "joined to that invincible and divine spirit." The donor at the foot of the Trinity in Santa Maria Novella has been recently identified as a certain Lenzi who was the official standard-bearer, the Gonfaloniere, of the city in 1425.[55] The first important public appearance of Masaccio must have been the lost *Consecration*, a scene of contemporary historical signi-ficance, with its portraits not only of the artist's friends but also of Brancacci, of the ambas-sador Ridolfi whose diplomatic master-stroke was the alliance of 1425, of personages like Niccolò da Uzzano, Giovanni di Bicci dei Medici, Bartolomeo Valori, and many others. Had the fresco survived, we should have had perhaps the finest possible illustration of that Florentine moral fiber which twice resisted the onslaught of Milan. Even in the power-ful figures depicted in the fresco cycle in the Carmine we can sense something of the back-ground of a political event which made dramatic demands on the citizenry. This is certainly

24

not to say that Masaccio was no more than the product *sic et simpliciter* of those forces, but only to point out how fully Masaccio reflected not only literary and philosophical Humanism and Brunelleschi's artistic Humanism but also, and as well, the political character of the Florentine state of his times.

This book will be concerned with other matters in what is to follow. It has seemed appropriate to the series in which this book appears to explore first the broad historical background with all its many implications for our understanding of Masaccio before going on to a more detailed study of the artist, his life, relationships, and works. The problems such a study presents are philological and may at times seem even finicky. As we follow certain tracks or strive to define the factors at play, it may sometimes seem as if we are straying far from our central subject and—to use a metaphor appropriate to the circumstances and *si parva licet componere magnis*—as if we are applying the microscopic vision of a Van Eyck rather than the synthesizing orientation of a Masaccio. And yet, there is no contradiction involved. What seems useful today is not another synthesis nor another critical definition of Masaccio —especially after the fine studies by Mesnil, Salmi, Pittaluga, Longhi, Argan and, most recently, Brandi—but instead an attempt to single out what problems remain and to bring together all the available data. The latter task is especially necessary because much time has elapsed since the last major effort, Salmi's monograph of 1948 in which he brought up to date his earlier study of 1932. New works by Masaccio have appeared since then, and various themes have been explored more searchingly and in fresh perspectives.

It is precisely from such a focus on facts and from the deeper understanding to be gained thereby that an up-to-date judgment on Masaccio can be drawn, not from those deductions which for long now have been crystallized in critical formulas. Indeed, even the Masaccio considered typical by contemporary criticism can now be seen to be a conception of a single moment and not for all time. This is easily proved: at the beginning of this century, nineteenth-century academic prejudices set up a barrier to admitting as authentic certain parts of the Pisa polyptych—they were considered too "vulgar"![57]—whereas today other prejudices are at work which oppose, for some strange reason, the recognition as Masaccio's of the little *Madonna* proposed by Longhi, of the side panel in the National Gallery, London, and—if I may—of the triptych at San Giovenale discovered by the present author.

The subject of Masaccio is therefore far from exhausted. It is pertinent to stress how, in view of the recent minutely detailed historical and biographical contributions of Procacci, of Meller's interpretations, of the study on the *Trinity* by Schlegel and Tolnay, and of the new fact of Masaccio's work at San Giovenale in 1422, it has seemed to me necessary to replace the old approximate evaluations of Masaccio's "circle" with—in terms borrowed from Nicholas of Cusa—a more many-faceted polygon. Herein lies the essence of this book, whether it be concerned with recapitulating what is known or in proposing new points or with freeing ourselves, where necessary, from certain well-implanted philological and critical errors of the past. We have been obliged to attack directly and unhesitatingly such errors, not because of any personal taste for polemics but instead in proportion to their authority, their wide diffusion, and their stubborn persistence. Finally, this is an essay in the literal sense of the word, no more than the groundwork for further study. It will be a matter of gratification for me if scholars concerned with further research of Masaccio will find this book some help in their efforts.[58]

BIOGRAPHY OF MASACCIO

Perhaps only an Ingmar Bergman could make a film on the life of Masaccio, a life in which there were scarcely any external events, and whose "plot" turned on deeply considered thoughts, not flamboyant actions, in settings of great beauty still deeply marked by medieval severity.

What happened in Masaccio's life was always simple but not necessarily humdrum or banal. He was appreciated by great Florentine leaders like Brancacci and probably also by highly-placed personages in the Roman Curia, perhaps even by Pope Martin himself, and he had ties of close friendship with such outstanding artists as Brunelleschi and Donatello. But it was a life without worldly pomp, unlike that of Van Eyck who, in Masaccio's own life-time, travelled Europe on a variety of missions, some of them diplomatic, did portraits of princesses, was received at his homecomings with public ceremonies. Nor in his life was there anything of romantic bohemianism à la Van Gogh or Gauguin or Modigliani. For all its historical significance, his life was indeed "sober and unadorned" in its exclusive concentation on art, a life very much like his own pictures.

What mattered most in such a life was, no doubt, simply the exchanges of ideas on a high intellectual and never superficial plane between friends named or nicknamed Pippo, Donato, Masaccio, Masolino. And there were meditations in solitude over the obsessive problem of what steps needed to be taken in what new direction to make reality of the nagging intuition that all the art and culture of Europe were moving towards something different. And there were also, part and parcel of what was simultaneously old and new, antique remains which everyone admired and commented on but whose real significance for the future was to be deciphered only within the artist's secret soul. And, further, there were secrets to be shared about new modern and truly scientific methods such as Brunelleschi's recent explorations of perspective which could be learned only through patience and hard work though they were discovered "not by a mathematician but by a painter."[59] And new buildings in a new style were going up, like the cupola or the Hospital of the Innocents, and these were worth study not only because of their great size or beauty but because they were models at one and the same time of something new and of something revived, plain for everyone to see and mysteriously harmonious. And statues were taking shape under Donatello's mallet which some day would count among the classical treasures of museums. And for Masaccio himself, there were colors which dried rapidly on the walls, fixing the first images of that new pictorial world men sought and which was nothing less than a more real equivalent of the real world. And there were panels prepared with gold on which his brush dashed figures which could well do without the gold and everything else that lingered on from medieval tradition. And finally, there were patrons of culture whose praise was the highest reward of any work, even if the actual payment was slight and public fame still wary. In the midst of all this was a young artist so rapt in the high problems he had set himself, such an "absent-minded and happy-go-lucky" person according to Vasari, that he neglected even his own well-being. Hence, the nickname "Masaccio"—Big Tom—which in Italian is depreciatory but which his friends must certainly have given him out of affection.[60]

It is not difficult to imagine how he was. In the Carmine, as Meller has noted, standing behind Saint Peter who heals the sick with his own shadow [Plate 52], are Masolino wearing scarlet

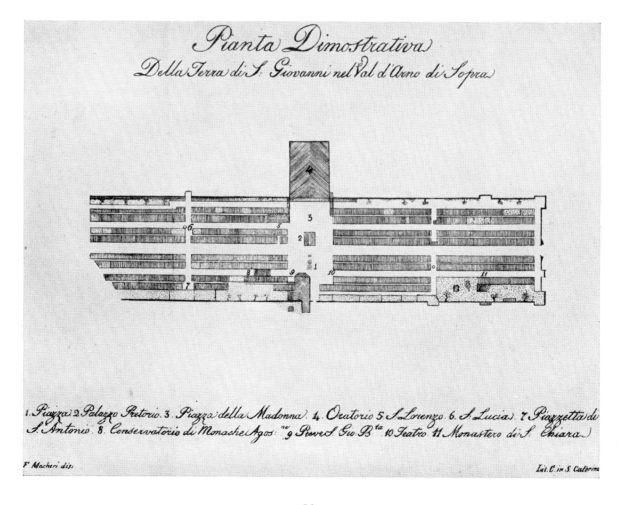

headgear, Donatello to the rear appearing as a very old man, Masaccio himself in the guise of the blond Saint John; the suppliants may well be portraits also, just as the houses are certainly those of some street in Florence of the time with the rusticated façade of a small palace and, farther back, less pretentious houses with their upper storeys projecting on struts, and all a little crowded and higgledy-piggledy in the old center of the city. (Even Charles V as Emperor declared in 1536 that the city pleased him "but it is all propped up everywhere," which induced people to rid their houses of these exterior supports.) This was, all told, the perfect setting for Masaccio, because he was a man of great simplicity but of virtually apostolic decisiveness and with a humanity both intense and intent.

Masaccio's life began in the Florentine countryside, in the green fields of the upper Valdarno. To visualize the setting of his early life, we ought perhaps to look for a more truthful, more sober picture, something more in the character of Masaccio himself, than the conventional literary description by the chronicler Giovanni Morelli (1371-1444) with all its graces and its laudatory intent. Morelli describes the Mugello Valley, but his words can serve also *mutatis mutandis* for Masaccio's Valdarno. Even a brief excerpt suffices to reveal yet another Florentine "form" in the making, a close-knit, neatly-patterned design that leaves its mark even on the natural surroundings.

First of all, it is located in the midst of a very beautiful cultivated plain where beautiful and delightful fruit trees abound, and it is endowed with all good things like a garden; coming closer, you will see in the midst of it a lively little stream [this would correspond to the rather more impressive headwaters of the Arno in Masaccio's birthplace]. A lovely sight, and there are other pools and shoals in the plain, which are fed by delightful rivulets that drop from the beautiful mountains. All around, like a charming garland, there are slopes and hillsides easy to climb and others which are greater and higher but no less beautiful... a landscape half-wild, half-cultivated... And there rise up here and there great fortresses erected by the commune of Florence to watch over and make fast its lands. The said castles are situated in beautiful and charming places... They are girdled by a fine wide and deep moat full of good water; the walls are high and thick and strong with impregnable towers soaring high supported by jutting buttresses, and these too are a delight to see. Within, the inhabitants are nobly lodged in the many houses which line the fine well-ordered streets where cunning and skilled artisans of every kind abound who know well how to receive and honour visitors from elsewhere. Around these castles, on the slopes and hills and heights, are scattered for some two or three miles many more humble dwellings of citizens on sites lovely and well cared for, with delightful views over-looking the pleasing farmlands.

The description is a bit idyllic, as were to be the landscapes of Fra Angelico and Gozzoli, but it offers an acceptable picture of the Florentine countryside where nature and man worked hand in hand to create a world both varied and pleasing. The landscape must have assumed this character, which even now it still retains, in the course of the century preceding

Masaccio's birth when the local feudal powers were broken and the Florentine middle-classes settled in great numbers on the land, diverting part of their wealth to the countryside where numerous sites had become available through the breaking-up of vast holdings.[63] Van Eyck has left us not only glimpses of the interiors of Flemish dwellings but also of Gothic cities of the North spread out along the great waterways (though his views of such cities are generalized and imaginary) and of broad sweeping plains. But one wonders to what extent Masaccio for his part deliberately rejected the task of depicting the splendor of his homeland, preferring to set his personages in a primeval and still barren world, turning his back on the enthusiasm for naturalism in landscape which, in his times, was sweeping all of Europe. There comes to mind the *Adoration of the Magi* [Plates 24-25] from the predella of the Pisa polyptych and now in Berlin, with its barrier of uniformly arid hump-like mounds which stretch away to the distant horizon. Perhaps these could be justified as a brilliant personal interpretation of the rugged but much more monumentally mountainous panorama of the descent from Consuma to Casentino, or of certain crests of the upper valley of the Arno near Reggello, or even—since the work was painted at Pisa—of western Tuscany towards Siena, in the vicinity of Volterra. But the fact is that there was already a tradition in Florence which ran from Giotto to Lorenzo Monaco of depicting the Nativity and the Epiphany in something like a Franciscan hermitage set among jagged rocks. The guides to the Holy Land, and the pilgrims who returned, may well have spoken of a land like a desert with swelling dunes. What is more, as a setting for the birth of Christ, such a landscape, still naked and seemingly barren, must have been understood as a symbol of death and rebirth.

The setting of the *Tribute Money* [Plate 46], however, is better defined, a valley almost locked in by steep hills and towering mountains which reach towards a sky striated with bright clouds. It may be that the gray expanse which stretches from above the head of the figure of Saint Peter, squatting at the far left, as far as the arm of the first apostle in the group, was once a vast curve of lake, broken by circling waves, which has lost its color and which may have been a more representative image than that blue pool, whose colors have not faded, from which Peter has taken the fish. However, the terrain together with its trees seems to descend towards this expanse after a declivity and the trees seem to reappear on the opposite bank. Salmi feels there is a reminiscence here of how the majestic chain of the Pratomagno mountains looms up suddenly as one enters the valley of the Arno, precisely in the region where Masaccio was born. Certainly this too is a very austere landscape, but one can still make out, despite the damage wrought by the fire, fine rows of trees which climb the swelling

12 - A CARMELITE SAINT
(from the Pisa polyptych) - *Museum* - BERLIN

hills in front of the bare, rocky mountain and also a thicker clump which once appeared below between the heads of the Apostles; the tree trunks which divide the middle plane in depth originally had delicate foliage, except for two which were quite bare; besides, there must have been at the extreme left a leafy branch intended as a light and airy but nevertheless effective screen for the end of the painting.

Finally, there is the example of the *Distribution of Alms* [Plate 56] with its glimpse of both town and country—large houses either simple and practical or more elaborate or elegantly modern and pretentious, and then a bit of countryside speckled with green from which rises, white and tall, the massy bulk of a small castle. All of this recalls any number of small towns in the valley of the Arno.

To conclude this parenthesis: in his landscapes, Masaccio seems to have preferred an austere cohesion which would agree with his overall stylistic vision and which moreover is consistent with a certain specifically Franciscan tradition that lingered on in Florentine painting.[64] However, in this also he went beyond the Gothic limitations, achieving a sense of space which transcends what Clark calls "the landscape of symbols."[65] And perhaps with time his own vision became less severe: there are more and more touches of naturalistic detail as he worked down from the upper tier of frescoes in the Carmine to the lower where the *Story of Theophilus* takes place before houses Brunelleschi might have imagined and in the green peace of a walled garden [Plates 60-61].

It would not be difficult to show how Masaccio's robust cohesion and concentration in treating landscape was carried on by Castagno as in the scenes in the upper tier of frescoes in Sant'Apollonia and the fresco with Saint Julian, and even by Piero della Francesca, for instance in the *Transport of the Holy Bridge* in Arezzo or the *Resurrection* in Sansepolcro. Even when Domenico Veneziano, in the *Adoration of the Magi* now in Berlin, made the first true introduction into Italy of Flemish microcosmic virtuosity, he took as his guide Masaccio's birth salver [Plate 75], adapting the circular framework of Masaccio's round panel with its geometric regularity and transplanting it from an indoor scene to a "*plein air*" treatment of nature.

Masaccio was born on December 21st, 1401—Saint Thomas's day, whence his name Tommaso[66]—in the upper town of Castel San Giovanni, the present-day industrious and lively town of San Giovanni Valdarno. Castel San Giovanni had been founded around 1295-1300, together with nearby Castelfranco and Terranova, half-way along the main road between Florence and Arezzo. Florence chose the site not merely to assert her sovereignty but also to provide a living demonstration of the Florentine republican way of life as opposed to the old feudal powers, particularly of families such as the Pazzi and the Ubertini: "... medio ferme spatio inter Arretium et Florentiam... concidit oppida, ut forent simul ornamento simul belli presidio; et alterum quidem in sinistra Arni ripa situm, cui nomen dedere a patrono civitatis." So wrote Leonardo Bruni, in Masaccio's time and in the best humanist fashion, recounting what was, after all, a recent medieval event as if it belonged to Antiquity—not that Masaccio himself would ever believe, like Mantegna, that present-day reality could and should be decked out in borrowed Roman trappings.

San Giovanni Valdarno has grown like any modern town but preserves traces of its original plan which was as rational as a Roman colonial center, with walls designed—or so tradition claims—by Arnolfo: a very elongated rectangle with four gates in the middle of the sides and with its crenelated walls reinforced by twenty-four towers. In the center, running the entire length of the castle, from the wall facing the Arno to the opposite wall facing the Chianti River, there opened a great piazza overlooked by two churches and, isolated in the center of the piazza, the Palace of Justice, next to which there used to be a great covered well, the so-called " well of Arnolfo," and a column which still bears proudly the *Marzocco*, the lion rampant, symbol of Florence. The principal street, bordered by porticoes with small arches, runs on either side of the piazza along the entire longitudinal median axis of the town from the gate towards Arezzo to the gate towards Florence. It was in this street Masaccio's family lived. Other streets were laid out in straight lines and separated regular, equal-sized parallel blocks of houses between which ran narrow alleys. The vicariate of San Giovanni had jurisdiction over a large territory, stretching from Pontassieve to Montevarchi, Bucine, and Laterina and from Cascia to Greve, but the inhabitants must have been loyal patriots: they still speak an unmistakably Florentine dialect, whereas in nearby Montevarchi one begins to hear the dialect of Arezzo.[67]

Sometime before 1383 there arrived in Castel San Giovanni from the commune of Gaiole in the Chianti region a certain Mone (that is, Simone) d'Andreuccio and his younger brother Lorenzo.[68] By 1393 the family—by then called Dei Cassai from the trade practiced by the two who were *cassai*, furniture-makers[69]—seems to have grown:[70] among the sons of Mone there was one Nanni, aged thirteen, who was to turn up in the records again in 1401 as "Ser Johanni," which indicates that at twenty he had already acquired the title of notary (his intelligence must have seemed quite exceptional in his family). In 1401 Ser Giovanni is found to be married to a Madonna Jacopa from Mugello[71] who within the year, at only nineteen, was to give birth to our Masaccio.

The Cassai owned at that time three plots of land, one of them partly planted with vines, and a house in the town.[72] This is the house facing the main street and with a courtyard in the rear, which is marked today by a commemorative plaque. In 1442, the records show, half of it belonged to Masaccio's brother Giovanni.[73]

In 1406 the young notary died, and in the same year was born Giovanni who was given his father's name but was more often called by the nickname Scheggia, that is, Chip, rather as we would say, a "chip off the old block." Ser Giovanni left nothing as an inheritance, and as was the custom of the time Jacopa took a second husband,[74] a certain Tedesco, an elderly pharmacist of Castel San Giovanni who was a widower twice-over with two daughters,[75] one of whom, Caterina, later married another artist, Mariotto di Cristofano. The latter, born in 1393 at San Giovanni Valdarno, was already active as a painter in Florence in 1419. Although he was, to all intents and purposes, a brother-in-law of Masaccio and Giovanni, nothing in his personality as an artist, which has been recently reconstructed,[76] allows one to suppose that he could have had any influence on the development of our painter.

Of Masaccio's boyhood, from the fatal date of 1406 when he was orphaned, we know nothing, but he could surely have counted on both his father's family and on his newly remarried mother.[77] But on January 7th, 1422 "Masus S. Johannis Simonis pictor populi S. Nicholai de Florentia" enrolled in the Guild of Doctors and Pharmacists (to which painters belonged) and thereupon became an independent painter in Florence with lodgings in the parish of San Niccolò on the left bank of the Arno.[78]

The recently discovered triptych of San Giovenale which is dated April 23rd, 1422 proves however that Masaccio could not have acquired such a profound feeling for Florentine culture without having already spent several years in the city.[79] The scene therefore has shifted from the little town in the Valdarno to the capital city. As reminders of home, Masaccio could look out on the hills dotted with olive trees just behind the wall that cramped in the quarter of San Niccolò, and on the other side of the Arno, upstream from the Ponte alle Grazie, there was a wide beach like those in the Valdarno where the river flows more swiftly. And yet it is unlikely that idle nostalgia could distract him from the exciting things being done in Florence itself by the two friends Brunelleschi and Donatello whose work he must have known and understood as early as 1422 as his triptych of that year demonstrates. We can follow him in fancy as he strolls along streets bordered by high somber palaces, such as the nearby Via dei Bardi where Niccolò da Uzzano lived, crosses a bridge to plunge into the heart of the city bustling with shops and a thriving populace, comes out at last on the Piazza del Duomo where, since 1420, the gigantic cupola had been rising dizzily higher and higher on its concentric rings and where Donatello had his sculpture workshop. There too, among the idlers around the church, could be picked up the latest news and gossip: how when Pope Martin visited Santa Maria Novella the Florentine youngsters sang mocking ditties at him ("Pope Martin's not worth a tinker's damn"); or how in 1423 they threw stones in the courtyard where Master Gentile da Fabriano kept "certa scultilia et picture maxime importantie"; or that the Duke of Milan was acting up again and threatening a new war; or again that peace and prosperity seemed just around the corner with the new maritime prospects opening up from Pisa to Leghorn.

Attempts have been made to discern the blight of poverty in the life of Masaccio, but this (and here we can only agree with Procacci) does not seem to be borne out by the facts (unless the modest economic lot so many of us still live in is considered stark poverty). Those were times of great prosperity for Florence, and some of the advantages of the economic miracles taking place rubbed off on all the citizenry. A mere count of the paintings executed by Masaccio in the few years of his life, beginning with the triptych of San Giovenale, suffices to show that he could not often have been out of work. For the polyptych of Pisa he was paid eighty florins (something around a million and a half lire today, roughly around 2400 dollars) [80] which was certainly not a lot but neither was it small pickings,[81] especially since he could, and seemingly did, work at other things at the same time. Nor do his childhood and adolescence seem to have been particularly deprived, since, after all, money must have been available to send him off to Florence to study, and we know that his brother Giovanni was supported by their mother until the age of seventeen.

In any event, two documents of 1426 and 1427, the most important surviving evidence for Masaccio, are a trustworthy guide to his economic conditions. They are concerned only with practical everyday matters, but for this aspect of our study are much more valuable than any imaginary reconstruction. It was not until 1424 that Masaccio enrolled in the Guild of Saint Luke, the painters' guild, and this leads us to wonder if perhaps he may not first have gone to Rome, following the traces of his two good friends Brunelleschi and Donatello, and if that journey did or did not coincide with the semi-jubilee year of 1425 as has been suggested (though there is a question as to whether or not the jubilee was actually celebrated).[82]

But the notary Ser Giuliano di Colino degli Scarsi from San Giusto left a memorandum concerning his chapel in the church of the Carmine in Pisa:[83]

13 - MADONNA AND CHILD WITH ANGELS (from the Pisa polyptych)
National Gallery - LONDON

14 - MADONNA AND CHILD WITH ANGELS (*detail:* the face of the Madonna) - *National Gallery* - LONDON

15 - MADONNA AND CHILD WITH ANGELS (*detail:* a lute-playing angel) - *National Gallery* - LONDON

My chapel in the said church was built by Master Pippo, son of Master Johanni di Gante, stone-carver of Pisa. It was begun on the 29th of November 1426 [Pisan dating; the common calendar would read 1425] and cost me about 140 florins. The panel of wood for the altarpiece was made by Master Antone di Biagiò of Siena of the chapel of Santa Cristina, and cost me eighteen florins. Master Mazo the painter, son of Giovanni of Florence, of the parish of San Michele Visdomini painted it, beginning on the 19th of February 1426; it cost eighty florins.[84]

Masaccio received this payment in several installments and certainly does not seem to have been as absent-minded about his creditors as Vasari claims: ten florins (about 300 dollars) on February 20th; fifteen (about 450 dollars) on March 23rd; another ten on July 24th "which I paid to Master Donatello, marble-worker of Florence" (a debt between friends?); twenty-five (about 750 dollars) on October 15th "and he has promised me not to undertake any other work before this is completed, and put it in writing," was the guarantee given by his brother Giovanni[85] and the sculptor Leonardo Pardini of Pietrasanta; three lire on November 9th "which I paid to a tailor who said he had made him a short jacket"; one florin likewise turned over to Donatello on December 18th "who gave it to one of his apprentices who was there"; while Andrea di Giusto, "the lad who worked for him," received thirty grossi (something over 60 dollars) on December 24th; and finally sixteen florins and fifteen soldi as balance due were paid to Masaccio on December 26th, 1426 "with the proviso that he should turn over the fully completed panel to me and that it should meet the approval of the said Master Antone" (the prior of the Carmine in Pisa). So we find Masaccio in 1426 turning up now and again in Ser Colino's premises or elsewhere to collect his money. It is clear that he spent Christmas in Pisa and, in fact, may well have passed a good part of the year there—although we cannot rule out the possibility that some of the work on Ser Colino's painting was done in Florence—and the sojourn in Pisa was perhaps not without profit for his keen perceptions. With Nicola Pisano, Pisa had been the cradle of an Italian figurative classicism to whose tradition Masaccio must inevitably have turned, and Nicola's son Giovanni had brought diverse elements together into a plastic expressionism. Eve Borsook has recently[86] pointed out certain reminiscences in Masaccio's polyptych of works done in Pisa by the two Pisanos.[87] Perhaps such comparisons can be carried even further to apply, for example, to the *Madonna* published by Longhi who dates it from precisely the time of the Pisan polyptych and in which perhaps there is something of Giovanni Pisano (compare Plate 38 and Figure 7);[88] one is even tempted to wonder if the classical character of certain heads in the *Tribute Money* does not derive from Nicola.[89] Procacci has discovered the tax bill of about April of the same year, 1426, presented by Castel San Giovanni to Maso and Giovanni then resident in Florence, but the document consists of no more than a single line.[90] There survives, however, a tax declaration written in Masaccio's own clear and careful handwriting (see above) on July 29, 1427 to the newly set up property tax office.[91] Well-known as is this document, it is worth reproducing in its entirety, since no summary or paraphrase could bring out its full flavor.

Before you, gentlemen of the tax office for Florence, the county and the district, we hereby declare all the goods and holdings in furniture and real estate of ourselves, Tommaso and Giovanni of the upper town of Castel San Giovanni Valdarno, currently residing in Florence.

In cash we have approximately six soldi.

Our family consists of ourselves and our mother aged forty-five; I, Tommaso, am twenty-five years old and my brother Giovanni twenty.

We live in a house owned by Andrea Macigni for which we pay an annual rent of ten florins, and [the house]

36

faces the street and is bounded on the second side by the said Andrea, on the third by the Archbishop of Florence, on the fourth by the said Andrea.[92]

I Tommaso rent part of a workshop from the Badia of Florence, for which I pay two florins a year, and which faces on the street and is surrounded on the second, third and fourth sides by the said Badia.[93]

We owe to the painter Niccolò di ser Lapo one hundred and two lire and fourteen soldi   L. CII s. XIIII.[94]

We owe to the gold-beater Piero six florins or thereabout   fior. VI.[95]

We owe to Lorenzo Adimari and his company three florins   fior. III.[96]

We owe to the lending agencies of Lioni and of Vacha for loans made there several times four florins fior. IIII.[97]

We owe to Andrea di Giusto, who has worked with me, the aforesaid Tommaso, the balance of his salary, six florin   fior. VI.[98]

Our mother should have one hundred florins from her dowry, forty from Mone d'Andreuccio of Castel San Giovanni and sixty from the heirs of Tedescho of Castel San Giovanni, her second husband   fior. C. Our aforesaid mother should receive from the heirs of the above mentioned Tedescho the income from a vineyard located by the fish-pond in the commons of Castel San Giovanni as well as the occupancy of a house in said Castel San Giovanni both bequeathed to her by the said Tedescho; we can say nothing of the income from the vineyard nor of its extent because we know nothing about it, neither does our mother have any income from the said vineyard nor does she live in the said house.[99]

So also as *homo oeconomicus*, as a man of extremely simple means, our painter was "sober and unadorned." There was the rented house in the Via dei Servi where he lived with his mother and brother, the workshop in Piazza San Firenze, a few debts, a claim for what was due to his mother from her rather unobliging relatives in San Giovanni Valdarno.[100] But on that hot day in 1427 Masaccio must have been easy in mind as he climbed the stairs of the Palazzo Davanzati to settle his accounts with the new tax system. Others waiting may have passed the time by scribbling on the walls the calculations that can still be seen there, but the young painter had other things to think about: the paintings he was himself executing on other walls, those of the Carmine...

According to Ugo Procacci, the best-informed expert on the Florentine tax rolls, at least among art historians,[101] the rates were fixed at five on the thousand for net capital minus living expenses (Giovanni dei Medici was taxed seven million on a taxable capital of almost a billion and a half; Palla Strozzi, the wealthiest of them all, was taxed almost nine million; Rinaldo degli Albizzi paid about a million on 210 millions). But it is not so clear if taxes were collected at set periods or every month or something worse (if figured annually, the burden would not have been so heavy),[102] and therefore it is not easy to explain why the first result of these special tax levies was to discourage almost completely all private patronage of artists.[103]

Whatever may have been the cause—whether it was because the Brancacci were no longer able to pay for their frescoes,[104] or because Masaccio was becoming aware of his own worth and so, "not feeling at ease in Florence" (Vasari),[105] wished to see if Pope Martin (who gave Gentile da Fabriano twenty-five florins—over 750 dollars—a month in 1427) might not show more appreciation than his fellow citizens,[106] or whether it was because Masolino urged him to join him in Rome—for one reason or another Masaccio left Florence, perhaps at the beginning of summer in 1428.[107] Who knows also whether he may not have thought of trying out for himself Brunelleschi's clever dodge of becoming suddenly unavailable until begged to return to a position more worthy of him. But destiny had other plans: Masaccio was to be allowed to speak his message with great power for but a little time. There would never be for him the full tide and triumphs of a Van Eyck. The thread of Italian painting was to unwind luminously from the art of Masaccio, but Fra Angelico and Filippo Lippi and the others, all the way up to Raphael and Michelangelo, were obliged to spell out in profound and painstaking study the lessons of the Carmine frescoes, so few were the works left by the short-lived master of them all.

The story ends in the Rome that Martin V was beginning to restore and beautify.[108] There we find Masaccio, a mere man among great ruins, but soon to be inscribed by Alberti among those "not to be placed lower than those who were ancient and famed in those arts." [109] And there Masolino once again could listen spellbound to the discourses of his friend—but not for long. Was he poisoned? That was the accusation bandied about later in Florence, and if it were true it would at least be an acknowledgment that he was a "dangerous" man, even if his assassins only aimed at getting rid of a too capable rival. But this is probably no more than a suspicion thought up—by analogy!—in the time of the Borgias: Manetti, who gathered his information directly from Masaccio's brother, does not even hint at it.[110] It was probably in the summer or autumn of 1428 that Masaccio died suddenly.[111] The news was brought to Florence, where we can imagine it being told to Brunelleschi caught up in work on his cupola and his other undertakings. One must always conclude with an anecdote, and the last is always the best. We know from the portrait by Masaccio himself the grim mocking face of Filippo,[112] and we know the love for cruel pranks, like the trick played on the woodcutter Grasso, that lay behind that terribly acute brain, and we know how his tongue was capable of cutting remarks. But now he said only, "We have experienced a great loss in Masaccio."[113] This is the first, the truest, perhaps the most decisive judgment ever rendered on Masaccio.

16 - SAINT PAUL (from the Pisa polyptych) - *Museo Nazionale* - PISA

ORIGINS AND ENCOUNTERS

"*Miraculous*"—that was Vasari's word for what was truly exceptional among the great artistic creations of the past, however much he may have thought them outdistanced by what came after or was not yet "perfect" as was, to his mind, the art of the Cinquecento. Miraculous were for example "the things by Giotto and by Andrea Pisano and Nino" (the fine line of classicism within the Gothic) or the lantern of Brunelleschi's cupola of which he admitted that "nothing better has yet been done in our times, nor will be, peradventure, in times to come."[114] The adjective "miraculous" itself implies a double meaning: one relative and concerned with history, the other virtually absolute. The second meaning corresponds perhaps to the extraordinary "modernism" Vasari sensed in Masaccio.

But anything which is "miraculous" sets special problems for both the art historian and the critic. Whatever is "miraculous" is also "mysterious" inasmuch as it must perforce be an emphatic and inexplicable departure from the narrow river-bed of tradition and environmental influences in which more conventional art, as if forced to it by its very nature, is bound to flow. But is the miraculous really an isolated phenomenon which generates itself and has no other roots? Or does it only appear as such because of our incomplete grasp of the intricate web of history? The temptation to ferret out antecedents and influences is hard to suppress: we are reared with a logic based on causal links, and we think it no more than right that it apply also to history, whatever accidents may admittedly intervene in the course of events. Does not the genius of the artist correspond to one of the many incarnations of the omnipresent original Genius which, conditioned but not totally determined, is responsible for each successive step in history? Is it not the same "miraculous" originality that we attribute to a great statesman or a great scientist?

Furthermore, the "miraculous" suggests that every great artist remains always on the same exceptional high level, so that any work or part of a work which does not reach the heights must be, we presume, the work of his studio helpers or pupils. But is this really true? What hand was ever born perfect and remained so always? Did Homer never nod? The truth of the matter is that, as criteria go, "perfection" simply will not do, it is all too relative. To limit ourselves to the case of Masaccio, not many years ago the admirable *Saint Paul* of Pisa was considered too "weak" to be by the master and was therefore assigned to Andrea di Giusto; Berenson was attacked for having urged the National Gallery of London to acquire the "rather vulgar" *Madonna* which now turns out to be the central panel of the Pisa polyptych; even today there are critics who carp at the Berlin birth salver painting or at the two saints of the side panels in London. On the other hand, if we turn the tables and decide not to fuss too much over questions of "autographs", "workshop" or "school" (the most difficult questions for historians today), just as much caution is needed: before rejecting as unauthentic the *Madonnina* recovered from Germany or the two small panels in Altenburg, the whole question should be studied more thoroughly.

There is, moreover, in the case of Masaccio the fact that his major work, the frescoes in the Carmine, have been much altered by time and by the fire of 1771. Any considerations and conclusions based on them must take this fact into account. Several other works which must have been of comparable importance though perhaps different in character have been lost: the *Consecration* in the Carmine cloisters, the *Saint Ives* in the Badia, the *Annunciation* in San Niccolò. Their loss reduces the number of facets of the artist's work that we can know, and yet every facet of his work had the most significant consequence for the Renaissance.

For our purposes, there were all too few works produced in that brief lifetime, briefer certainly than that of Van Eyck who worked on until 1441. Moreover, in a certain sense, the art of Masaccio took off from a less favorable and more humble base than that of Van Eyck. While Van Eyck could find "within certain limits a point of departure in Franco-Flemish Gothic" (Salvini), especially in the miniature with its rich potential of naturalism, Masaccio found nothing better in Florence than the local late-mannerists of the Trecento and the new mannerist exponents of International Gothic who gravitated around the barren planet of Lorenzo Monaco. Even when Brunelleschi and Donatello returned from Rome, their mysterious antique "treasure" contained nothing specifically relevant to painting, and they themselves learned only slowly how to utilize what they had discovered. In 1422 Van Eyck began the decoration of the palace in the Hague for John of Bavaria, Count of Holland, and then entered the service of Philip the Good, Duke of Burgundy; beginning with the *Adoration of the Mystic Lamb* he was fully equipped with a highly perfected technique of painting in oils. In 1422 Masaccio was still limited to the old technique of tempera when he painted the little triptych for San Giovenale at Cascia on commission from some bourgeois of Florence. Already set apart from his contemporaries, he had in his private sketchbook only the addresses of his friends Brunelleschi and Donatello, Masolino's too perhaps, but all the rest was still blank. From the start there was something "apostolic" about Masaccio, and the proof is that he began or wished to begin, with a minimum of what had come before him, uniquely conscious as he was of the power of his inner revelation. In the mirror of history, Masaccio's painting appears in the simplest garb as compared with the splendor of Van Eyck's: the severe tunic of one of his figures in the Carmine as contrasted with the sumptuous brocades of Van Eyck's Chancellor Rolin.

Art historians have not failed to inquire into the beginnings of Van Eyck, finding a possible solution in the miniatures of the Book of Hours of Milan. For Masaccio, however, until recently they found themselves confronted with a difficult alternative. It seemed quite probable and, indeed, human that Masaccio should have gone through an initial gradual phase of development.[115] But in that case historians had to take into account the fresco in Montemarciano [Figure 4] which has only a vague and general resemblance to Masaccio's work and which, on close study of its details, proves disturbingly coarse or disappointingly feeble. Lindberg in 1931 finally decided to attribute it to the minor painter Francesco d'Antonio: a later echo, therefore, of Masaccio and not his own still raw first effort.[116] At least one art historian felt free to wax ironic about those who hoped "to discover Masaccio as a tadpole, embryo, amoeba or the like and to watch him climb step by step through all the biological processes all the way up to glory." The same art historian promptly turned around and took the opposite position by declaring "that if there ever was an artist who emerged from the brain of painting fully armed and sure of his way, it was Masaccio—and for that reason, any pre-history of Masaccio as a painter makes no sense." [117] This comparison of Masaccio with Minerva who, spear and all, was produced by Jove is, of course, not to be taken literally, the more so as it is in contradiction with its author's entire methodological approach. Rather it should be interpreted as a perfectly justified postulate that a genius like Masaccio who turned out his masterpieces by the age of twenty-five must have revealed his fundamental gifts right from the beginning. Until recently there was, moreover, a stumbling-block in the whole unsolved problem of chronology. Those who believed in the authenticity of the Montemarciano fresco were forced to date it no later than 1420, as remote as possible from all the other paintings, and to suppose that the young Masaccio would have whiled away his time in a country town thinking and painting in a country manner without making contact with what was happening in Florence. Others, like the writer quoted above, who considered Masaccio's earliest work to be the panel from the church of Sant'Ambrogio with Saint Anne and the Madonna could not, as scrupulous historians, date it earlier than 1424, thus leaving unexplained several years in which it was perfectly possible that Masaccio might have gone through a formative phase.

It must be said that the recently discovered triptych of San Giovenale at Cascia dated 1422 [Plates 1-6][118] may confirm, rather than refute, the best arguments of both parties. It gives proof of Masaccio's gradual development but at the same time reveals him as already possessed of an unmistakable individuality. Thus the appearance of this new evidence has finally made it possible to fix at least one firm landmark in the early progress of Masaccio. Quite apart from my own modest contribution to this discovery, I think there are good reasons why the attribution of this triptych to our painter has had such prompt and virtually unanimous and outspoken acceptance despite the heavy responsibility that such acceptance bears; there are also good reasons why its very few opponents have limited themselves up to now to the most cautious opinions.[119]

If nothing more, these attitudes themselves help confirm the attribution to Masaccio of the San Giovenale painting. The fact is, it suffices to compare the Madonna in the central panel with the Madonna in the Pisa polyptych [Plate 13] to be convinced that both are creations of the same personality, though he had matured between 1422 and 1426. But there is also the fact that in the thrones of the two panels there is the same fundamental conception of strong spatial construction. The back-rests of each of the thrones are in two parts, and this is a sign of a new sensitivity to the proportional relationships between sections. However, in the San Giovenale throne the lower part is smaller than the upper and rises only as far as the level of the arm-rests which grow out of it. In the Pisa throne, on the other hand, it is the upper part which is smaller, and its columns, likewise smaller, are doubled, unlike those below; in its way this motif recalls both the façade of Brunelleschi's Pazzi Chapel and the Brancacci tomb in Naples by Donatello and Michelozzo, the latter of whom was working in Pisa at exactly the same time as Masaccio.[120]

Moreover, in both paintings the entire space is rhythmically stratified by the same treatment of the human form, both in depth and height. As for the successive strata in depth from front to back, in the Pisa panel there is a certain similarity, despite the obvious limitations, in the separate planes of the angel musicians in the foreground and those kneeling behind the throne to Donatello's approach in the contemporary relief in Siena of the *Banquet of Herod* done between 1423 and 1427. The San Giovenale panel includes fewer elements—the Madonna and Child and two small angels seen from the rear—and its perspective is different, with

17 - SAINT ANDREW (from the Pisa polyptych) - *Lanckoronski Collection* - VIENNA

18 - CRUCIFIXION (*detail:* torso) -
Museo di Capodimonte - NAPLES

19 - CRUCIFIXION (from the Pisa polyptych) - *Museo di Capodimonte* - NAPLES

a very high central focus point and a much wider spread of the throne on its dais with its series of projections; the result is an exaggerated depth[121] extending all the way to the back-rest which forms a final decisive niche to shut off space in depth. However, in the vertical plane, in both the Pisa and San Giovenale paintings, from the eyes up, the head of the Madonna rises in identical fashion above the back of the throne so that even the upper area of the arch is exploited and thereby rendered spatially meaningful by virtue of the penetration of a volume into it. In the same way, the arms of the angels in the San Giovenale panel dip into the space in front of the throne and bring it to life.

Examination of the two panels in terms of volumetric geometry shows that they are conceived as two projecting structures with different perspective treatments. That of San Giovenale has a very high vanishing point, giving the effect of a view from above down and of objects sliding down in a widening plane, and this is still tied to the Gothic empirical approach. On the other hand, the Pisa painting has its vanishing point midway up the panel, with the result that all the foreshortenings are reinforced and the forms are condensed in volume. But both paintings are constructed with scientific consistency and with the same basic striving for a firm grasp of space and of the physical, spatial reality of the bodies. When we move on from a consideration of the elementary structural framework to the details in which the figuration is articulated and defined, again we find that in both paintings the pensive face of the Madonna reveals the same psychologically intense feeling of the burden she must bear. The Child in both is a sturdy male completely nude who looks at us with piercing eyes, intent upon the grape He is eating (the flimsy veil over the Child in the San Giovenale painting was obviously added by Masaccio later, probably to placate the parish priest). In each of the paintings the angels in the foreground are altar-boys dressed in similar tunics of a rose color modeled partly by light, partly by shadow. The demonstration could be carried further with a comparison of the saints in the right-hand panel of the San Giovenale painting with those in the Pisa polyptych [Plates 11-12] in which even closer similarities can be found since the details themselves are less complex. Such a comparison can also be extended to other works of Masaccio, and this opens up a whole new series of philological arguments, but the present writer has already done this on two occasions[122] so that it seems unnecessary to go over the ground again.

However, the little triptych of San Giovenale has a special significance.[123] It employs a language which is, in many respects, quite new and, moreover, highly meaningful in its innovations although (quite unlike Van Eyck's *Mystic Lamb*) there is nothing obvious and

20 - CRUCIFIXION (*detail:* Christ) - *Museo di Capodimonte* - NAPLES

21 - CRUCIFIXION (*detail:* Madonna) - *Museo di Capodimonte* - NAPLES

striking about it, which explains why the painting remained unnoticed throughout so many years in a little church in a rather isolated valley of the Valdarno. Over and beyond the special treatment of perspective and space and the sober psychological intensity already mentioned, the innovations include the Christ Child Himself. The Child who eats grapes —an allusion to the Eucharist—had never previously appeared in religious iconography and derives, as we shall see, from an antique model [Figure 12].[124] Moreover, without the later addition of the veil, the Child would have been completely nude—a positive manifestation of naturalism this—something else never known before, at least in Florence. And this is the first painting known which flaunts its membership in the avant-garde by the use of humanistic Roman lettering which can be made out on the plinth of the base but which has almost disappeared from the evangelical salutation written out with careful attention to foreshortening around the curve of the dais of the throne. New also is the naturalism (a term one need not be ashamed to use although it has long been out of fashion) with which objects and persons are rendered: the well-rounded crosiers and the hermit's crook, books like the fine one held in the foreshortened right hand of Saint Juvenal, and hair, lashes and eyebrows (though these are lacking in both the Madonna and Child)[125] and beards and eyes (the aged Saint Anthony Abbot's are bloodshot) down to the fine detail of nails touched with red, almost as if to show how the warmth of the blood flows even to the extremities—"and let all the members of the dead down even to the fingernails be dead and every slightest part of the living be alive," was the advice of Alberti a few years later.

But the overall effect is modest, like the striped green floor on which the scene is set. Though the throne is majestic and richly adorned with Cosmatesque inlay and the haloes are carefully worked out in various florid designs, the painter nevertheless resisted the seductions of mosaic pavements and gold brocades so much in vogue in his time. What he sought was rather a certain air of austerity, and this is reflected also in his treatment of the draperies. However logical, these do not indulge in the fashionable exuberant calligraphic opulence which even Van Eyck could not resist in the *Mystic Lamb*.

From a sociological standpoint, what taste does this represent: folk, middle-class or high-bourgeois? Elsewhere the present writer has considered this question on the basis of Antal's principles[126] and has come to the conclusion that the little triptych was designed to satisfy the tastes of everyone present at its inauguration. The peasantry would have approved of its seeming traditionalism and its easily-understood, unambiguous language. The landed bourgeoisie would have found reflected in it their own cultural attitudes which were in the process of maturing, that is, clarity and naturalistic logic and a completely human rendering

44

of the religious subject (without her mantle, the Madonna with her embroidered rose tunic is nothing more than a gentlewoman of the times dressed in contemporary costume, virtuous but not ideally beautiful); they would have been aware too of the importance given to those fundamental objective factors, space and time, which the new rationalistic thought tended more and more to re-evaluate:[127] not only is space scanned rhythmically by the stripes in the pavement but also a corresponding and quite objective "*tempo lento*" seems to emanate from the painting.[128]

As a result of apparently contradictory sociological factors already pointed out by Antal, what seems simple and popular in the triptych may turn out to be instead the expression of a high social and cultural level. A more humble painter, as we know from the many surviving works of the time, would have indulged the popular fancy for showiness, whereas the austere elements we have singled out in Masaccio's polyptych are due, rather, to an ambitious artist who may well have found support for his own grave view of the world in the tastes of certain refined upper-class circles. Though both societies—Florentine and Flemish—were alike in their economic well-being, the traditional sobriety of Florence may well have expressed itself in this manner rather than in pomp and splendor such as that of a Van Eyck.

Produced by a youth of twenty, the triptych of San Giovenale quite naturally betrays a certain crudeness, with Gothic holdovers in the left-hand panel [Plates 2-3] where the two saints, Bartholomew and Blaise, appear to be stuffed into their garments and where the hands of Saint Blaise do not grasp the symbols of his sainthood in convincing fashion. Further, although this may be due to the painter's high viewing point, the feet of Saint Bartholomew are not foreshortened within a plane—an innovation Vasari attributed somewhat naively to Masaccio—but are in "the old rude manner which... made all the figures stand on the tips of their toes." In any event, the innovation itself may have been not merely an application of the new science of perspective but, in addition, an attempt to stress symbolically how firmly planted on earth were certain religious personnages.

Also, the treatment of color in this panel lacks a certain refinement, as in the strident clash of reds between the tunic of Saint Bartholomew and the cope of Saint Blaise. It has been suspected[129] that this left-hand panel might be the work of an assistant, but this is contradicted by the fact that both panels show the same stylistic and technical treatment of details such as the bishops' crosiers and mitres and the grayish whites of the bishops' gowns and gloves. The same hand painted both the Saint Blaise on the left and the Saint Juvenal on the right, and the latter is the most progressively conceived figure in the triptych; whatever

22 - CRUCIFIXION (*detail:* Saint John) - *Museo di Capodimonte* - NAPLES

23 - CRUCIFIXION (*detail:* Saint John, lower half) - *Museo di Capodimonte* - NAPLES

difference there is, is due entirely to Masaccio himself who matured with each new day's work.

As a matter of fact, the left-hand panel is of utmost importance for what it tells us of the origins of Masaccio's style. Certainly for anyone who wishes to seek out the antecedents of this triptych the first and best clue is to be found in the chapels Giotto painted in Santa Croce. In the *Trial by Fire* of the Bardi Chapel, the throne of the Sultan [Figure 10] is decorated with inlay-work which emphasizes its various parts in a way very similar to what was done later in San Giovenale. However, there is an even more immediate precedent in the round painting in the same chapel with its symbolic depiction of Obedience [Figure 9] in which the back of the throne is analogously horizontal. There is no doubt that the garments of Saint Juvenal were inspired by the figure of the Sultan with his costume in purplish red, grayish white and gilding, and the Sultan's head resembles those in the left-hand panel of the triptych, particularly Saint Bartholomew's. In the Peruzzi Chapel, other figures, especially those in the *Resurrection of Drusiana* and some of those on the right, offer obvious prototypes for the saints in San Giovenale.[130]

Here, then, our triptych confirms Berenson's intuitive judgment that Masaccio was "Giotto reborn":[131] right from the outset, the young painter studied and drew inspiration from Giotto. It is an accepted fact that the late Giotto of the frescoes in the Santa Croce chapels, with their rich and mature pictorial complexity, constitutes the most advanced point reached by the Trecento in relation to what art was to become in the following century, just as it is known that, for example, Masaccio took the division of the wall into marbled panels in the *Story of Theophilus* [Plates 60-61] from Giotto's *Burial of Saint Francis* in the Bardi Chapel, a motif which, reworked in Renaissance idiom by Masaccio, was to become one of the most typical of the entire Florentine Quattrocento vocabulary. Here, however, we run into a most ticklish question—whether or not the revolutionary Masaccio respected the achievement of Giotto—and this is related to the whole problem of the delimitation of the Renaissance in time. Battisti has given us a subtle and precise key to the critical awareness of the great painter of the preceding century that even the founders of the Renaissance—Masaccio and his friends—must have had,[132] an awareness that remained stable and positive over and beyond all their other polemical positions. Giotto the artist "not for the delight of the eyes of the ignorant" but rather "for the intellectual pleasure of the learned" (Boccaccio); Giotto who "translated the art of painting from Greek into Latin and made it modern" (Cennini); Giotto who "rendered art natural" and together with his disciples was "as wise as the ancients" (Ghiberti): Giotto must have seemed the precursor if not, indeed, the founder

24-25 - ADORATION OF THE MAGI (from the Pisa polyptych) - *Museum* - BERLIN

—for painting at least—of that Humanism of the arts that Masaccio and his friends propounded. They could find in him both what was new and what was classical, since he was anti-medieval and opposed to the folk tradition but, at the same time, remote from the decadent court-influenced style of the second half of the fifteenth century which was the product, essentially, of the triumph of the Gothic over Giotto's principles.[133] It is not mere chance that the famous painting now in the Louvre with five portraits of the "renewers of art" [Figure 3]—originally attributed to Masaccio but now given to Paolo Uccello— should include Brunelleschi and Donatello but, for painting, no less than Giotto.[134] In fact, Masaccio's glory was somewhat put in the shade by the earlier glory of Giotto, and it was only Leonardo who succeeded in making the more recent painter esteemed higher than the older one.[135] Some of Giotto's legendary glory was due to the fact that his name was linked with that of Dante. True, literary men of the Quattrocento went so far as to question the supremacy of the poet because of his use of the vernacular and because of his Aristotelian-Thomist philosophy,[136] but Brunelleschi devoted much of his precious time to reconstructing mathematically the three worlds of the Divine Comedy. It seems likely that the grandeur and vivid imagery of the great poem were still deeply appreciated, if not by the Humanists themselves at least by the circle of artists with a broader and more popular culture to which Masaccio belonged. In this respect, Longhi has expressed an intuitive grasp of the relationship between Masaccio and Dante.[137]

Giotto was therefore one pole, the lodestar of tradition which guided Masaccio's development. The other pole comprised Brunelleschi and Donatello. Not that those two were like Dante's Ulysses who desired to go beyond where men had ever gone: the exploration of the fabulous world of Antiquity was not a matter for one brave man but was joined in by all the adherents of Humanism. Yet the path they chose was not the easy one of hunting up old manuscripts or of jotting down sketches of relics of the past in their Gothic-styled drawing books, like Gentile da Fabriano or Pisanello or Ghiberti.[138] Their way was more direct and more perilous, aided only by the intellectual instruments they had to invent for themselves day by day. Perhaps there has never been a moment in the history of art so close to the risks that science runs: what would have become of the Renaissance if Brunelleschi's cupola had collapsed? With Brunelleschi and Donatello as guides, there was no way of shirking the ultimate rigorous and difficult experiment: to leave behind the safe shelter of the Gothic style where others whiled away their art. History today sings Masaccio's praises and what he did seems in retrospect so very easy, but it was not so in 1244. To expect a youth of twenty to bring about *ab imis* a renewal of all of Italian painting—friend as he may have been of Brunelleschi and Donatello who were themselves only just finding the way—is to ask too much. No one has a right to find the triptych of San Giovenale disappointing.

In that triptych, the influence of those two great revolutionaries is easily made out. From Brunelleschi derives the coherent and full application of the first formulation of the laws of perspective [Figure 19]: the lines of the pavement move from the lateral compartments to the central focal point of the Madonna's neck and coincide now and then with the perspective lines of the throne, intersecting on their way key points such as the gloved right hands of the two bishops, so that we have, as it were, invisible anchor lines of perspective which bind together the three panels. What we are struck by is not the foreshortening of the hands or feet, as in the Child, or of objects such as Saint Juvenal's book—this was a skill already known—but rather the deliberate insistence on such foreshortening in order to demonstrate general, fundamental laws: the hands of the Virgin not conceived flatly and in idealized fashion, as in Masolino's Madonna in Bremen, but in two different and thoroughly worked out profile positions; the convincing shelf made by Saint Juvenal's right hand which holds the book; the articulation of Saint Anthony's hand grasping the staff as seen from a frontal plane. What is missing in the triptych, however, is a rhythmic scansion in the foreground-to-background perspective: the pavement is marked by no more than rather unusual perpendicular stripes which are not even parallel to the surface, a way out which Masaccio must have taken in order not to relapse into the old worn-out empirical approach and which is a significant clue to the stage which Brunelleschi would have reached in his research by that year, probably not having as yet succeeded in finding the exact proportions which exist between points in depth.

Brunelleschi's influence is also at work in the treatment of the throne which is no longer merely vertical but is neatly rounded off by horizontal framing. It explains also the unusually wide form of the ogival arches in each of the compartments—indeed, I cannot think of any arch other than that of the central panel here which so clearly recalls the profile of the sections in the cupola which, at that very time, was rising above the cathedral.

As for Donatello, the Virgin—proudly set in the true center of both the breadth and depth of the triptych with a volume which entices the eye to circle its contours and which is contained within the throne as in a niche—is certainly a discreet pictorial equivalent to his own Saint George with which it also has in common the twisting of the contour lines towards the center (as in the right arm and the draperies) and, indeed, even the conception of the head as an ovoid (the laying-out of planes in the head also recalls that in Donatello's Saint Louis). Further, Donatello's marble David anticipates the Madonna here in the complete absence of eyebrows, and there are still other traces of his influence: the scissors-like opening of the Virgin's mantle, the awkward stance of the Child (compare this with Donatello's Isaac for the Campanile), and—again like scissors—the way Saint Juvenal's hand grasps his crosier (compare this with the Saint Louis); what is more, I am certain that the flattened relief of the figure of Saint Juvenal can be explained only by Donatello's relief of Saint George and the Princess, and the head of Saint Juvenal is probably related to that of the Prophet which, precisely at that time, Donatello was sculpting for the Mandorla Door of the cathedral [Figure 11].[139]

Giotto, Brunelleschi, Donatello were the essential factors in the development of Masaccio: Giotto as the base, Brunelleschi and Donatello as the other two sides of that simple but extraordinary triangle which is the "form" of Masaccio. Giotto—whose greatness was beyond dispute for the Florentines—provided the fundamental point of departure; Brunelleschi, the new spatial-harmonic theory which was perhaps the rediscovered ultimate mathematical secret of Antiquity; Donatello, then in the first phase of his sculpture, something like an explosion of multiform energy in which naturalistic and classicizing elements more and more came to dominate vestiges of Gothic expressionism until 1422 (again the crucial date) when in his Saint Louis for the tabernacle of the Palace of the Parte Guelfa he cast in his lot completely with Brunelleschi's Humanism albeit in his own particular version, sentimentally romantic and therefore sometimes anti-classical, pictorially dynamic, expressive of a restless and free imagination (and this too may be relevant to Masaccio's own untrammeled individuality).[140] Both of them, Brunelleschi and Donatello, had returned from their somewhat mysterious but epoch-making visit to Rome as great connoisseurs and coiners of an archaeological vocabulary of images. But it may not have been that vocabulary which intrigued Masaccio most: he adopted it for the Madonna's throne in the Pisa polyptych[141] and perhaps also for the lost side panels but not for the Saints or the predella; in the Carmine it appears only in the painted grooved pilasters which frame the episodes and a little also in the Theophilus fresco; in the *Trinity* of Santa Maria Novella it is much used, but the real influence there was Brunelleschi's new architectural style—the *Trinity* is, in fact, a kind of "homage to Brunelleschi"—and that style was deliberately intended to extend Humanist principles to the visual arts.

Upon analysis, however, the triptych of San Giovenale quite naturally turns out to have other ancestors than the three indicated. Every young artist finds himself in a particular environment, subjected to particular circumstances from which, only little by little, he succeeds in freeing himself by making his own choices and eliminating more and more of the traces of what he has rejected. Those traces remain discernible in those parts of his youthful work not yet remoulded into a personal idiom. This is the case in the triptych, in the left-hand panel which—for all that it is the weakest—is also, for that very reason, the most interesting for what it reveals.

Had that panel alone survived, we should certainly not think of Masaccio but rather of some minor artist in the tradition of Bicci di Lorenzo (compare Figure 20)[142] or even of Giovanni dal Ponte because of the heightened psychological vitality in the rather grim heads with their heavy hair and beards, but even this is more evident in the opposite panel. If nothing else, this gives us an acceptable clue to the stylistic origins of our painter which merits further exploration. In the years between 1417 and 1422 in which we presume Masaccio first came to Florence, the workshop of Bicci di Lorenzo was already one of the most active in the city,[143] turning out pictures for the middle classes and the provinces. It was a flourishing studio which must often have taken on new apprentices who could subsequently build up their own clientele, particularly in the smaller towns outside of Florence. Bicci di Lorenzo, born in 1373, succeeded to his father who belonged essentially to the Orcagna tradition to which the son remained more or less faithful in the *Annunciation* of Porciano (now in Stia) done in 1414. But the two pieces of his triptych dated 1423, now in the museum at Empoli [Figures 18 and 20], show that in the intervening years he had learned something of the slow and more human rhythm Ghiberti had introduced into his first door for the Baptistery. Nor is the Madonna in the central panel at Empoli of negligible quality. She wears a mantle of a fine luminous azure and her flesh is milky-hued. She sits on a throne which at least strives for a certain novelty and a secure construction: its concave back-rest is finished off horizontally like that of the San Giovenale triptych (and, what is more, like that of Ghiberti's two saints in the first door) although there is a compromise with the Gothic in the thin twisted columns. The entire picture, with its throne and figures, has however a more conventional and verticalistic rhythm than our triptych.

Bicci, however, was himself also an architect, the author of the projects for Niccolò da Uzzano's palace in the Via dei Bardi, for the palace intended for the University of Florence, and for the church of Sant'Egidio in 1419. For the old family palace of another magnate, Giovanni di Bicci dei Medici, he executed a fresco series on the Great Men. Certainly he was no supreme master, although his own works must be distinguished from those of his

26 - ADORATION OF THE MAGI (*detail:* horses and grooms) - *Museum* - BERLIN

27-28 - CRUCIFIXION OF SAINT PETER AND BEHEADING OF THE BAPTIST (from the Pisa polyptych) - *Museum* - BERLIN

29 - BEHEADING OF THE BAPTIST (*detail:* the executioner) - *Museum* - BERLIN

various collaborators in the workshop such as Stefano d'Antonio and Bonaiuto di Giovanni, but he was, on the whole, a highly regarded and very active professional painter. Moreover, when one considers the date of his birth, it is clear that he must have been somewhat open to what was new without however really comprehending it, as can be seen in his painted monument for Cardinal Corsini from around 1422 in the Cathedral with its hints of a Humanist approach and of perspective treatment, or in his *Consecration* in Sant'Egidio which is perhaps an early echo of Masaccio's lost fresco on the same subject. Later he came under the influence of Gentile da Fabriano and Fra Angelico and participated, albeit in a minor role, in the work undertaken by Domenico Veneziano in Sant'Egidio where he came to know Piero della Francesca who, ten years later, was to succeed him in painting the chapel of the high altar at San Francesco in Arezzo.[144]

With considerable reservations, I venture to hazard the hypothesis that Masaccio and perhaps also Masolino may have spent some time in Bicci di Lorenzo's workshop, as did in 1421 Andrea di Giusto who later became for a while assistant to Masaccio. If our comparison of the left-hand two saints of Masaccio's triptych with those of Bicci has proved on the whole acceptable, there is also, I think, some hint of past association to be made out in the earliest known work of Masolino, the *Madonna* of 1423 now in Bremen, and the contemporary *Madonna* by Bicci in Empoli [Figures 22 and 18]. The gentle decorative modulations of outlines, the undulation of the gilded hems of the mantles, the long tapering hands stretching out from under the mantles, the doll-like faces of the Virgins, the Infants with their puffy sausage-like flesh, all seem to me to prove a common source, even if Bicci still employs long Gothic lines and, in the Child, a certain angularity in contrast to Masolino's more concentrated, delicate and soft quality. Then too, there is something in common between the expression of one of the personages in Masolino's *Story of Tabitha* in the Carmine and that of one of the apostles in the *Last Supper* in the chapel in Santo Stefano in Empoli which, as indicated in the preceding note, I feel can be attributed to Bicci [Figures 26-27]. For the purposes of our argument, the comparison is obviously not invalidated even if the painting is really by Bicci's helper Stefano d'Antonio. Finally, it seems worth noting that among the apprentices in Bicci's workshop in 1421 we find, along with Andrea di Giusto, one Giovanni da San Giovanni who may well be the young brother of Masaccio as Cohn also believes.[145]

As for the Masaccio of 1422, when one compares the San Giovenale triptych with that of Bicci at Vertine in Chianti from 1430 [Figure 21]—which includes the same personages except for two of the saints—one can measure the abyss which already sets off the youthful work in San Giovenale from the routine level of minor personalities. But if one tries to imagine how Masaccio might have painted even earlier, say in 1417 when he was a lad of sixteen first trying his hand, there is no sacrilege in supposing that his work would run along the lines of, for example, a *Madonna and Child* now in the museum in Warsaw [Figure 24], which is close to Bicci in style but, to judge by the photograph, more energetic and less facile.[146] This has been said, it should be understood, only to indicate a possible direction in the search for the earliest Masaccio and certainly in no way to suggest that work with its unfortunate, clumsy Infant could conceivably be ascribed to Masaccio.

Having presumed that Masaccio may have served his apprenticeship in the workshop of Bicci di Lorenzo, it may be of some value to stop for a wider view of the environment in which painting in Florence at the start of the fifteenth century was produced. True enough, our young painter seems to have preferred his own company, but even negative reactions are meaningful—and perhaps Masaccio's were not all that negative.

Certainly right from the outset our painter was not one to frequent the Monastery of the Angels where the monks made a pious pastime and specialty of executing miniatures and embroidery but where also Don Lorenzo Monaco—who was nevertheless undoubtedly the greatest painter then living in Florence—continued to produce his mystical paintings. Don Lorenzo, like the monks, spun his own kind of ancient precious thread. As had been done throughout the Trecento, he wove together the Florentine tradition with the choicer tradition of Siena, that of the Lorenzettis and of Simone Martini. But the loom he used was new in sentiment and form and his rhythm was fleeter, attuned to the International Gothic style through the widespread diffusion of miniatures. And yet, lines that cut like scythes or flex drawn bows; colors that are clouded or clashing or iridescent as the subtlest veil with never a quiet, normal modulation; steep inverted perspectives, desert-arid rocks, castles like crystal, and churches dredged from dreams; graphic symbols such as those green tufts which represent water; lunar lights and flashes in the night—what else could this provoke in Masaccio (remember, the *Adoration of the Magi* in the Uffizi dates from the fatal year of 1422) but the most clear-cut opposition? What Masaccio sought was not ecstatic visions but, rather, a rationalized view; secular and earthy realism in the unambiguous light of day rather than mystic transport or nocturnal phantasms; physically real and existential plasticity and not the fine-drawn, ultimate spiritual parching of what is material; above all he sought a meter which would serve to scan the true, slow but sovereign harmony of nature. Florentine common sense and the classicistic rationalism of the new culture not only must have alienated Masaccio from the fascination of that melancholy and monkish art but must also have inspired him to the most sharp-tongued blistering rejection of it. If he turned his back on Don Lorenzo, for similar and, indeed, better reasons Masaccio must have found nothing in common, at first at least, with the other coteries, neither with the now aging exponents of the Trecento in Florence nor with the younger group given over to the new-fashioned International Gothic. Agnolo Gaddi and Spinello Aretino were dead as was the crude and clumsy Giovanni del Biondo and also, more recently, Niccolò Gerini. The outworn angular spiky style of the sterile academic followers of Orcagna lingered on in a Lorenzo di Niccolò but somewhat softened and more personal, as well as in the rather more unctuous Mariotto di Nardo. The Master of the Madonnas and the Master of the Straus Madonna and the more provincial Cenno Cenni continued each in his own way the tradition of Gaddi while remaining open, nevertheless, to the new international current. And the aging Ambrogio di Baldese and others like him carried into the new century, in the façade of the Bigallo of 1386 and the Datini Palace in Prato of 1411, a vein of dry narrative-painting whose only worthwhile result was Paolo Uccello's extraordinary frescoes in the Green Cloister. Of the cosmopolitan *nouvelle vague*, the foremost exponent was, naturally, the Master of the Bambino Vispo who, returned probably from Spain, was commissioned in 1422 to do a work for the cathedral of Florence much more important than the San Giovenale triptych which dates from the same year. There was also Alvaro Pires, a Portuguese who came to Pisa, but the new style also affected the sensitive Fossello di Jacopo Franchi, the more formally competent Master of the Griggs Crucifixion, the rather harsh Master of 1419, and the more energetic Giovanni dal Ponte. Nothing better—or at least not for Masaccio—among all the many specialists of non-religious subjects, of narrative painting on marriage chests and birth salvers, or of Triumphs and mythologies and battles and flirtations in gardens: the Master of the Judgment of Paris had the odd habit of painting figures which seem to perch on stilts.[147]

This was the kind of painting most in favor in Florence between 1420 and 1430 (Antal has a sociological explanation for this) and one can understand how isolated Masaccio must have felt. If the only painter with whom he had anything in common was Masolino, we can well imagine what ties of friendship drew them together and what they had to say about their many colleagues of undeniable refinement but today of interest only to the most specialized historians (though history, which tends to see things in crude simplifications, has exalted Masaccio and reduced all the others to minor and often anonymous delights for the erudite). Must we then resign ourselves to believing that the newcomer from the Valdarno had to settle for a stubborn, contemptuous and total isolation, a kind of total void? Such over-simplified notions are always suspect, so we must take a closer look, on the basis of many indications already given by other historians, at Masaccio's origins and at the influences exerted on him.

Starnina, who died between 1409 and 1413, not long before Masaccio came to Florence, no longer seems negligible though much in him remains to be explained despite the knowledge we have acquired in the past thirty years. Only a Berenson with his singular approach to history could completely ignore him, not even mentioning him in the revised edition of his list of Florentine painters. For our part, what we know of Starnina suggests that he may provide one of the most fruitful clues to what can be called the pre-naturalistic phase which we can discern more or less well in Florentine painting prior to Masaccio, that is, between the beginning of the century and 1420 in line with the general European trend (Broederlam worked in the last decade of the fourteenth century). True, Masaccio himself had no need of such antecedents; moreover, his genius did not consist in the invention of naturalism but rather in its systematic transfiguration into something else. In any case, the question arises as to whether the first wave of this new interest in the objective world may not have come to Florence through Starnina in particular who returned from Spain in the very first years of the century, and whether he may not have been the most authoritative exponent of this trend in opposition to Lorenzo Monaco and the others.

Nor are there lacking motives and pretexts to justify our insistence on Starnina. In the first place, according to Vasari, Masolino himself was his pupil, and Vasari's genealogies may well have drawn on well-founded traditions and observations and, in any case, were certainly not haphazard. The more so since in his turn Starnina is said to have been the pupil of Antonio Veneziano, so that the line is that of painting of a particular sensitivity to color and atmosphere ("figures... immersed in transparent air, in a mild azure light"—Toesca said this not of Masolino's work at Empoli but rather of Antonio Veneziano),[148] painting which tells its story with fresh vivacity and is somewhat alien to the tight and narrow Florentine tradition, owing more to its contacts with other regions (Antonio with Northern Italy, Starnina with Spain, and Masolino with Hungary, Rome and Lombardy—and one wonders if perhaps he had not travelled elsewhere before 1423, the year in which he enrolled in the guild in Florence, no longer a young man). Anyone who compares the red-ochre underdrawings, the *sinopias*, of Antonio's tabernacle of the Torre degli Agli with the remaining fragments of those of Starnina in the museum at Empoli [Figure 31] and with those of

30 - BEHEADING OF THE BAPTIST (*detail:* a young soldier) - *Museum* - BERLIN

Masolino at Empoli [Figures 39-42] will observe in all of them the same anti-linear conception which implies that the forms were meant to grow and take on definition through paint laid on in delicate chiaroscuro, without preliminary guiding lines and linear constructions such as were usually employed in Florence.

Here we cannot go into the whole confused question of Starnina. It must suffice to note that if the frescoes in Gaddi's style in the Castellani Chapel in Santa Croce from around 1387 can be considered as a youthful work of Starnina's—Vasari so attributes them but without proof—and if we recall that Gaddi had contacts with Antonio Veneziano and that Starnina was at one time identified with the rather banal "Co-Worker with Agnolo," then it is possible to make sense of the conclusion drawn by Vasari in his biography of that artist, that Starnina was "very hard and rough in his dealings" but after returning from Spain (where documents prove his presence from 1398 to at least 1401) he was transformed into a man both "gentle and courteous"; this personal metamorphosis may well have been reflected in his style. The word "courteous," however, should not be allowed to set us off on a false track. On the sufficiently well-established basis of the remains of his work in the Chapel of Saint Jerome in the Carmine, completed in 1404, Starnina does not appear to indulge in the elegant vagaries of the Late Gothic style. Instead, he shows a solid and clear sense of construction, secure enough to bring into line any analytic and decorative borrowings he may have made from the contemporary manner. Nor is this contradicted by Toesca's vague recollections of the traces surviving until his time of the fresco with Saint Denis on the façade of the Palace of the Parte Guelfa in Florence (apparently painted by Starnina in 1406 when Pisa was taken) which "reveal an extreme Gothic style"; what Toesca saw was no more than a few fragments of the under-drawing with pieces of drapery, scarcely enough evidence for a stylistic judgment.[149] The surviving fragments in the Carmine are more reliable [Figures 28-30]. The saints' figures are conceived somewhat perpendicularly; the architectonic perspectives of their tabernacles are complicated but precise; their heads are drawn in foreshortening from below; objects such as the lily-banner striped by the shadow of Saint Reparata are accurately rendered and well colored; hands have firm grasp and eyes are penetrating; and there is throughout a pictorial sense which attenuates the hardness of the drawing. From the two engravings by D'Agincourt we can learn something of the lost frescoes of the life of Saint Jerome [Figure 29]: buildings drawn in empirical perspective but fulfilling adequately their scenic function; attention to psychology; portraits of contemporaries among the figures; a treatment of opulent drapery which rivals that of Lorenzo Monaco. However, unlike the latter's practice, everything here is treated with an intensity appropriate to its naturalism (of the surviving fragment with Saint Jerome's bookshelf I will not go so far as to say that it represents a deliberate programmatic position as does a later painting in Brussels, the *Jeremiah* by the Master of the Annunciation of Aix). The episode of the school-master spanking the child who rides piggy-back (described by Vasari) was to be taken up again by Gozzoli in San Gimignano. The sources have this to say:

And because he had dwelt for some time in Spain and France, he depicted in the said chapel certain fashions in garments of those countries [Billi], with very happy invention and an abundance of fashions and ideas in the attitudes of the figures... *Gherardo appears to have delighted in these touches of nature*... the works which he did there at S. Girolamo greatly pleased the Florentines, because he had expressed in a lively manner many gestures and attitudes which had not been attempted by any painter before his time [Vasari].

If asked to pin down the stage reached by Starnina at the Carmine, by analogy at least I would name Broederlam as the boundary *post quem* and Hubert van Eyck and the Master of Flémalle as the other *ante quem*, although it was Spain, not Burgundy or Flanders, that Starnina visited, and this is in itself typically Florentine. In this regard, Coletti wrote that "his deepest inspiration was probably the great example of Maso, and it is understandable that he should have opened the way to Masaccio."[150] This is even more understandable today, on the basis of the San Giovenale triptych, when we can compare Masaccio's Saint Anthony Abbot with the same saint by Starnina in the Carmine, however fragmentary the remains [Figure 28], or Starnina's Saint Benedict [Figure 30] with the younger painter's Saints Blaise and Bartholomew: there is much alike in the hands, the archaic but already logically conceived drapery, the books, and the like.

As for the *Thebaid* in the Uffizi, in his study of 1940 Longhi pointed out the Masaccio-like character of certain details. But despite that scholar's customary keen insight and despite the obstinate insistence of certain among his most die-hard admirers, the *Thebaid* is certainly not to be ascribed to the Fra Angelico of 1420 who was the first to incorporate into his art the lessons learned from Masaccio. A bit farther on we shall consider the first true productions of Fra Angelico in their proper chronological place according to the most recent studies. However, here already we must ask if anyone can still believe it possible to attribute the *Thebaid* to a Masaccio-influenced Angelico (whose luminous chromaticism is so different from this and whose feeling for perspective is so much more profound) or if it would not be more reasonable to relate it to the Starnina frescoes in the Carmine as has been done so convincingly by Procacci. In my humble opinion, the *Thebaid* is probably a late work by Starnina from around 1405 to 1413, a work which had notable and demonstrable influence in its time as, for one, in the illustrations of his voyages by Fra Pietro della Croce, now in

Buffalo, which are dated 1417, a very embarassing date for certain historians' theses. A work such as the *Thebaid*, which Lanzi thought should be attributed to Pietro Lorenzetti and Berenson to Maso di Banco,[151] is obviously not yet in the style of Masaccio nor is it any kind of foredestined prelude to him in particular; rather, it is better understood as a bridge between the greatest Tuscan painting of the early fourteenth century and that of Florence in the fifteenth century. Paolo Uccello, who has been presumed to be a pupil of Starnina, certainly learned from this unique painting with its masterful depiction of animals and nature, and so did Fra Angelico. This is significant precisely because it shows a certain continuity between the two great centuries, a certain fidelity to a Florentine tradition. And finally I believe that Starnina must have played an important role at the beginning of the fifteenth century in establishing that bridge, a bridge which Masaccio and his most immediate successors in the drastic renewal of art, men like Castagno, eventually felt strong enough to burn behind them but which had been, nevertheless, of the greatest utility to the development and progress of Florentine art.[152]

There is, however, another hypothesis which is not without its points, although it is less and less favored today: that of the influence of Arcangelo di Cola da Camerino. Little is known for sure about his life.[153] Documents exist for the years between 1416 and 1429. In 1420 and 1421 he was in Florence, at the beginning of 1422 he left for Rome at the invitation of Pope Martin V. Had he already developed in 1400-21 a leavening and luminous chiaroscuro like that of the Emilian painters which could have been taken over, transformed and used by Masolino and passed on by him to Masaccio?[154] The triptych of San Giovenale of 1422, a date close to that when Arcangelo was in Florence, does not show any evidences of this nor even of any characterization of the personages resembling Arcangelo's; the figure of Saint Juvenal, which shows most modeling and chiaroscuro, is sufficiently explained as a re-interpretation of Giotto's color harmonies plus the relief technique of Donatello with its attention to light-catching surfaces.

Indeed, one suspects that things took place the other way around. On the basis of the only work by Arcangelo for which we possess a definite date, the triptych of the Monastery dell'Isola from 1425 which has been burned but is known from photographs, his other surviving works all seem to belong to a later period, between 1425 and 1430 at least, when he would have returned to Tuscany and come under the influence of Gentile and been affected by the first innovations of Masaccio and Masolino. Without attempting to untangle the confused state of the list of works attributed to him—which has turned out even to include paintings by Bicci di Lorenzo and Domenico di Michelino—we can limit ourselves to noting the resemblances between the Frick diptych and the very similar Madonna in Bibbiena; in these the influences of Gentile and Masaccio are obvious, and in the triptych in Mexico City and the Cassirer tabernacle the influence of Masaccio seems more marked. These are, in fact, the best of Arcangelo, still cautiously exploiting the florid Gothic but of a progressively finer taste. When he attempts more obviously to speak Masaccio's language with the dialect of Trecento Rimini, as in the predella in Modena, the results are certainly not very brilliant.

But in the same year of 1422 that the triptych of San Giovenale was painted, there arrived in Florence the greatest modern painter Italy of that time could boast of: Gentile da Fabriano.[155] And yet, as far as concerns Masaccio, what came of this was no more than a distant contact which remained without sequel, or perhaps even, to put it bluntly, a firmly negative reaction.

Born around 1370, Gentile was at the height of his maturity and prestige in 1422. Behind him were his works for the Ducal Palace in Venice and the Broletto of Brescia as well as an invitation to Rome from Martin V. In addition, he had a vast experience which ran from copies from the Antique to the most recent miniature painting of Europe, and he had assimilated everything that contemporary Italian art had to offer. Thus, concealed in the garments of one of his angels we can find a maenad from some sarcophagus, a female saint is dressed in the latest fashion, and the range of his citations and allusions is as immense as are the multiple but perfectly synthesized combinations he draws from them. The *Adoration of the Magi*, for example,

is a work of extraordinary complexity which brings together the most advanced experiments of Italian painting of those years, and what is especially notable is the seemingly effortless skill with which this painter from the Marches incorporates into his own language elements from Lombardy (the women behind the Virgin), from Siena (the Holy Family derives from Taddeo di Bartolo) and from elsewhere, a skill which points to a gift for synthesis—in his aspirations towards a style which would no longer be merely regional—which, if not equal, is certainly similar to that which was later to distinguish his countrymen Raphael and Bramante [Arslan].

His contemporaries, unlike us, knew not only his religious paintings but also his portraits, narrative scenes and even a storm scene. Alongside him stood not only a Jacopo Bellini but also the young genius Pisanello. Gentile: that his very name speaks of that affable and most aristocratic art, courteous and courtly in every sense, is not the random reflection of a modern writer like Piero Bargellini but of "the divine Michelangelo who, in speaking of Gentile, used to say that his hand in painting corresponded to his name" [Vasari].

31 - CRUCIFIXION OF SAINT PETER (*detail:* one of the executioners hammering) - *Museum* - BERLIN

32 - BEHEADING OF THE BAPTIST (*detail:* a soldier looking on) - *Museum* - BERLIN

If the greatest and most superbly severe and laconic descendant of Masaccio could pay homage to Gentile, in conversation with his friend Vasari in sixteenth-century Rome when the historical appreciation of art of the past was in its infancy, it is not surprising that a man of great worth such as Palla Strozzi himself should have turned his attention to this celebrated master from outside Florence of whom the Pope himself must have spoken with admiration when he was a guest at Santa Maria Novella. Palla Strozzi, the father-in-law of Felice Brancacci, Masaccio's patron, was an enthusiast for Classical culture, but besides the fact that in 1422 Masaccio was still a very young and unknown beginner, the idea of a puritanical and therefore, logically, pure art could not yet even have been imagined, as is proved by the entire trend of European painting of the time.

History is not conditioned only by isolated factors but also by precise temporal successions. This explains why even Antal[156] was more attentive to the play of the complex social stratifications affecting taste than to the tidy course of historical time which itself is subject to the whims and conditions of artists and their patrons. It so happens that 1422 was a year of exceptional prosperity for Florence resulting from the events of the preceding year when Livorno was purchased and the Magistrature of the Sea instituted. In that same year, 1422, the Count of Urbino was created a Florentine citizen, a distinction sought at that time by many Italian lords and which testifies to the high prestige of the Republic which now, like ancient Rome, could confer citizenship as a high honor on the great feudal aristocracy. It was an especially propitious year for dreaming of faraway places (the Orient where maritime interests hoped to find new trade outlets) and, likewise, for dreams of chivalry such as hover over the *Adoration* of Santa Trinita—and to commission such an exceptionally sumptuous work. It was completed in May of the following year, 1423, when the situation began to worsen with the beginning of the war with Francesco Maria Visconti. It is true that the Quaratesi polyptych was finished in May of 1425 after the rout of Zagonara of the preceding summer, but it is also a fact that Gentile left Florence in 1425, probably because, among other reasons, he could no longer find there a steady and thriving market. Perhaps also, besides the fact that Lorenzo Monaco died, there may have been a need for economic retrenchment which would explain why he did no more than the cusps and predella for the triptych the Strozzis had ordered for the sacristy of Santa Trinita as a companion-piece to Gentile's *Adoration* (the work was finally completed by Fra Angelico as a *Deposition*). As Procacci has remarked,[157] it was probably no longer considered good taste to display one's wealth in those troubled times of the Republic, even if Palla Strozzi himself did own one-sixth of the total patrimony of Florence as the tax registers of 1427 show.

Gentile was, in fact, a painter for plutocrats. It is more than probable that the cost of the *Adoration* must have exceeded considerably the 150 florins (equivalent to several million lire today) which the documents show, since it was executed with the most lavish care and Gentile's fees were already high. This is the more likely since we know that Palla Strozzi was still in debt to Gentile for those 150 florins after the picture was finished, which suggests that Gentile had been receiving large sums on account to cover his expenses while in Florence. Gold on embroideries, on objects, on ornaments, even on lozenge-shaped designs to bring out their relief and to create a greater illusion of realism; horses, dogs, apes, camels, leopards, birds; clusters of flowers on the pilasters; corteges, fields, castles, cities, watercourses, ships; nocturnal scenes or sunlight realized in gold, streaming over the countryside; city squares; turbans, brocades, gowns with flowing trains... Gentile dazzled the Florentines with an art unfamiliar in the homeland of Giottesque austerity, a treasure of naturalistic observation of the modes and manners of a more cosmopolitan society. That shortly afterwards Masaccio should have triumphed appears so much the more a virtually miraculous victory of the spiritual element—aided, of course, by the Milanese menace from outside and by the heavy tax burdens within. Certainly the Florentines never got over their nostalgia for Gentile's kind of art which left its mark even on a Fra Angelico, a Domenico Veneziano and on the minor painters of marriage chests; thirty and more years later, under the Medicis, Gozzoli was to take up again the gold and polychrome thread. But by then the frescoes of Masaccio stood on the walls of the Carmine as a silent warning, more meaningful to the painters than any sermon or any sumptuary laws. By that lesson in austerity fixed in a masterwork, even Botticelli, Ghirlandaio, Filippino Lippi were to be held in check a little, and Florence never produced a Crivelli or a Pinturicchio. On the other hand, was the lavish splendor of the *Adoration* no more than a mirror held up to the self-illusions of chivalry, to the vanity of the *jeunesse dorée* of the Florentine nobility and upper middle classes? Or was it not also somewhat the expression of the (so to speak) imperialist functions that had been assigned to artistic manifestations in Florence?[158] Palla Strozzi was not alien to such reasons which appealed not only to his personal pride and his pride of caste but also to his sense of patriotism. And there remains the fact that it was in Florence and not elsewhere that Gentile was able to paint this most splendid and most accomplished among all of his works.

The whole question of the credits and debits of Gentile's sojourn in Florence is, moreover, complicated and far from clear, and is so much the worse for *a priori* attempts to ferret out a supposed influence of Masaccio and Masolino on Gentile, an influence which was probably nonexistent or, at best, feeble in view of the relative immaturity of both of them up to at

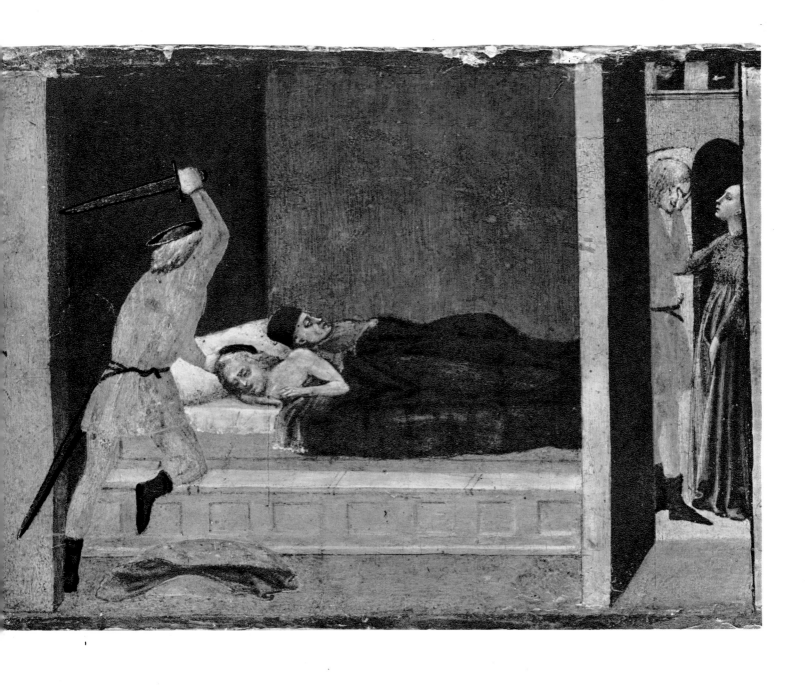

33 - CRIME OF SAINT JULIAN (from the Pisa polyptych) - *Museum* - BERLIN

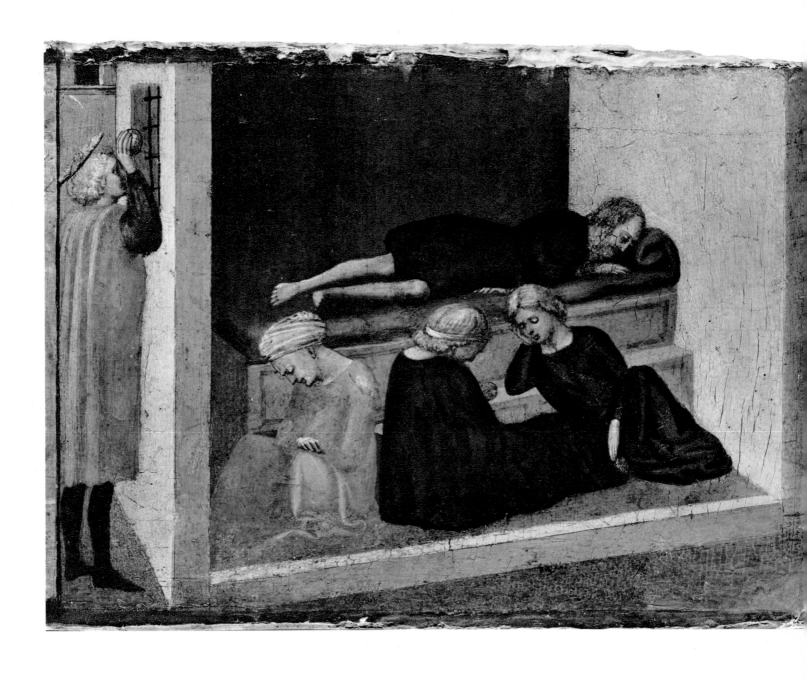

34 - SAINT NICHOLAS AND THE THREE GIRLS (from the Pisa polyptych) - *Museum* - BERLIN

least the end of 1424. The delicate flowers on the small pilasters of the *Adoration* may have been suggested by the way Ghiberti at that time was framing the first door of the Baptistery, and Ghiberti may have inspired the flowing and well-balanced rhythmic feeling in the small Prophets in the cusps (in which there is good reason to note an influence on Masolino but not vice versa). But point-by-point demonstrations and confrontations are problematical with a personality as strong as that of Gentile, and it would be wisest to limit oneself to the supposition that the general atmosphere of Florence, with its classicizing and rationalistic trends, may have aided him to discard his Gothic traits and to modernize his style somewhat. An influence of the sculpture around the principal door of the Cathedral can be discerned in the perhaps contemporary monumental *Madonna* in New York, despite the little angels, the singing birds and the fretwork throne with its florid back-rest. Further, the scrolls of the small Prophets in the *Adoration* have Humanist lettering, as do Masaccio's inscriptions in San Giovenale and Masolino's in the Bremen *Madonna;* these are the first three Italian pictures in which such characters appear, and this trait relates them to the same Florentine Humanist circle.

The *Adoration* was probably the most advanced picture in all of Italy at the end of 1422, and Gentile's limits in it are limits that only the radical extremism of Masaccio was capable of smashing through. The *Adoration* is not lacking in modern elements but its weakness —relative to the Renaissance and to history in general—lies in its failure to make a decisive break with the great line of tradition. Thus, despite all its treatment of depth, the excellence and abundance of its animal studies, facial types, illustrative episodes, foreshortenings and the like, there remains a Gothic ambiguity in its treatment of space and a Gothic technique of construction based on the addition of quantities; moreover, a two-dimensional approach prevails in the soft modulation which weakens the sense of volume and tends, rather, to draw the eye to the surface calligraphy. The ultimate ideal of such art is Gothic tapestry: the only animal missing from the *Adoration* but completely symbolic of the work itself, of the attitude of the painter and of the taste of the patron, is—precisely—the peacock. Renaissance painting was to be quite different, with its illusion of deep projection, its carefully worked out subordination rather than coordination of all elements (as Grassi has said) with everything clearly stated: the aim was to be to "make a hole in the wall," as it has been defined, and not merely to decorate the wall. This is *trompe d'oeil,* perhaps, but with all the moral significance of a window opened up on reality: history and no longer fable. The only animal that, for their part, Masaccio and his friends could take as a symbol was *homo sapiens.* In a certain sense, it might even be said, as Battisti declared recently, that Masaccio and Gentile stand for the two contrasting aspects of Florentine life: "the opposition between public morality and private morality." [159] Gentile would thus be, in sentiment at least, a symbol of domestic intimacy with all its stubborn respect for tradition: walls paneled in warm-toned wood or frescoed to imitate patterned cloth or green gardens, adorned sometimes with tapestries or leather, in rooms where furniture and beautiful objects were crowded in comfortable promiscuity. Masaccio, on the other hand, is like the unadorned geometrical severity of palace-fronts which show blind lozenged faces to the city's eyes, like public life and public duties, like the ideal principles which served to guide the city itself.

Masaccio versus Gentile? Perhaps there is some point in saying that the Santa Trinita *Adoration* was the principal inspiration for the *Adoration* from the Pisa predella [Plates 24-25]—but in a negative sense only. This, says Masaccio, is how an Adoration of the Magi should really be painted: broad space accurately set down but nude and desolate; the cortege reduced to the minimum with no more than two pages for each King, one to stand by him and the other to watch the horses; the Holy Family solitary and proud with the Madonna, perhaps against her will, made to sit on a gilded folding-chair brought by the Kings instead of on the Family's own uncomfortable pack-saddle; the ox and ass in the stall intent on what concerns them, backs turned to the scene; no crowding together to give the illusion of a great throng but instead a clear and spacious disposition of the figures; long shadows cast by the sun to indicate a precise time of day; and the two bourgeois in their gray capes who directly sum up the social level of the picture—sober, practical-minded, matter-of-fact people. Not that there are lacking saddles in ivory, gold objects, fur-trimmed garments, but what dominates is an extreme simplicity. Perhaps in 1426 Palla Strozzi, like his son-in-law Brancacci, may have come to understand that this type of painting was much closer to the conciseness of Classical languages, to the concentration typical of Antique art as known from sarcophagi, and indeed to Republican Neo-Stoicism.

Disdainfully proud in his rented half of a workshop, there was nothing that Masaccio could have cared to borrow from the great Gentile (for Masolino, the case was different) except perhaps the detail of the veil stretched—but with utmost logic—across the brow of the Sant'Ambrogio Madonna which recalls that of the Quaratesi Madonna which at that very time Gentile was painting for Masaccio's own parish, or ex-parish, of San Niccolò.[160] As a matter of fact, the Sant'Ambrogio painting, the so-called *Metterza Saint Anne*, seems to me precisely a challenging reply, even before the Pisa *Madonna*,[161] to that second masterpiece executed for Florence by Gentile [Figure 15]. Plasticity as against linear treat-

35 - PRAYER IN THE GARDEN and SAINT JEROME PENITENT - *Lindenau Museum* - ALTENBURG

ment and shaded volumes, solid substance as against gentle rhythms, closed rectangular masses in projection as against delicate calligraphy incised on a background of precious patterned velvet, the pride of commonfolk as against an aristocratic dream-world, decisive gestures and firm grips as against languid bloodless hands, throats capable of speech as against necks burnished like ivory, bulging eyeballs... Even of the Infant's sex there may be more to say than that "it certainly must have made a great impression in its time, but after all it is no more than an iconographic detail of minor importance" (Brandi); as a matter of fact, it has all the impact of a vulgar word, though less scandalous for being spoken of a child, but that child is something more than the primped-up grimacing princeling who sits on the lap of the Quaratesi Madonna.

Not that Gentile hesitated to depict a naked child; it was he who exploited this motif in Florence, even if he himself did not import it, as can be seen in the *Madonna* in New Haven.[162] Relevant to this is a sheet of drawings in Bayonne by Gentile's pupil and friend Pisanello with a sketch of an antique Dionysiac torso which may have been employed by Gentile for the *Adoration* and in which I have finally located the most probable source of the Infants eating grapes Masaccio painted at San Giovenale and Pisa; the drawing [Figure 12] was of some antique sarcophagus or paleo-Christian mosaic with nude Amors harvesting grapes.[163] So Gentile, with his baggage of bits of Classical sculpture and sketchbooks, would have had no reason to frown at such iconographic innovations. However, even when he painted assassins in a detail of the *Adoration* or beggars in the predella, his attitude was not that of a forthright and novel realism such as Masaccio's, and such figures, like the rest of his painting, are tinged with the old air of fable and legend.

But even setting aside the paintings for Sant'Ambrogio and Pisa, it is absolutely certain that Masaccio made still another reply to the Quaratesi polyptych and in the same church of San Niccolò, although some time later I think. Anyone who has noticed how "a dense and heavy shadow" (Grassi) falls across the green Majolica-tiled paving behind the four saints in Gentile's polyptych [Figure 16] shutting off all spatial depth so that the elegant figures seem blocked forever at its edge; anyone who has admired the admirably worked cope of the Saint Nicholas of which Gentile seems to say: "this is what painting is—a limning on gold-leaf, a precious embroidery, a fiction all on the surface from which you must not ask any useless and unnatural excess of depth, whether spatial or objective or ethical..."; anyone who has looked at the very beautiful dream-like episodes of the predella (which at the start of our century Schmarsow took to be by Masaccio), especially the pilgrims and invalids at the tomb of Saint Nicholas whose extreme subtlety has been beautifully pointed out by Longhi;

36 - PRAYER IN THE GARDEN (*detail:* the bitter cup) - *Lindenau Museum* - ALTENBURG

37 - SAINT JEROME PENITENT (*detail:* the saint and the angel) - *Lindenau Museum* - ALTENBURG

anyone, I say, who knows these things should turn his imagination to an attempt at reconstruction of the lost *Annunciation* by Masaccio which once adorned the same church.

Such an attempt would inevitably refute Longhi's hypothesis that the lost painting was nothing else than what is now known as the Goldman *Annunciation* by Masolino. Here is how Vasari describes the lost painting:

> ...besides an Annunciation, there is a house full of columns beautifully drawn in perspective. Besides the drawing of the lines, which is perfect, he shaded off his colours so that they are gradually lost to sight, a fact which proves him the master of perspective.

This is exactly what we should expect from a Masaccio so steadfastly opposed to Gentile, as Parronchi has seen very clearly;[164] this is also what we are led to expect on the basis of the birth salver in Berlin [Plate 75] which also has much in common with the stupendous *Annunciation* crowning Piero della Francesca's polyptych in Perugia [Figure 13]. These were what that rugged Florentine Masaccio, who started out virtually with a *tabula rasa*, turned out as his reply to Gentile and even to the first marvels of lighting and perspective of Flemish painting: the new Renaissance-style architecture sweeping out in all its magnificence to invade space with its wedge of perfect perspective; natural daylight shining forth as a symbol of a new and positive attitude towards life and blinding out the pallid luster of a Gentile. It was in this way that the obscure apprentice turned " architect and sculptor in paint" triumphed over that "wonder-working floriculturist and weaver in colour" (Grassi)—and it was a triumph of the austerity of the Florentine State with its dedication to Humanist culture over that private Florence which still dallied in over-refined and languid dreams of the past.

True, it was one of Gentile's specialties to make evanescent figures like those angels in Siena

> painted... with a color so transparent and thin and with such delicate contours in Siena yellow that, if anyone looked at them without fixing his gaze, he would not make out even the things openly represented [Tizio, 1425].[165]

However, the fading into distance Vasari remarked on in Masaccio's *Annunciation* was another kind of optical marvel, one of rational character conceived according to aerial perspective. Perhaps, as Parronchi supposes, it was a matter "of the effect described, as examples, in Theorem 109 of Book IV of Vitellione's *Perspectiva*, according to which, when an object is struck by strong reflected light, another object placed close to it will seem to be a continuation of the first object *propter reflexionem lucis fretae ab illis corporibus quae non permittit eorum distantiam discerni.*"

38 - MADONNA AND CHILD - *Palazzo Vecchio* (Collection of works returned from Germany) - FLORENCE

39 - EXPULSION FROM PARADISE
Church of the Carmine - FLORENCE

But by that time Gentile had left Florence, perhaps was already dead if the date of Masaccio's lost *Annunciation* really falls around 1427 or later, as its apparently full maturity suggests. In this mute and negative encounter between Gentile and Masaccio, two geniuses who had no language in common with which to communicate, exponents of two cultural generations in arms against one another, there is one truly curious and poignant aspect: their common end on the soil of Papal Rome within one year of each other, and with Masaccio perhaps still hoping to succeed Gentile at San Giovanni in Laterano. And in the *Baptist* in London [Plate 78] executed during Masaccio's last days in Rome, with its wasted and hirsute but still energetic prophet who anticipates the ascetic figures of Donatello, there is yet another occasion to contrast the *sans-culotte* Masaccio with the aristocrat Gentile if one recalls, as Masaccio certainly did, the melancholy Baptist Gentile painted for San Niccolò [Figure 16]. But if the ground on which Masaccio's figure stands is flowered—something Gentile especially loved and which shows his influence—it is nevertheless so irregular that the Saint's foot must stretch its tendons to implant itself. Out of that nucleus of concentration on the essential which was Masaccio's main resource against the most dangerous opponent of the Renaissance who went so far as to dare to invade Florence, heart of the Renaissance, there had by the time of this painting been developed the Florentine science of the anatomy of physical movement: it was clear to whom, in the long run, would go the victory... even though Gentile left behind a vast reign with countless faithful subjects, and even though the river-nymphs dear to the Humanists shed floods of tears over his tomb in Santa Maria Nuova in Rome— which was certainly more than they did for that difficult, grave, and even discourteous and pushy young Masaccio.

There is another name to be considered, however, the name traditionally linked with Masaccio's as his teacher: Masolino.[166] But it should be remembered that more than twenty years ago Longhi quite accurately pointed out that Vasari never did state flatly that such a relationship ever existed, not mentioning it in his biography of Masolino where one might have expected it to be stressed, and in that of Masaccio himself saying no more than that "he began to practise at the time when Masolino da Panicale was engaged upon the Chapel of the Brancacci in the Carmine of Florence, and he followed as closely as possible in the footsteps of Filippo and Donato, although his art was different." This indicates only that they were contemporaries, a perfectly obvious fact since they worked on the same scaffolding, and that Masaccio's real teachers were Brunelleschi and Donatello.[167] Recently Procacci has, with reason I think, taken up again the hypothesis already put forward by Repetti

40 - BAPTISM OF THE NEOPHYTES (*detail:* the two youths) - *Church of the Carmine* - FLORENCE

41 - BAPTISM OF THE NEOPHYTES - *Church of the Carmine* - FLORENCE

and by Magherini-Graziani that Masolino was not a native of Panicale in the Valdelsa, as Vasari states, but of the manor-lands of Panicale which are part of the zone called Renacci in the territory of San Giovanni Valdarno:[168]

It is therefore logical to think that already in his childhood—it is well known at what a tender age boys were recruited for the masters' workshops—Masaccio may have been placed as an apprentice with his already famous compatriot who would certainly not have overlooked the natural gifts of the lad. This also explains the continuous lifelong collaboration between the painters of different ages and of diverse artistic aims but linked together by that love which binds together people who come from the same place, especially when they have left behind their tranquil birthplace for the restless life of a big city.

In any event, likely as is, in general, this solidarity between compatriots—"men of Valdarno as we both are, we should help each other"—it can be demonstrated more precisely. Did Masolino really teach Masaccio how to prepare colors? Or could they not both have learned in the same workshop (Bicci's perhaps, as we have suggested) or Masaccio elsewhere? Why did Masolino not take Masaccio with him to Hungary? One thing certain however since the discovery of the San Giovenale triptych is that already by 1422-1423 the two had set off on profoundly different paths: Masaccio was as we have described him, and Masolino was as we find him in the Bremen *Madonna* [Figure 22], a very beautiful work but of quite different character. And since the Bremen painting, by virtually general agreement, is the earliest certain work of Masolino's known so far, then the attempt on the part of German art historians to discover among the paintings of Masolino the *Frühwerke* of Masaccio, basing themselves on the presumptive results of stylistic analysis, can be eliminated once and for all. From at least as early as 1422, Masaccio can no longer be confused with Masolino.[169]

There is something else these two do have in common: the early influences on each of them are so obscure that not even the documents and under-drawings discovered by Procacci have cleared up the problem. In 1423, when Masolino painted the Bremen *Madonna* (for the Carnesecchi family for whom he later did the triptych of Santa Maria Maggiore)[170] and enrolled in the Guild of Doctors and Pharmacists, he was already forty years old. Of what he had done in those forty years we know nothing beyond Vasari's statement that he helped Ghiberti on the first door for the Baptistery (and this even is controversial) and that he was a pupil of Starnina and, finally, that his father was a house-painter.[171] And yet in the Bremen *Madonna* and the remains of the frescoes of the following year in Empoli Masolino is already the Masolino we know: Gentile da Fabriano, Masaccio, the general progress in culture add no more than external traits to a nucleus which appears from the first fundamentally original and well set.

66

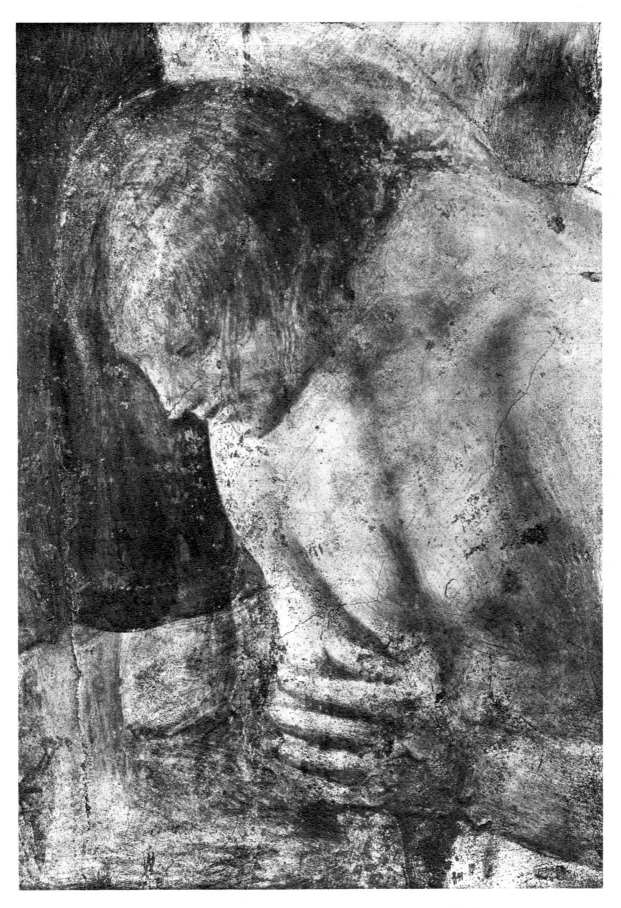

42 - BAPTISM OF THE NEOPHYTES (*detail:* the baptized man) - *Church of the Carmine* - FLORENCE

In relation to contemporary painting in Florence, the position of the Bremen *Madonna* is just as eccentric, though in a different way, as that of Masaccio's work in San Giovenale. In the carefully modulated line which profiles the meditative image and heightens the elegance of the winding borders of the draperies, Masolino has very little in common with Lorenzo Monaco and the others, despite the iconographic derivation, including the cushion. In the Child with his little bottom exposed by the shirt, and in the tender Madonna, the naturalistic aspect is clear-cut, out of the ordinary and even bold, rendered with much grace and simplicity. Chiaroscuro is used to achieve a soft plasticity in harmony with the forms set in profile, avoiding spiky projections and foreshortenings. All this is quite different from Masaccio's Madonna in San Giovenale. The light in Masolino's painting is warm, rosy tints even touch the cheeks of the Christ in the cusp of the frame, the vari-patterned ground is not based on perspective lines, the cushion is virtually pure contour, and even the Humanistic letters of the inscription are very much rounder and softer than the higher, thicker and more varied letters of Masaccio.

In the Chapel of the Cross in Santo Stefano at Empoli, executed in 1424, the red ochre under-drawings and the few surviving fragments of fresco suffice to prove that Masolino was already the novel and fascinating narrator he later showed himself in San Clemente in Rome and at Castiglione Olona [Figures 39-42].[172] On the lateral walls at least, there seems to have been a sort of high plinth and figured on it some kind of portico or crypt with double arcades seen straight on [Figure 42], treated in perspective with its colonnades. Beneath this there seems to have been shown the kneeling members of the confraternity which commissioned the chapel.[173] This was a remarkable invention, and although it is less worked out, as well as placed at the base instead of above, it is analogous to the portico in the *Annunciation* on the outside of the chapel in San Clemente in Rome and, in a way, also anticipated the painted altar in Masaccio's *Trinity* at Santa Maria Novella in Florence [Plate 67]. This seemingly three-dimensional plinth must have lent a sense of depth even to the fresco above it. In the fresco, the surviving under-drawings reveal edifices of simplified, anti-Gothic structure treated in perspective, cone-shaped mountains at the horizon like those in the painting of the *Foundation of Santa Maria Maggiore* now in Naples, and figures linear but elegant in type: in the scene of the testing of the Cross [Figure 41] the women wear the long trains fashionable then in Lombardy. The Beheading of Chosroes [Figure 40] is quite similar to the Beheading of Saint Catherine in San Clemente, except that in the latter the chiaroscuro is more obvious and softer as compared with that of the under-drawing where it is thinner. Comparison with Agnolo Gaddi's cycle on the same subject in Santa

Croce reveals an enormous difference, even in iconography: Masolino's scenes are concentratedly simplified without the abundance of details and angular formalism of Gaddi, and Masolino's softer treatment is evident in the few fragments of fresco remaining on the under-arch of the entrance and on the small window [Figure 14]. Chosroes' executioner extends his left leg and arm to direct and balance the blow, and the hand is seen in foreshortening, which indicates keen observation of reality.

A dangerous and even heretical question therefore presents itself: in these works, are we not perhaps on the threshold of the Renaissance? There can be no doubt that in the fresco cycle at Empoli there is a new sense of space which is unlike the preceding static approximation typical of Gothic style and which, if not yet in measured perspective, is at least a dynamic approach to perspective (the effect is heightened, moreover, by the painted plinth). There is also a much warmer naturalistic verisimilitude if one thinks of the spring-like light-blue airiness in the two surviving circular frescoes with female portraits. And there is a new feeling for the human figure which is seen with fresh eyes liberated from the preceding Gothic formulas. The very fine female heads are set in typically Renaissance circular tondos [174] in which the volumes of the faces themselves create a feeling of space explored in all its extension and in which the material appears like a light and pleasing concentration of a cosmic atmospheric vitality. In these there is apparent the creation of a new type of mirroring of nature unknown in even the most effusive and sensuous paintings of the Trecento, a mirroring *sui generis*, not aiming for effect but purely intuitive.[175] So even Masolino's procedures, however modest, delicate and ingenuous they may seem, appear to cast off the past and seek for some kind of regeneration. To be sure, they differ markedly from Masaccio's at San Giovenale, for the younger painter provides firmly tightened structures for his new world, clear-cut expositions, inexorably sharp images. With Masolino however, as can be seen also in the fine under-drawings of the vault with their figures that dissolve in tenderness, both sweet and free, his first intuition of the future seems to have been that of a light and a space suffused with ethereal but vital particles of matter, in which the beings depicted are nothing more than condensations of these particles in single creatures which move us precisely because of their gentle and ephemeral configurations seeming to flower in the soft breath of a cosmic zephyr. Indeed, no paintings are more springlike than those of this chapel dedicated to the True Cross, the symbol which is repeated over and over from the vaults to the entry arch and which is carried by each of the saints; in the hands of a Lorenzo Monaco it might well have expressed something different, an obsessive contrition. Perhaps it was also in such aspects that the world could be viewed with fresh eyes, with

43 - STORY OF TABITHA (*detail:* the street in foreshortening) - *Church of the Carmine* - FLORENCE

44 - STORY OF TABITHA (*detail:* the houses on the piazza) - *Church of the Carmine* - FLORENCE

45 - THE TRIBUTE MONEY (*detail:* Saint Peter paying the tax collector) - *Church of the Carmine* - FLORENCE

46 - THE TRIBUTE MONEY - *Church of the Carmine* - FLORENCE

the freshness that was to be thenceforth the common aspiration of the times and which is seen here as a kind of gentle pictorial optimism, a dawning though still primitive impressionism, a spatial metaphysics both humble and Arcadian. True, this is not yet Masaccio's style, but perhaps it is something more—or in another sense less—than the true International Gothic style of Gentile, Pisanello, Michelino, Stefano or the Salimbenis who were still wandering in the nocturnal shadow of the refined and tortuous Gothic dream. It has no exact equivalent in the various naturalistic trends in Europe at that time, because the fundamental base of Masolino remains still the ancient sober essentiality of Florence's Giotto. When one thinks of what Masolino was doing in 1423 and 1424, one cannot escape the conclusion that, even if Masaccio had died at San Giovenale in 1422, Masolino's subsequent work at the Carmine, in Rome, in Castiglione Olona would not have been much different. But did he owe his initial impetus to the earliest works of Masaccio and perhaps even to Gentile's arrival on the scene? To me at least it seems so. Not that one would wish to equate his sensitive, thoughtful and empirical intuition with Masaccio's forward-looking iron control and systematic procedures, his decisive and lucid deliberate self-affirmation. But if Masolino was still caught up in a dream, it was an early morning dream and like such dreams so much the more realistic. Masolino's position at the threshold of the Renaissance was glimpsed even by Vasari who as early as 1550 remarked that it was "in many respects wholly foreign to the manner of Giotto" and who, in the second edition, added no new information but, significantly, some further reflections:

I have frequently examined Masolino's works, and have found his style very different from that of his predecessors... Masolino further introduced a softer air into the faces of his women, and gave brighter clothes to his youths... and he was fairly skillful in perspective. But the matter in which he chiefly excelled was coloring in fresco, his paintings being colored and shaded with such grace that the flesh-tints possess an indescribable beauty. If he had been a perfect designer... he would have been numbered among the greatest.[176]

With this interpretation of Masolino in mind, there is no reason to delve more deeply into the question of his relations with Masaccio over which so much ink has already been employed. I remain convinced[177] that the close collaboration between these two must have taken place between November 1424—when Masolino finished his frescoes in Empoli in which there is no trace of Masaccio's influence—and September 1st, 1425, the day on which Masolino left for Hungary. I further believe that the collaboration may have begun through the simple fact that Masolino needed a helper to complete his commissions—the Brancacci Chapel, the Sant'Ambrogio panel—before the date set for leaving Florence, in order to obtain the payment due and to avoid the penalties which were then customary for breach of contract.

Masolino returned in July of 1427, but there is no proof that he took up the work again at the Carmine nor even that he may have worked in Florence then nor in Figline as some documents suggest. Then he must have left for Rome where, in 1428, Masaccio joined him, again as a collaborator, but the younger man died suddenly and too soon to do more than the side-panel of the triptych for Santa Maria Maggiore and perhaps something else, part of the *Crucifixion* in San Clemente.[178]

Profoundly different as they were, the two men were able to collaborate because their styles had more in common with each other's than with that of any other painter of the time. Masolino was along in years and already highly appreciated, as we know from the fact that Pippo Spano invited him to Hungary, and also because the very large sum of 1000 florins was foreseen for the chapel at Figline he was asked to paint. Masaccio was young, probably not yet fully formed as an artist. It is logical, therefore, to assume that Masolino was in charge of the work and Masaccio his associate but also his subordinate. They must have had mutual respect: the notion of Masolino terrorized by Masaccio, of Masaccio exasperated by the stupidity of Masolino seems to me no more than yet another dramatic over-simplification. Indeed, Meller, with his usual subtlety, has gone beyond this, proposing that theirs was a friendship which extended to mutual homage, to a common stock of images and even to a somewhat equivocal exchange of such images. In the Carmine fresco of Saint Peter healing the sick [Plate 52], Masolino is, beyond doubt, portrayed wearing a red hood alongside Donatello and Masaccio himself, no small tribute on the part of Masaccio to his friend who must have been far away in Rome by that time, since this was one of the last frescoes to be done. For the portraits presumed to be of Felice Brancacci, both artists made very similar heads, Masolino placing his portrait in the fresco of Saint Peter preaching, Masaccio varying his slightly by adding a beard and moustaches and slightly correcting the perspective of the line of the eyes and placing him in the fresco of the Tribute Money as that disciple whom certain scholars take to be a self-portrait. In any event, the physical traits of a companion may serve an artist as model for a more generalized type: the head of Masolino's Eve may well be modeled after Masaccio's (and *honi soit qui mal y pense!*).[179]

Also, one must have come to the aid of the other at times, though not, as has been claimed, in the three heads of youths to the left in Masolino's *Saint Peter Preaching*,[180] because they seem to be part of the same "day's work" as the head of the Saint which is, beyond doubt, by Masolino[181] (in fresco painting, one can distinguish the areas worked on in a single day because the area moistened but not used must be cut away before the next day's work—this is what is called a *giornata*, a day's work); besides, they do not in any way resemble the two

47 - THE TRIBUTE MONEY (*detail:* Christ and the Apostles) - *Church of the Carmine* - FLORENCE

48 - THE TRIBUTE MONEY (*detail:* Saint Peter and the fish) - *Church of the Carmine* - FLORENCE

youths in the corresponding fresco, the *Baptism of the Neophytes*, by Masaccio [Plate 40] whose modeling is harsher and whose profiles are more chiseled, more linear with their hooked noses and tight bitter mouths; moreover, the strip of fresco preserved intact behind the Baroque altar reveals a more biting graphic firmness. Nor can these heads in the *Baptism*, by any stretch of imagination, certainly not on stylistic grounds, be attributed to Filippino Lippi.[182]

But we must concede to Longhi that the head of Christ in the *Tribute Money* [Figure 65] may well be by Masolino since it lacks that peremptory quality present in every detail ever painted by Masaccio. It is true that it was painted *after* and not before all the other heads —technical analysis proves this[183]—but this is anything but proof to the contrary. Why did Masaccio in the course of his work skip precisely this head? To ponder over it further? Or was it to avoid criticism (like that his friend Donatello had to endure for making his Christ too proud, too peasant-like) that he turned over this detail to his milder co-worker? Or did the latter insist on placing, as it were, his own seal on the *Tribute Money* to prove that he and no other was in charge of the entire project? In all events, if the head is really by Masaccio, then in this particular he shows himself a true disciple of Masolino.

On the other hand, for the background of Masolino's *Story of Tabitha* [Plates 43-44], we must again follow Longhi [184] in conceding the intervention of Masaccio. Masolino had never shown before and never showed again such admirable, precise and highly sensitive feeling for background, whereas we know that Masaccio had already painted, in the lost *Consecration*, a view of the Piazza of the Carmine and was to continue this same treatment in the lower tier of frescoes in the Brancacci Chapel, as is evidenced in the *Saint Peter Healing with his Shadow*. Here also the technical data warn us against too rashly awarding everything good to Masaccio, everything bad to Masolino. Whichever it was who conceived the far from perfect box-like room at the right also deserves credit for the very beautiful adjacent sun-bathed street in foreshortening; [185] and probably all three working-day portions up above, including even the portico to the left with all its defects, were painted by the same person: Masaccio. It is more difficult, however, to make a distinction between the few vivid tiny figures added to the background on small blobs of plaster [186] because at least those in the center, the three women and the child, seem more like Masolino's work than Masaccio's. But collaboration always involves possible influence. The attempt has been made to discern that of Masaccio on Masolino in the latter's *Pietà* in Empoli, although the monumentality and sorrowful intensity of that painting need not necessarily be due to Masaccio but could, in fact, be a tragic expression arrived at by Masolino himself. This fresco is, in fact, the

71

logical culmination of the rest of Masolino's work in the chapel and particularly that revealed by the under-drawings in the vault. As for the sturdier character of the *Madonna* in Munich compared with that in Bremen, this again need not be due to Masaccio but equally as much, and even more incontrovertibly, to the late-Gothic intensification in the treatment of drapery typical of a Jacopo della Quercia [187] and to a heightened chiaroscuro certainly inspired by Gentile. In the Sant'Ambrogio *Madonna* [Plate 7], the Saint Anne's outstretched hand is foreshortened, and for this reason it has been proposed to assign this figure to Masaccio himself although it must certainly derive from the Christ at the apex of Gentile's *Adoration of the Magi*.[188]

Where then can we discover Masolino really bowing before the iron hand of Masaccio? Not in the Carmine itself, in the *Adam and Eve*, a most beautiful fresco (whatever the schoolboys may say against it) with its sensuous idyll within a Gothic shady grove... last fleeting moment of blissful innocence before the agonizing whip of reality slashes down upon Masaccio's two sinners. Nor even in the stern gaze of Saint Peter preaching, a scene of grim humor with its listeners who have nodded off. But it can be found in the *Resurrection of Tabitha* with its many reminiscences of the *Resurrection of Drusiana* in Giotto's Peruzzi Chapel frescoes which Masaccio must have praised so highly. Here, indeed, Masolino undoubtedly appears forced, over-charged and almost a little grotesque, his fundamental stylistic equilibrium lost, except for the two youths in whom is preserved the serene character of the *Preaching* and the soft modeling of the Munich *Madonna*. And if such stylistic deviations and lapses reflect a critical moment, a kind of allergic reaction to the contact with Masaccio, we must ask ourselves why such failings appear also, though in different manner, in the unfortunate two angels at the bottom of the Sant'Ambrogio *Madonna* [Plate 7] while the angel facing the one ascribed to Masaccio, for all that it forces itself to compete with Masaccio's, nevertheless is as acceptable as the angels in the Munich *Madonna*. In my opinion, this occurs precisely because here Masolino was forcing himself not simply to imitate Masaccio but even to assimilate into his own quite different, much less harsh system certain elements typical of the younger painter: the profiling of the arm of the angel to the right recalls that of the first Apostle on the left in the *Tribute Money*, the distorting, bleaching-out lighting on the angel to the left may be Masolino's personal interpretation of the violent lighting in Masaccio's frescoes, especially in that of Saint Peter fishing, a lighting Masolino now attempts to graft on to a figure of the type of the sorrowful Saint John of the Empoli *Pietà*. I have had occasion elsewhere to expound my idea that the face of the Child in Masaccio's Sant'Ambrogio *Madonna* is contemporary and kin to that of the Apostle directly behind the neck of Saint Peter in the *Tribute Money* [189] and that therefore the two works must have been executed, in part at least, at the same time.

The fact remains that Masolino promptly became himself again in the Carnesecchi triptych. The heaviness of line and a certain sparseness that in the *Resurrection of Tabitha* seemed weaknesses are now reabsorbed into Masolino's spontaneous elegance with its deliberately archaic and somewhat naive character. To Masaccio's eloquent modeling, Masolino opposes the sharply incised contours of his images. If, along with Salmi and Parronchi, we can concede that in a work by Andrea di Giusto there is a reminiscence of Masolino's lost *Saint Catherine*, done as a side-panel for the Carnesecchi triptych,[190] the figure with its flowered garment as painted by Andrea more closely resembles Gentile in style. Masolino therefore must have fought on two fronts and with different weapons: against Gentile with characteristic Tuscan sparseness, against Masaccio with decorative idealization of figures.

But we need not follow Masolino beyond 1425 when he left for Hungary, because his entire vocabulary was firmly established by that date, nor was it affected by his second collaboration with Masaccio in 1428 in Rome. True enough, he became more analytical, giving in to the as yet confused demands—half-Humanist, half-courtly—of the period after Masaccio's death and of the non-Florentine environments in which he worked then. It must be said, however, that the attempts to equate Masolino and Masaccio with Hubert and Jan Van Eyck are based on a too vague analogy. Hubert may be distinguished from Jan by his still-medieval religious feeling, but that can certainly not be said of Masolino who from the outset rejected the gravity—whether ascetic or luxurious—of Lorenzo Monaco, Gentile, Pisanello and the Italian Late-Gothic style, without however taking the shortcut of sterile agitation typical of the Master of the Bambino Vispo and his like, just as he also was not willing to climb to unforeseeable heights with Masaccio. Masolino possessed neither the fanaticism nor the deep-lying heroic ethics nor the genius, as rigorous as it was audacious, of his young friend but only his own exquisite lyrical intuitive sensitivity. From the Gothic world he retained nothing of the solemnity of a Hubert Van Eyck but only the ultimate curious, sensual, entertaining, day-dreaming moods which were already a sign of the waning of the Middle Ages (even when his figures look sinister and stern, as they often do, we fail to be convinced). From the Renaissance he appropriated superficially—but early in his career—the first main bases: perspective, naturalism, daylight atmosphere, an architectonic approach derived from Brunelleschi, and an interest in archaeology. Nevertheless we must be consistent: we cannot praise Masolino to the skies within the late-Gothic context and then write him off as a simpleton in Masaccio's context. In any event, he fits badly within

73

the Gothic context, whereas within Masaccio's he is, admittedly, neither a forerunner nor a peer of the young revolutionary but certainly the first to go along with him, though on a more modest plane.[191]

Finally, among the various personages introduced into this chapter we cannot neglect three who in the decade following the death of Masaccio were to become the outstanding leaders of the very first rank, even if, in Masaccio's time, they played only a minor role and in one case perhaps no role at all. These are Paolo Uccello, Fra Angelico and Filippo Lippi, all of them still youths of more or less the same age as Masaccio, Uccello having been born in 1397, Fra Angelico about the same time according to the latest hypotheses,[192] Filippo Lippi soon after the start of the century, at the latest in 1406.

What contacts might they have had with Masaccio? Here again I must express convictions in part contrary to the highly suggestive proposals made in the well-known study by Longhi. In the light of the most recent data, it is quite possible that Masaccio and Fra Angelico never met on any occasion whatsoever, or at any rate almost never. Guido di Pietro was already recognized as a painter in 1417-1418 when he executed a panel for the Gherardini Chapel in Santo Stefano al Ponte, but at that time Masaccio, even if we admit that he may already have come to Florence, was no more than a youngster fresh from the country. Then, between 1418 and 1423, Guido took orders and became Fra Giovanni in San Domenico at Fiesole and must then have been locked up not only within those gentle monastery walls outside the city but also in the fervid and ascetic inwardness of his novitiate. Presuming that his years as novice and student could have paralyzed at least partially his life as an artist "for a maximum of five or seven years,"[193] until around 1425 there must have been an interruption and a retardation in his work as a painter.[194]

In fact, in the triptych of *Saint Peter Martyr*, which must be dated at the beginning of 1429, his vision is closer to that of Gentile da Fabriano than to Masaccio's. In the altarpiece for San Domenico in Fiesole probably from around 1429-1430, the principal influences appear to be Lorenzo Monaco and Masolino. In the tabernacle for the Linen-Weavers from 1433, there lingers still the influence of Ghiberti. For the rest, elsewhere I have tried to show how thick and slow was the filter through which Fra Angelico absorbed Masaccio's influence: there are no clear evidences of that influence (along with that of others) until, at the earliest, 1433-1434.[195] The little panel in the Des Cars collection, for example, must have been done after Fra Angelico arrived at his maturity which culminated in the tabernacle for the Linen-Weavers Guild, and that small painting has much of Masaccio in it, but a Masaccio of a saintly good humor, and is stylistically close to the *Naming of the Baptist* in the Museum of San Marco. During Masaccio's lifetime, Fra Angelico seems to have carried on with his enamel-like quite traditional style derived from Lorenzo Monaco and—perhaps also—from Ambrogio di Baldese whose work in the Gherardini Chapel he completed while he was still young and before taking orders. His painting in that period appears grave and solemn because the essential process took place not externally but within the soul of Fra Giovanni and was intensely spiritual and religious. But if Fra Angelico had accepted earlier the influence of Masaccio, would this not have signified a too-ready acceptance of worldly values? We should then have had only a gifted disciple of Masaccio, but not, perhaps, the Blessed Angelico. In short, the contact between the two, the decisive contact at any rate, did not take place during Masaccio's lifetime, and it is no less touching for having taken place a few years later when this pure soul pored over the work of Masaccio on the walls of the Carmine and took from it the means to incarnate the truth of the Faith in an idiom befitting the Renaissance.[196] What is curious but quite natural is that, in all events, Masaccio the layman was "sober and unadorned" while Fra Angelico was "delightful and devout and highly ornate with the greatest facility" as Landino impeccably characterized each of them.

If there was a precocious disciple of Masaccio, it was that other monk of quite different temperament, Filippo Lippi. In 1421 he pronounced his vows at the Carmine, in 1430-1431 he was already listed in the registers as painter and therefore must have begun much earlier than 1432, the presumed date of his fresco *The Confirmation of the Carmelite Order*. Here I do not wish to insist on my suggestion of a few years back[197] that the small panel in the museum at Empoli has reminiscences of Masaccio's polyptych for the Carmine of Pisa and that it dates somewhat earlier than the usual date proposed, after 1432; moreover, it was in the Carmine of Pisa that there was a Sainted Bishop done in fresco which was attributed to Masaccio but which Vasari, on his own responsibility, proposed to ascribe to Lippi. Furthermore, it is perfectly legitimate to imagine the young Lippi as one of the most interested onlookers at the work going on in his own church of the Carmine, and he certainly must have spoken with Masaccio—indeed, one wonders if Masaccio may not have portrayed that bright young monk as one of the two young friars alongside the older Carmelite beside the throne of Saint Peter, but this is a question better explored by Meller.

The chapel in the Carmine had just been newly painted by Masaccio, and being very beautiful, greatly delighted Fra Filippo, who frequented it every day, and was always practicing in the company of many youths who spent their time in drawing there. These he far surpassed in skill and knowledge [Vasari].

In the Carmine, besides the *Confirmation of the Carmelite Order*, Fra Filippo did various things in fresco, all now lost, such as a Saint John the Baptist with stories from his life and also

the figure of St. Martial, near the organ, which brought him great renown, as it would bear comparison with the paintings of Masaccio... He had so far acquired the manner of Masaccio, making his things in a similar manner, that many declared that the spirit of Masaccio had entered into the body of Fra Filippo [Vasari].

There is no need here to go over Vasari in detail and to follow him to the letter: the *Confirmation of the Carmelite Order* suffices to measure how penetrating and personal were Lippi's interpretations of Masaccio, even though we have no way of judging either the quality or the chronology of his lost frescoes for the Carmine. However, there seems to be much truth in Vasari's affirmation that Lippi took advantage of the fame he had acquired by following in the traces of Masaccio to escape from the monastery where, in fact, he no longer appears in the records after 1433. In the Trivulzio painting, possibly from 1432, Lippi borrowed elements not only from Masaccio but also from Donatello as well as from Luca della Robbia who had begun his singers' pulpit in 1428; and in the *Madonna* of Tarquinia of 1437 he managed to parallel and synthesize the first Flemish achievements. These two facts attest to the remarkable temperament of the man, and it is noteworthy that in his famous letter of 1438 the boldly forthright Domenico Veneziano paid homage only to him and to Fra Angelico. Be that as it may, Filippo Lippi owed to Masaccio his initial inspiration as a painter and even perhaps his escape from monastic life.[198] There were other more remote indirect consequences of the encounter between the two painters: Lippi's introduction of the new Renaissance concepts into Padua between 1434 and 1436 and even we might say, in one sense at least, the birth of his son Filippino. Around 1482 that son, Filippino, took on the task of completing the frescoes in the Brancacci Chapel,[199] and while I cannot share Fiocco's enthusiasm for them, I can appreciate their effort to conform to the style of fifty years before—and to that of Masaccio especially: perhaps the first great example of "restoration" in the history of art and evidence of the veneration for Masaccio not only on the part of the Lippis but also of the Florentines—it was, in a way, an act of familial piety towards an ancestor.

Finally, because everything concerning Domenico Veneziano is still completely problematical and obscure up to 1439, and because we cannot share the hypotheses of some who insist on attributing to him some of the finest works of Masaccio such as the Berlin birth salver, the side-panel in London, and the insertion in Masolino's *Crucifixion* at San Clemente in Rome,[200] this chapter can conclude—like Longhi's famous study of Masaccio—with Paolo Uccello, but not in terms of a "paradoxical fabricator of coffers" as it was put there, since in that case the paradox is the critic's, not Uccello's.

Apprenticed to Ghiberti at ten, perhaps a pupil of Starnina and therefore in contact with Masolino, in 1415 at the age of eighteen enrolled in the Guild of Doctors and Pharmacists and in 1424 in the Company of Saint Luke, Paolo di Dono could very well have been a young painter with high ambitions and fierce determination at the time Masaccio was performing his great deeds. That consummate masterpiece, the equestrian portrait of Sir John Hawkwood in the cathedral of Florence, is dated unequivocally 1436,[201] so there is no reason to presume that it was not until 1455 or 1460 that Uccello's genius affirmed itself, a genius which for all its eccentricity was by no means slow in developing. Moreover, an eighteenth-century inscription attributes to Paolo and dates at 1416 the tabernacle from the locality known as Lippi e Macia at Novolo. Recently detached, this fresco's under-drawings have been exposed and reveal a fine, soft manner which is admittedly still Gothic and very close to Starnina and the successors of Antonio Veneziano [Figures 34-36]. As Procacci has seen, with his customary acumen, this eighteenth-century attribution to Uccello of a work otherwise difficult to place is an indication not to be ignored.[202]

Elsewhere, with reference to the Saint Peter in mosaic on the façade of San Marco in Venice done by Uccello in 1425 and known to us from a painting by Gentile Bellini, I pointed out that as early as this date there appear traits owed to Masaccio.[203] Likewise, there is much to say for Parronchi's recent attribution [204] to Uccello of the very beautiful *Nativity* of the predella panel catalogued as number 1648 by the National Gallery, London, until now assigned to the School of Masaccio or to the Master of the Castello Nativity. For Parronchi, this *Nativity* belongs to Masolino's Carnesecchi altarpiece of 1425—the sources state that Paolo collaborated in the predella and in the Annunciation at the top[205]—and this too seems convincing, although I hesitate to pronounce positively on Parronchi's proposed reconstruction of the entire altarpiece, especially when he insists that it was crowned by the Goldman *Annunciation* which, for him, is not by Masolino but by Uccello working at that time in a style close to Masolino's.

There was, however, in fact an *Annunciation* by Paolo in that altarpiece which was carried out with such great subtlety in perspective that "a small and insignificant space on a plain surface may be made to appear large and remote," and there was even "a more difficult thing in some columns foreshortened in perspective, which bend round and break the sharp angle of the vaulting where the four Evangelists are" (Vasari). Hence, since the Carnesecchi altarpiece was executed in 1425, the year Paolo left Florence for Venice, we must assume that it included this remarkable piece of perspective—which could certainly not have left Masaccio indifferent, especially since his companion Masolino was working on the same altarpiece. There can be no doubt: Masaccio and Paolo must have met, and it was perhaps the most difficult of all Masaccio's encounters because conversation between them must have been like two sword-blades that clash, like the two theories of perspective they stood for: Masaccio upholding Brunelleschi's theory, Uccello the notions of the Middle Ages and of Ghiberti.[206] True, Paolo Uccello also was reconstructing a world, but he reconstructed it according to his obsession with perspective, sometimes in pure stereometry, at others with fantasies, sometimes inspired by the polyhedrons he drew endlessly in foreshortening, at still others by the birds who sang in his cages. Basically, in carrying to extremes the system which was being propounded at the time, Uccello demonstrated its fundamental cerebrality, its truly paradoxical ultimate consequences.[207] Masaccio, however, sought absolute certainty. For this reason, the two painters must not have understood each other, or perhaps they understood very well that their paths, turned as both were to the future, were in fact fatally diverse. Is it accidental that Paolo Uccello is omitted from Vasari's extensive list of painters who profited from the lesson of the Carmine? Or is it because he was really—as Vasari understood very clearly—one of the creators of the Renaissance along with Masaccio and the others? And perhaps the Carmine frescoes therefore had nothing to say to him, though from time to time he exploited Masaccio's art of giving real weight to the human figure. I am inclined to think Parronchi is right in supposing that the *Trinity* of Masaccio, with its perfect and highly objective perspective and its human figures equally objective and signifi-cant, may have been a reply by Masaccio and by Brunelleschi to the subtleties of Uccello in the *Annunciation* for Santa Maria Maggiore. In conclusion, then, we can say that there must really have been an encounter between Masaccio and Paolo Uccello, even if we must call it—with due respect to the second term—an encounter between a philosopher and a sophist.

49 - THE TRIBUTE MONEY (*detail:* Saint Peter and four Apostles) - *Church of the Carmine* - FLORENCE

DEVELOPMENT AND DIRECTION

Now that all the pieces have been set up on our chess board, we can trace Masaccio's progress after the triptych of San Giovenale. We shall not, however, immediately propose a chronological sequence which might appear subjective and questionable but instead take our time to ponder the various possibilities, a procedure both more useful and more objective. Thus, we shall first consider the lost *Consecration* as most writers have done, although it may not, as now seems likely, be the first work in terms of time. Similarly, other works will be considered out of sequence in order to place them in relationship to the most significant forward moves of the painter.

With this in mind, we can only hope that our survey will not seem equivocal and obscure in its conclusions, and that the reader will not be too disappointed at not finding here detailed descriptions of each work, since these have been done so well and so often in the past. In their place, we have chosen to focus on historical and critical annotations and discussions although these, unfortunately, may not always be as extended as they should be. What counts here, then, is not description of works already known to the reader but, instead, a chain of reasoning regarding the problems those works still present.

THE LOST CONSECRATION   To challenge the attribution to Masaccio of the San Giovenale triptych dated 1422, the date of 1423 has been proposed for the lost *Consecration*,[208] but this seems, to us, a completely hypothetical dating. We know only that the church of the Carmine "was consecrated in 1422 on the 19th of April at the request of Messer Francesco Soderini by Monsignor Amerigo Corsini, first archbishop of Florence, and present also were Messer Antonio del Fede of the Carmelites, bishop of Soana, and Messer Benozzo Federighi, bishop of Fiesole."[209] The ceremony was commemorated by Masaccio in a monochromatic fresco in green earth—*terretta verde*—over a door in the cloister, but not necessarily immediately after the event. The fresco, tragically enough, was destroyed, it now appears certain, around 1600[210] and not 1612 as has been claimed. At the latest, this fresco must have been done shortly before Masaccio set to work in the Brancacci Chapel,

50 - THE TRIBUTE MONEY (*detail*: a young Apostle) - *Church of the Carmine* - FLORENCE

51 - THE TRIBUTE MONEY (*detail*: the legs of the tax collector) - *Church of the Carmine* - FLORENCE

that is, late in 1424, or even later, in view of the presumed maturity of its conception which seems to have been comparable to that of the *Tribute Money* or the *Story of Theophilus*.

What exactly do we know about this lost fresco?[211] It "depicted the Piazza of the Carmine with many figures" (Manetti), that is, according to Vasari, "a great number of citizens in mantle and hood who are taking part in the procession" (among whom, as is known, were Brunelleschi "in sabots," Donatello, Masolino, Brancacci, Uzzano, Giovanni di Bicci Medici, B. Valori, and L. Ridolfi).

...and not only did he draw all these notabilities from life, but also the door of the convent, and the porter with the keys in his hand. The work possesses many perfections, for Masaccio's knowledge enabled him to put five or six people in a row upon the piazza, judiciously diminishing them in proportion as they recede, according to the point of view, a truly marvellous feat, especially as he has used his discretion in making his figures not all of one size, but of various stature, as in life, distinguishing the small and the stout from the tall and the slender, all foreshortened in their ranks with such excellence that they would not look otherwise in real life [Vasari].

On the basis of the surviving drawings of details [Figures 43-47], it does not seem that Masaccio's fresco had anything like the crowd scene in Bicci di Lorenzo's *Consecration of Saint Giles* [Figure 48] but depicted instead a strung-out procession with a certain amount of open space and no great depth and with the church of the Carmine in the background. The plane of depth must not, however, have been pushed back so far as to leave exposed the paving of the piazza beyond the crowd.[212] Certainly, at the time it was done, Masaccio would not have attempted anything like the immense open space in the Perugino fresco in the Sistine Chapel. However, the *Consecration* must have had something in common, *mutatis mutandis*, with the *Resurrection of the Son of Theophilus* with its heads outlined against the walls of the Carmine (the rows of figures by Filippino Lippi may well have been inspired by the lost Consecration). Perhaps also in a more or less central point one saw the procession curving to the rear to enter the portal of the Carmine.[213]

On the other hand, taking into account the drawings and Vasari's description which mentions only the procession, it does not appear likely that there were depicted any solemn liturgical moments of the liturgical proceeding or groups of kneeling figures as in Bicci's *Consecration*. For this reason, it seems justified to reject as irrelevant the drawing in the Accademia of Venice Salmi refers to [214] as well as the small panel of Giovanni del Ponte since both have the celebrant of the rite enthroned and this would make the scene similar to Bicci's homage to the Pontiff in his *Consecration*.[215]

As for the drawings of the *Consecration* known to us—Uffizi [Figure 47]; present whereabouts unknown [Figure 43]; Folkestone [Figure 45]; Casa Buonarroti, Florence [Figure 46];

52 - SAINT PETER HEALING THE SICK BY HIS SHADOW - *Church of the Carmine* - FLORENCE

Albertina, Vienna, by Michelangelo [Figure 44] [216]—they all suggest a group proceeding from the left in three rows, after which the cortège is interrupted by two figures turned in the opposite direction while a third takes up again the movement towards the right; there is also another small group turned towards the left but motionless, among which perhaps (as indicated by Michelangelo's drawing) is the doorkeeper mentioned by Vasari (or at least a doorkeeper), although his keys hang from his belt and are not held in his hand as Vasari described them. [217] The diversity of physiognomies in the fresco, singled out for praise by Vasari, is confirmed by the drawings; for example, in the group to the left, there is a tall figure who stands out, although not in the foreground, and next to him, facing forward and squeezed in, the head of a short man, and the personage on the right drawn by Michelangelo must have been of massive build.

How excellent was, in fact, this *Consecration* famed in its time for its "great artifice"? [218] Certainly pictures of public ceremonies of religious character and including portraits must have been known already in fourteenth-century Florence. Nor is it likely, as far as one can gather from the few references in the sources, that the appeal of the *Consecration* lay in the perspective view of the Piazza of the Carmine, especially coming after the two recent and highly praised small panels of Brunelleschi with views of the Piazza of the Baptistery and the Piazza of the Signoria. [219] What was commented on most was the procession itself and how closely it resembled what really took place. Further, there were the portraits, no longer inserted in the margin, as it were, as in religious paintings, but directly involved as chief actors in the scene. And mention was made also of the feeling of movement in the procession, of an action caught as it was occurring, and of the strong characterization of the individual figures all united within a single perspective. It is evident that in his *Consecration* [Figure 48] Bicci di Lorenzo did not understand the art of continuous variation which, on the basis of the drawings known, we can presume to have been a feature of Masaccio's fresco. That must have seemed like a break with the tradition of a uniform procession of figures which had prevailed in medieval painting ever since the Byzantine period and which was, in its essence, highly symbolic and anti-individual.

Moreover, examination of Bicci's method of working from the red ochre under-drawing to the final fresco (as illustrated in Procacci's *Sinopie e affreschi*) verifies Procacci's thesis that for the Trecento and early Quattrocento the under-drawing, the sinopia, was the definitive preparatory drawing and that the painter proceeded rapidly and directly in his task of covering it with the final fresco. For the few variants Bicci chose to introduce between the drawing and the painting, and for his poorly defined treatment of details and generalized,

53 - SAINT PETER HEALING THE SICK BY HIS SHADOW (*detail:* the cripple) - *Church of the Carmine* - FLORENCE

54 - SAINT PETER HEALING THE SICK BY HIS SHADOW (*detail :* Saint Peter, Saint John and an old man) - *Church of the Carmine* - FLORENCE

unindividualized characterization, such a rough and ready practice sufficed. This could not have been the case with Masaccio's *Consecration*. Portraits such as those in the *Saint Peter Enthroned* or as were said to be in the lost fresco cannot be improvised while stuccoing and painting on a scaffolding. It must be remembered also that, except for Michelangelo's, all the surviving copies in drawing of that fresco are themselves weakened by the overall facility of sixteenth-century mannerism which is fundamentally opposed to Masaccio's "great artifice," to the punctilious, studied precision in all details which was typical of the true Renaissance.

The *Consecration* must have been, in this respect, a kind of manifesto. The new sense for history was mirrored not only in its general subject, a specific contemporary event of historical importance, but also in its pinning down this action with a great number of excellent and highly individualized portraits. The principle of perspective applied to the procession was, in any case, a general principle of logic and spatial cohesion, but to it was added another principle, that of individual characterization: it is typical of Masaccio to take off from a radical starting point but to end up with an adequate and fully responsible realization in concrete terms of what he aimed at. This was basically related to Brunelleschi's approach which progressed from an overall conception of the cupola of the cathedral to the ultimate definition in purely technical terms; it was typical likewise of the new philological attitude of Humanism which tended more and more to textual criticism.

However, by using the medium of green earth the *Consecration* was forcibly limited to chiaroscuro with none of the advantages of color. In this also it stopped far short of the complete objectivity of Van Eyck, laying down, instead, the primarily linear basis typical of Florentine art. Finally, if we were able to count the "many" or "infinite number" of citizens depicted in the fresco, it is likely that they would turn out to be fewer than the adjectives suggest; it is probable that this impression was given by the vigorous power of synthesis that was Masaccio's and which was characteristic of the early Renaissance. In any event, this procession—company or platoon as it may have been—was enough to create a grand effect. It is obvious that some discretion should be used in speaking of Masaccio as unappreciated by his contemporaries: the *Consecration* could not help attracting the attention of the Florentine oligarchs who found themselves portrayed there with a forceful presence no less than that of their own personalities, and perhaps the *Consecration* was in part responsible for the enlisting of Masaccio to work on the near-by Brancacci Chapel.

55 - STORY OF ANANIAS (*detail:* the faithful poor) - *Church of the Carmine* - FLORENCE

ATTRIBUTED PORTRAITS   In Vasari's time there still existed a series of portraits by Masaccio in the home of Simon Corsi,[220] but today it is most difficult to judge of Masaccio as a portrait painter properly speaking, though this he probably was.

The portrait of a youth in the Mellon Collection at the National Gallery, Washington [Figure 53], does not seem to me to belong to Masaccio for two reasons. One of these is the insistence on minute decorative details which is entirely alien to Masaccio, not so much in the collar of speckled fur as in the tiny twist of white collar at the back of the neck or, again, in the folded line of the top of the head-dress or the button-hole in the cloth over the chest. The other reason is the excessively calligraphic treatment of the outlines as in the bulging forehead, a linearism which suggests, instead, Paolo Uccello. Salmi seems to have made an excellent suggestion in remarking in this portrait a Flemish influence, but that automatically excludes Masaccio.[221]

On the other hand, the male portrait in the Gardner Museum, Boston [Figure 49],[222] seems to me much more robust, the more so since close examination of it in photographs seems to reveal that the original outline of the profile has been filed down and sharpened and initially may very well have resembled the two portraits in the *Baptism of the Neophytes* [Plate 40]. And yet the flattened-out planes in the face are too smooth and tenuous for Masaccio (with the exception of the ear which is very well studied) as are also the somewhat too narrow bust and the banal succession of collars. Nevertheless, it is not beyond possibility to think that this might be a youthful work, prior even to the *Consecration*. The plum-colored cloak is in Masaccio's chromatic scale, and the turban with its bright note of flame red and extending so far as to be cut off by the frame helps give strength to the somewhat reduced profile; moreover, there is in the profile itself a certain incisive psychological force which is both emphasized and redeemed by a formal grace.

In any event, the X-ray photo the museum has so kindly provided [Figure 51] reveals that the true original profile is clearly related to that of the portrait generally attributed to Paolo Uccello in the museum at Chambéry as had already been suspected, with good reason, by Enio Sindona:[223] this is borne out by the narrow line of the eye, the eyelid marked by a fold, the prominent eyebrow as well as by the conspicuous lips and the fine sharp chin. However, if there is no need to doubt that the prototypes of this style of portraiture go back to Masaccio—a style which became widely diffused, as in the two portraits of the Olivieri in the United States (of which the two young gentlemen in Masolino's *Story of Tabitha* may be, in some sort, a reminiscence)—in order to attribute to Masaccio the portraits in Boston and Chambéry, as Berenson did, it would be necessary to date them much earlier, perhaps not much beyond 1422, the date of the San Giovenale triptych. But when one looks at the portraits in Masaccio's known works—the two youths in the Carmine with their cloaks lacking any excess ornament such as multiple collars, or the two bourgeois in the Berlin *Adoration*, or the portrait presumably of Lenzi in the *Trinity*, and all the other portraits that can be singled out in the Carmine frescoes—one has the impression that Masaccio's conception of a portrait must have been much more synthetic, severe and robust than these two works discussed.

THE METTERZA SAINT ANNE   If we admit as a possible date for the *Consecration* something in the vicinity of 1424, the progress made by Masaccio between the San Giovenale triptych and the rest of his work remains somewhat obscure. However, it is worth noting that Brandi considers the panel for Sant'Ambrogio, known as the *Metterza Saint Anne*, [Plates 7-10] as dating from very shortly after the San Giovenale triptych.[224] This seems not without justification at first glance, especially in certain details: compare the head of the Virgin of the triptych with that of the angel to the right in the panel; also, there is much in common between the heads of the two Infants, notably in the treatment of the hair. But the dating of the Sant'Ambrogio panel,[225] even apart from all the suppositions advanced earlier in this book in connection with Gentile and Masolino, is inevitably conditioned by the chronology of Masolino, and I believe that Masolino's share in this painting dates from at least late 1424 and certainly after the Bremen *Madonna* of 1423.

As for the plastic concentration of the image which occurs between the two works, Brandi contributes his usual subtle observations, such as "one has the impression of a telescope unscrewing from one part to the other: from the hand of the Infant we pass to that of the Madonna and from there to the leg and the other hand in a plastic continuity" [compare Plate 9]. What seems noteworthy also is that precisely here, in this figure of the Infant, there begins a certain dilatation, a certain widening-out, of the form of the more prominent parts such as the face and the right hand, almost as if they were flattened against a wall or an invisible pane of glass. This is a procedure by which the line acquires tension but only in function of its plastic role, and it corresponds to a more general stylistic treatment transmitted from Donatello to Filippo Lippi especially. Now, this is also a procedure which anticipates the style of the Carmine frescoes where the three-quarter profiles are markedly flattened out, most conspicuously in the *Tribute Money* [compare Plate 49] and somewhat, but less so, in the *Baptism of the Neophytes*.

Further, in the San Giovenale triptych one has the impression that space is conceived quite

56 - STORY OF ANANIAS - *Church of the Carmine* - FLORENCE

57 - STORY OF ANANIAS (*detail:* houses and countryside) - *Church of the Carmine* - FLORENCE

58 - STORY OF ANANIAS (*detail:* the mother) - *Church of the Carmine* - FLORENCE

naively and limited to its most terse extension, whereas in the *Metterza Saint Anne* it becomes instead a denser medium, especially because of the light source from the left which models the chiaroscuro strongly and accentuates the play of color, as in the veil of the Madonna and the green gown of the angel. There is a thoroughgoing condensation of means: the lighting; the form whose verticality is rendered somewhat squat by the low perspective point; the color which has become deeper in tone; the foreshortening which has become more insistent, more decisive, as if it too were pressing towards the viewer (note the curvature of the base of the throne); the material which has become more of a plastic and autonomous mass instead of a basic volume conceived linearly. All this creates the impression of a certain vulgarizing, of a more earthy, popular notion of the Madonna and Child in contrast to the rather noble figures in the San Giovenale work. What compensates for this loss of nobility is, however, an accentuation of the impression of pride, of hieratical dignity charged with energy. Like a gaseous substance which, compressed, increases proportionately its pressure force, this seated woman with her herculean child whose hand sketches out a benediction is an image of utmost compactness and solidity which is at the same time infused with a terrible potentiality: gaze fixed on infinity or transfixing the viewer, hands fully capable of grasping, like that of the Madonna on the leg of the Child which is deliberately rendered inelegant but strong. If one compares this Virgin with the Saint John the Evangelist of Donatello which is still shot through with vestiges of flowing Gothic linearism or even, as has been done,[226] with Brunelleschi's cupola in which the static quality triumphs, it is plain to see that in this painting Masaccio achieved a decisive originality even when compared with the attainments of his two great friends.

EVIDENCE OF PERSPECTIVE STUDIES   Another hypothesis worth following through, in tracing Masaccio's development after the San Giovenale triptych, is that he may then have devoted himself to deeper study of the problems of perspective which, at that same time, were the most obsessive preoccupation of Brunelleschi himself (although perhaps it is not necessary to follow Parronchi in dating Brunelleschi's two famous urban views as late as 1424-25, after the arrival of Toscanelli in Florence).[227] It is undeniable that the formal change which occurred between the paintings for San Giovenale and for Sant'Ambrogio was the result of a changed conception of space: the artist grasps space more decisively, not merely laying it out but, instead, making the figure master of the space in which it is set. This plastic force is obtained through the use of a closer viewing-point which is placed considerably lower than the center of the picture (clearly seen in the *Saint Anne* in the bit of the right arm of the throne which is exposed) and which results in greater prominence both from below and from above of the things depicted; in fact, the hand of Saint Anne is already clearly conceived in *sottinsù*, that is, in perspective foreshortening as seen from below. The painter shows that he is now capable of manipulating as he wishes the perspective setting, and we know from Vasari that in the lost *Saint Paul* of the Carmine and *Saint Ives* of the Badia he had applied rigorously his skill in foreshortening from below.

Moreover, the birth-plate in Berlin and the *Trinity* in Santa Maria Novella demonstrate a remarkably full understanding of perspective, from which we can conclude that Masaccio had by that time engaged in serious study of the problem and, in this aspect also, had left far behind the rough solution employed in the San Giovenale painting. If its attribution were not so uncertain, light might be shed on this point by the little *Exorcism of a Possessed Man* in the Johnson Collection, Philadelphia [Figure 55].[228] The fact is, not only are its figures too incurably shaky, whether they be by Andrea di Giusto as is probable or by someone else, but also one cannot possibly imagine Masaccio's acute and precise mind constructing such a perspective setting. There is a lack of logic in the relationship of the three naves of the Renaissance-style temple with the bulk of the cupola behind them as well as in the definition of details: where, for example, is the alignment of the right nave in relation to that of the left which runs from the pilaster of the great arch of the façade? To say nothing of smaller details, such as the gawky houses in the background or the arches and bull's-eye windows so clumsily squashed into an incorrect perspective.

Nevertheless, the initial conception of the Johnson Collection painting is too complex and subtle to have come from Andrea di Giusto alone or from some other minor painter, and it is legitimate to suppose that it is at least a partial copy of that

scene of small figures now in the house of Ridolfo del Ghirlandaio, in which besides the Christ delivering the man possessed, there are some very fine buildings so drawn in perspective that the interior and exterior are represented at the same time, as he took for the point of view not the front, but the side, for its greater difficulty [Vasari].[229]

If we presume that the Johnson Collection painting is not, in fact, the picture Vasari described (because Ridolfo and Vasari, after all, had certain standards) but is some sort of copy done after Masaccio's lost work, then the latter must have been an exercise in painting an edifice of complex architecture with its walls stripped away and open to analysis such as had been one of the *tours de force* in perspective of the Florentine school in the Trecento, as is for example Taddeo Gaddi's *Presentation of the Virgin* in the Baroncelli Chapel. But here the exercise becomes infinitely more complicated since the perspective is dictated by a viewing-

59 - STORY OF THEOPHILUS (*detail:* the invocation of Saint Paul) - *Church of the Carmine* - FLORENCE

point placed radically at the side and with two lateral principal vanishing points (as in Brunelleschi's view of the Piazza of the Signoria), while the scale of figures is adjusted to a central axis running in depth towards a third vanishing point, space itself. The small groups of personages in the background, each with four figures, virtually a human counterpart to the quadrangular pilasters of the edifice, are another example of an invention so subtle as to justify ascribing it to an original by Masaccio, from which also must have come certain fine analyses of the passage from dark shadow into light which can be glimpsed in the interior of the temple.

THE PISA POLYPTYCH   Just as the triptych of San Giovenale gives the only certain data, as regards both style and chronology, for determining what Masaccio was and did at the start of his career, so also the polyptych from Pisa, whose date is settled by documents as 1426, four years later than the triptych, offers us the only other certain point for a study of how and when the artist arrived at his brief but formidable maturity.

Four years only, and yet, to recognize the San Giovenale work as Masaccio's required all the specialized skills of the art historian and the confirmation furnished by the date which was discovered under a strip of the frame, whereas the Madonna of the Pisa polyptych [Plate 13], for all its relationships to that of San Giovenale, belongs clearly and unmistakably to the Renaissance, from the throne on to every detail.

The scheme Salmi proposed for the reconstruction of the polyptych, whose surviving parts are now widely dispersed, [Figure 58][230] may perhaps have involved too many separate sections according to recent observations by Shearman,[231] but in any event it is clear that the overall organization as a polyptych no longer had any direct influence on the pictorial content as such. The frame itself was no more than an external boundary which was still in Gothic style, just as the gold background in the paintings, wisely retained by Masaccio to create a stylistic unity with the framework, constituted something like a compact interior curtain before which figures entirely Quattrocento in conception took their places. The fact that the lines of the cusp, in the central panel of the Madonna, cut off the arms of the throne at the top is good proof of the lack of relationship between the exterior arrangement and the interior space of the painting itself: a Gothic painter would normally have included the entire throne within the limits of the panel. For this reason, I think also that the bottom of the panel remains as it was originally, with the angel lutanists cut off below the knees; Shearman however believes they were initially full-length, but in that case there would have been an excessive vertical extension of the panel. Moreover, such a cutting-off of the lower extremities of the angels to make a sort of three-quarter figure is similar to that of the Saint Paul and the Saint Andrew which were in the cusps of the side panels.

What exactly was there initially in the Pisa polyptych? A Madonna [Plate 14] whom, for my part, I simply cannot think of as coarse but, instead, as nobly beautiful although a little mature and veiled with melancholy,[232] as if subtly foreseeing the tragedy ahead. A Christ Child, blithely unconcerned but proud, greedily intent on devouring His bunch of grapes while looking at us. And around their completely Renaissance-style throne already discussed above,[233] four small angels among whom two play lutes,[234] and these are all on a smaller scale than the divine protagonists.

The four large saints to the sides of the throne have been lost; the low dais in Renaissance style must have continued into their compartments. There remain four small saints for the side pilasters [Plates 11-12], two of them intently reading sacred texts, the other two clutching their mantles, alert and energetic. From the upper compartments there survive the Saint Paul [Plate 16], haughty, almost derisive, with book and sword, and the Saint Andrew [Plate 17], corpulent in body with his head virtually stuffed between his shoulders, carrying his cross. Probably originally there were several more saints. The initial arrangement, with each in a separate compartment like statues in niches on a cathedral façade, can be imagined by recalling the Piero della Francesca polyptych at Sansepolcro or even Mantegna's polyptych of Saint Luke in Milan, though there would have been even more saints. It may be that Masaccio was inspired by some ideal arrangement such as that of the façade of the cathedral in Florence on which, in his time, work was proceeding feverishly. As a matter of fact, it is rare to find in late Gothic Florentine polyptychs such complex monumentality (though there is the example of the work by Giovanni del Biondo for the Rinuccini Chapel in 1379): this was perhaps the third point in which Masaccio, apart from any particular contingencies, may have wished deliberately to cling to and even accentuate the traditional scheme.

The innovations in the Pisa polyptych were entirely a matter of style, independent of overall schemes, framework and the like. However, it has been so frequently analyzed and praised that there is no need here for more than a recapitulation. More than anything else, there is its evident maturity: a confrontation between the three Madonnas—those of San Giovenale, Sant'Ambrogio, and the Carmine of Pisa—indeed gives one the impression of three milestones. In the San Giovenale triptych, there is an early attempt to give some kind of coherency to an image which continues however to be conceived according to a fundamental Gothic scheme. In the Sant'Ambrogio Madonna, the image is rejuvenated, acquires, one might say, an ulterior dimension, becomes completely real, but is nevertheless constructed as a kind of elementary demonstration, being more or less frontal and compact as if built up by one piece on another. In the Pisa polyptych, the artist feels such security that the form can be relaxed, the drapery can move in beautiful folds quite independent of the figure itself, the Madonna's hands no longer need to clutch the Child, and her head can be inclined. The light coming from the left is more precise but also more subtly and analytically modulated. The complicated, almost minute articulation of the throne into little columns, joinings and frame has the precise function of breaking up the light, while the wavy tooth-combed decorative motif on the dais—as compared with the perfectly smooth pediment in the Sant'Ambrogio painting with its platform entirely in light and the front of the step in shadow—is further evidence of a subtle and continuous rhythmic scansion of the light. Such concern with infinitesimal details was, indeed, indispensable to the new fundamental spatial-existential character of figurative art.[235] Along with this, it was necessary to make the forms function with ease within the picture in order to bring about ultimately an atmospheric relationship between the gold of the frame and the gold of the background. Only thus could there be achieved in the polyptych the full realization of a figurative presence no longer merely decorative or monumental but now scientifically "natural," rich in immanent value, fully humanized.

Further, the polyptych made its effect also and at the same time through a broken-up, articulated but nevertheless continuous movement not only in the light but also in the space in which the plastic image is set, as well as through the perspective approach whose more profound aspects were, at the time, another of the secrets that Masaccio alone, at least among the painters, had grasped. The three small scenes of the predella have somewhat too much insistence on vertical lines, so that once the eye has passed the angel musicians it tends to follow the angle of the *sottinsù* perspective foreshortening from below, aided in the ascent by the small saints at the sides and even more by the Saint Paul and Saint Andrew, to arrive at last at the Crucifixion. In the latter [Plates 18-23], the Magdalen is not only a dramatic wailing figure "like a transfixed butterfly" (Brandi) but also functions as a transition to the central panel below, thereby avoiding the too sharp break which would have occurred if beneath the feet of Christ there were only the wood of the Cross. The Tree of Life crowning the Cross was only recently brought to light in restoration;[236] previously there had been an ugly tablet with the letters INRI. It seems to symbolize in its solid spherical form that concentrated but dense and fully vital approach to figuration we have already noted in the polyptych.

It is here that Masaccio reached one of his greatest heights, and with a genuine virtuosity

60-61 - STORY OF THEOPHILUS (in part completed by Filippino Lippi) - *Church of the Carmine* - FLORENCE

in the treatment of forms. When, at the exhibition of religious art in Arezzo in 1950, Masaccio's *Crucifixion* was for the occasion juxtaposed to that of Piero della Francesca for the Sansepolcro polyptych, even Piero's very powerful masterpiece [Figure 56] seemed to be surpassed by that of Masaccio. Piero appeared less decisive, as if the gestures of his two suffering figures took place in an emptier space: he seemed by contrast more melodramatic, less refined—a startling thing to say about Piero! But in Masaccio's work there are extraordinary things: the ideal mandorla shape made by an invisible line passing through the profiles of the two standing mourners to rise as high as the Tree of Life and taking in the Crucifix and the nailed hands; and the complex of triangles which make up the composition; and the Christ, stoic, His head not drooping but raised up, the whole body projected forward by the perspective foreshortening from below, and its suffering tenseness made more acute thereby while at the same time still remaining heroically dominating. In the Madonna, starkly upright, compact, majestic, no more than the slightest signs—the wringing of the hands, the grimace on the elderly face [Plate 21]—are needed to reveal how racked she is with grief, and her halo with its pattern of leafed twigs seems almost a crown of thorns. Of great beauty also is the figure of Saint John with the halo in a design like twined ribbon, completely Renaissance in style, which surmounts his bowed head, the head of a mourner absorbed by sorrow, his features distorted by grief [Plate 22], his body wrapped like a column in the blue tunic, his feet spread out at an angle for a more solid stance [Plate 23], and the flow of the mantle with the double fold which rises to the bowed shoulders and the twisting arms, so much like Donatello but already beyond his attainment. Even the ground on which they stand has its beauty, sprinkled here and there with tufts of grass, and now and again speckled by shadow.

We have already had occasion to speak of the *Adoration of the Magi* likewise from the predella, which is at one and the same time austere and refined [Plates 24-26]. Now, however, considered in context, we have reason to suspect that the barren hills in the background were intended to correspond, in some way, to the backdrop of gold in the rest of the polyptych, a means Masaccio would have chosen in order to avoid having to treat his scene in depth, keeping it instead front stage, in the foreground. Further, the dense streaks of long shadows on the ground are another example of the treatment of space and light already discussed. Finally, it must be said that the panel must not be interpreted merely as austere, as is usually done, but also as a demonstration of a new attitude towards figuration which required clarity, logic and sobriety but which already contained within itself its full potentiality for the treatment of detail. And then there is the group of horses with their very beautiful coloring like inlay and their trappings, saddles, caparisons, curling manes and braided tails—a lesson not lost on Piero della Francesca; and the action of the kings and their small retinue, the kings leaving behind their crowns as they advance and kneel and prostrate themselves to kiss the Infant's feet;[237] and finally, made to stand out prominently by the space left above the prostrate figure of the first king filled only by the cleft in the rocky hill, there is the Holy Family receiving the homage of the great in front of the humble cabin where animals, unconcerned, cluster quietly about the manger.

It must be granted that this picture is undoubtedly both analytical and circumstantial in the way in which it calls attention to details of costumes, to gold objects, to a blade of straw even, and its color which is unpretentious but refined and precious with accents of gold, azure, red, gray, white and other. In the other episodes of the predella, this same force and also this same concern with details and narrative flow continue: Saint Peter martyred between the two pyramidal boundary-markers [Plates 27-28 and 31] remains superbly proud despite the painful position, but the two executioners who are hammering, their bent heads bristling with shaggy hair like helmets (for all that there is an apparent error in their proportions which makes them larger than the Saint, although one must allow for foreshortening), are figures of such fluent anatomical conception that it is not surprising that certain drawings by Pollaiuolo of young students were once attributed to Masaccio. In the *Beheading of the Baptist* [Plates 27-30 and 32] the martyr is again a static figure, on his knees, head bowed in prayer awaiting the fatal blow; once again the executioner offers a marked contrast, with a movement so violent that the short skirt of his tunic billows out, his whole body ready to snap back like a spring under tension, and the line of his leg is already purely functional as if in anticipation of Pollaiuolo and Ercole de' Roberti.

The episodes of Saint Julian and Saint Nicholas [Plates 33-34] perhaps betray too much the hand of an assistant, usually considered to be Andrea di Giusto but perhaps Scheggia according to Salmi, or even Cola d'Antonio who painted the Saint Julian on the altar frontal.[239] They are both set in interiors with a bit of narrow lane outside squeezed between the wall and the frame. The heavy sleep of Saint Julian's parents in their bed covered by blankets is caught with a profound sense of veracity, and in the Saint Nicholas episode the cube of the room viewed from the side also contains sleeping figures, the three poor girls obliged to spend the night huddled on the floor while the bare-legged old man sleeps on, serenely unaware of the joyous awakening ahead.

91

OTHER WORKS OF THE PISAN PERIOD   We said that the polyptych of Pisa is one of the fixed points for the study of Masaccio's works. It is much the more surprising that the small *Madonna* [Plate 38] published by Longhi in 1950[240] and dated by him around 1426 should have been tacitly ignored by various scholars and that certain of them should have become convinced only after the discovery of the triptych of San Giovenale, perhaps because the latter evidences a capacity for finely detailed and lovingly appreciated naturalism unsuspected in Masaccio but present also in this small work.

However, in chronology, the small *Madonna* is more closely related to the Pisa polyptych, as Longhi has indicated. It suffices to compare their similar solutions for the left arm and hand of the Madonna which, foreshortened, support the Infant without having to exert force, as was the case in the earlier *Metterza Madonna;* or the circular neck-opening emphasized by a wide gold border used for the small angel musicians which likewise is used for the Virgin and the other two angels in the Pisan *Madonna*, though the motif does not appear elsewhere; and also the figure cut off near the knees as in the Paul and Andrew of Pisa, a low cutting-off point in itself unusual;[241] and again, as in the Pisan work, the mobility with which the image is infused, the easy but exquisite complications of the drapery, especially on the Virgin's right side, this too accentuated by the gold border. True, the Madonna and Child have a great sweetness about them, the mother tickling her son with a hand still somewhat claw-like as in the *Adoration of the Magi* in Berlin, the Child smiling while He grasps and feels the mother's arm. True also, the Child is in swaddling-clothes and over his salmon-pink flesh He wears a little shirt transparent as a veil, a veil which gives rise to a cobweb of light like that on the hood of the Pisa Madonna and which recalls Masolino's *Madonna* in Bremen (as all of this picture does in some way) and the Child also wears a little necklace of black beads with a coral pendant. It is likewise true that the color is warm-toned with passages of chiaroscuro. But to say that, because of these details and traits, this delicious little masterpiece—half-way between a Lorenzetti and a Giottino on one side and a Giovanni Bellini on the other—cannot belong to Masaccio is to reveal a rather rigid notion of the sentimental, imaginative and expressive possibilities of that painter. And since, in any case, this work is undeniably a masterpiece, we should like to know who, if not Masaccio, could have executed it; up to the present its detractors have been able to offer no alternative.

Another case of curious preconception is represented by the two small panels in Altenburg [Plates 35-37] which, I believe, constituted initially a small domestic altar. These were simply fobbed off on "the workshop of Masaccio" or even assigned to a Paolo Schiavo, but Oertel

62 - STORY OF THEOPHILUS (*detail:* Theophilus and the courtiers) - *Church of the Carmine* - FLORENCE

63 - STORY OF THEOPHILUS (*detail:* faces of bystanders) - *Church of the Carmine* - FLORENCE

deserves credit for having recovered them for Masaccio himself.[242] The formal traits suggest a date shortly after the Pisa polyptych: in the *Prayer in the Garden*, the Christ is something between the Saint Paul of Pisa and the bald man with the large purse in the Ananias episode in the Carmine, and the deep-set eye of the penitent Saint Jerome resembles, as Oertel noted, that of Saint Peter in the same fresco. I prefer to think, however, that one of the workshop hands must have intervened in these Altenburg panels, perhaps Andrea di Giusto because of the haloes which are similar to those in his predella at Ripalta (compare with Figures 1-2), but it is not possible to attribute to Andrea di Giusto alone such a high level of invention as that of this altarpiece to which Masaccio himself must have contributed much.

One can only suppose that familiarity with the Gothic-expressionistic pulpit by Giovanni Pisano in the cathedral of Pisa [Figure 7] may have suggested to Masaccio this in some way similar virtuoso treatment. The small panels of Altenburg seem to affirm this in their crushed draperies and their somewhat flattened, laminated forms: qualities which seem rather harsh but consistent with the decided fervor—the fanatic devotion, even—characteristic of the two panels, evidenced in the two angels plummeting down in opposite directions, the one in the top panel a flame-red streak against the gold sky whose red is echoed in the lower panel (proof of the original unity of the altarpiece), in the altar-cloth and in the cardinal's hat in the foreground, vain emblem of pride cast away on the rocky soil. Further, the streak of light on the blue sleeve of the angel extending the palm to Saint Jerome can be found again on the body of the crippled man in the *Saint Peter Healing by his Shadow* in the Carmine which has an analogous audacious formalism, similar also to that of the present-day Florentine painter Rosai.

But there is great beauty in the drapery of the mantle of the praying Christ, and in the triangle of stone-like forms made by the three sleeping apostles, with the light which curls in delicate glints over the yellow mantle of Peter or sheers across the rosy mantle and shoulder-cape of young John, of whose head almost nothing more is seen than a mass of hair. And the circle of rocks stretches away towards the horizon behind the Christ as if to stress the immensity of His solitude, but around the three sleepers they form a close-pressing mass which slopes down to form a unity with the three figures. Similarly, the tortured hollowed-out crags in the lower panel seem to repeat the gesture of the penitent who beats his breast. And on the foreshortened cubical altar, the black embroidery of the altar-cloth is related to the horrid black insects swarming on the ground. The so-called School of Masaccio turned out no comparable inventions of this quality, not even, certainly, that mediocre painter Paolo Schiavo. On the other hand, I suspect that, different as it may be, the altar-piece of

Altenburg may have inspired Fra Angelico's panel on the same subject in Forli, so much like it in its fluent and intimate emotion, even if Angelico's ideal world there was vegetable, with ears of wheat and fronds tossed by the night wind, whereas the world of Masaccio, in the Altenburg altar-piece, is that of the proud dark petrified torment of rock.

Much more doubtful is the *Madonna of Humility* in Washington [Figure 50],[243] a doubt which has always been connected with this picture despite the fact that Berenson was wholeheartedly for its authenticity as were many scholars in the 1930's. Brandi has remarked that if the painting was in the reserve deposit of the Vienna Kunsthistorisches Museum (and I do not know how it got there) and the very competent directors of that museum were willing to get rid of it, there must have been good reasons for this. There have even been rumors that there might exist some sort of documentation for it and even perhaps a photograph taken while it was still in Hungary in which it looked more Late Gothic than Masaccio-like, a sensational bit of information even if it must be taken with all due reserve under the circumstances; in any case, perhaps the archives in Vienna, if the painting really was there, may have some evidence in photographs or documents of the work which that museum got off its hands, and there is always the possibility of X-ray study.

However, leaving these possibilities to the side for the moment and judging superficially only, as one without direct acquaintance with the work, there is something which does not seem quite bona fide about the Washington painting. In the first place, there is the matter of the spatial "framing" created by the two planes of drapery. Then, there is a discord between their richness (the vertical one is in garnet-red shot with gold and there is, besides, a sumptuous cushion) and the decided humility of the Madonna, a humility which is, moreover, *sui generis*. The discord is further marked in the uncomfortable mixture between a Giotto-like "Franciscanism" on the one hand and the exotic Buddha-pose on the other. At any rate, from what we know of what Masaccio did elsewhere, he certainly never painted Infants so unfortunately tubular and weak-chested. As for the Madonna's face—I have in mind its appearance at the time Berenson published it [Figure 52], since which time restoration has given the two figures sharper, more Masaccio-like expressions—it seems to be a cross between the ovoid head painted by Francesco d'Antonio at Montemarciano, wrongly attributed to Masaccio, and the face of the Virgin in the Pisa polyptych, and the look of an English lady of around 1930: the halo is out of proportion and badly foreshortened and seems made of malleable sheet iron rather than precious metal; the arrangement of the veil and mantle on the right shoulder is scarcely conceivable; the dove in flight, so much in

64 - STORY OF THEOPHILUS (*detail:* Saint Peter enthroned) - *Church of the Carmine* - FLORENCE

65 - STORY OF THEOPHILUS (*detail:* the Carmelites) - *Church of the Carmine* - FLORENCE

66 - THE TRINITY (*detail*: the chapel) - *Basilica of Santa Maria Novella* - FLORENCE

67 - THE TRINITY
Basilica of Santa Maria Novella
FLORENCE

keeping with all the rest, has long been held to be a falsification (though the recent restoration turned up a jolly little halo for it).

Even if we concede that there is a similar pose of the Infant in Fra Angelico's so-called Bosco ai Frati altarpiece (and in the *Madonna* of Pontassieve) and if we add that in Donatello's *Madonna* in the Boston Museum, dated around 1425-30, the arm and right leg, with the toes peeping out from under the vest, are rather similar though more marked in profile, what exactly does this mean? Certainly there is something in the Washington *Madonna*—Brandi thinks it may be by Paolo Schiavo—and certainly that something is typical of the period, but what we doubt there may be (and we do not hope for anything more than to be disappointed) is anything that deserves the name of Masaccio.

THE BRANCACCI CHAPEL   From the bare wide piazza in the working-class quarter on the left bank of the Arno where rises still stark and unfinished the façade of the Carmine—so appropriate to our artist—we enter the church whose interior was redone in the late eighteenth century by Giuseppe Ruggieri and Mannaioni. The redecoration was done with good taste, but the stuccoed architectural details, the figures by Romei and their frescoed surrounds by Stagi, the parade of late sixteenth- and seventeenth-century altarpieces, even the Corsini Chapel which is admittedly among the finest achievements after the Renaissance, with its cupola by Giordano and marble reliefs by Foggini and Permoser, all this is out of keeping with what Masaccio and his friends created. The more so because the Brancacci Chapel frescoes are not pompous and showy, not even in the scale of their figures which in the lower tier are smaller than life—though somehow the measure of the Early Renaissance is conceived on a quite different scale, in some way mysteriously grander than any other. In the chapel itself [Figures 59-60], swarming as always with tourists from everywhere, the guides continually pronounce the three names Masolino, Masaccio, Filippino Lippi, the trio whose share in the work was for long a troublous question though it has now been well resolved. In our preceding discussion, we treated the more subtle though not definitive distinction suggested by Longhi and expressed our opinion on the chronology, so that we shall not have to return to that matter, although at the end of this study we shall propose certain additional arguments. For the moment, we are concerned only with examining and commenting on the frescoes each in its turn.[244]

In the *Expulsion from Paradise* [Plate 39],[245] Masaccio had only a rather narrow vertical surface to work on, and the area available may have been further reduced in height relative to the other scenes because of the Gothic capital which, it may be presumed, crowned the supporting pillar of the lower arch. For this reason, perhaps, the Gate of Paradise had to be reduced to a thin and rather schematic sort of stage side-wing with the high narrow slit of the opening surmounted by a much too small crenellated battlement; the result, however, was a gain in essentiality. From the shadow which, alone, defines the opening, stream forth a few gilded rays, and they suffice to symbolize the divine force and will which expelled the human couple after the Fall. This motif, the shadow in the opening, is of an extreme but very suggestive simplicity and was often used again by Quattrocento Florentine painters, among others by Domenico Veneziano in the predella panel with the martyrdom of Saint Lucy as well as by Fra Angelico, Filippo and Filippino Lippi.

Because of this symbolic presentation, the angel does not need to intervene materially in the expulsion, like a guardian of law and order as in the Gaia Fountain relief of Jacopo della Quercia (which dates from before 1419 and should be kept in mind as a possible source for Masaccio, especially for the movement indicated by the crossing legs), or as in the relief on San Petronio in Bologna (whose Eve, wracked with shame, may in fact be an echo of Masaccio's). Instead, armed with a sword in the right hand, the angel does no more than repeat the command, indicating with the left hand the bitter road to the travail of the world. The angel is serenely inexorable albeit sweet-faced—which is unusual for Masaccio—and though the face has been ruined by repainting its expression suggests nevertheless a certain commiseration for the guilty pair. Foreshortened, this figure helps to enrich both the composition and the color, its arm sketching out a circle which seems to embrace the two figures below, which are neither in simple profile nor entirely parallel, enclosing them in a kind of invisible niche of which the gesture itself constitutes the upper cornice. Likewise, the obviously symbolic red of the angel's gown and wings introduces a single but brilliant note in the very restricted chromaticism of the scene. It should be noted that the vest floats out like a cloud beneath the angel in flight, an observation probably made from nature (had this spreading out of the garment in downward flight because of the resistance of the air been observed during the paradise scenes in the sacred representations—what we call miracle plays—staged in the Piazza San Felice, and perhaps also at the Carmine, by Brunelleschi?).

In the two small hillocks is displayed a capacity for exploiting the symbolic possibilities of the background equal to that of Giotto in similar cases: the first, behind Adam, with its steep drop, certainly alludes to the Fall and reinforces, by its line parallel to Adam's left leg, the impression of movement; the second and smaller hillock, behind Eve, in its turn continues the line of her left leg and suggests that life will go on, but painfully and

68 - THE TRINITY (*detail:* the Crucified Christ) - *Basilica of Santa Maria Novella* - FLORENCE

never fully. The diversity between the two elements seems also to reflect the antinomy of male and female in the couple. These two nudes on the wall of a church must have seemed sensational and shocking to the time, with their realism and lacking even the dubious covering of vine-leaves added later. The attempt to find classical sources for them has not been very fruitful: for Eve, no more than the Greco-Roman Venus Pudica, probably known to Masaccio through the figure of Temperance on Giovanni Pisano's pulpit in the cathedral in Pisa; for Adam, with his torso showing that he is breathing in deeply (chest inflated, belly contracted) as would occur in weeping, it has been thought that there may have been a late Hellenistic model. These are, however, extremely vague associations, and while awaiting further evidence it seems opportune to suggest others rather more tangibly relevant to the Florence of Masaccio's time. For example, the rather crude squarish body of Eve set on stubby legs is traceable perhaps to certain reminiscences of late Romanesque-Gothic sculpture visible also in Brunelleschi's work where, as in the relief panel of 1401, they counterbalance the cultivated classicism of the style with a very original naturalism: the Isaac in the panel is much less Apollo-like than Ghiberti's, and the pathos of the head [Figure 64] seems very much related to that of Masaccio's Eve. As for Adam, with his inflated thorax, there is no point in seeking some Marsyas or Laocoön as prototype: there is a perfectly valid precedent in Donatello's Crucifix in Santa Croce.

At this point it is relevant to recall the lost painting of a nude man and woman once in the house of Palla Rucellai. But it is impossible to deduce anything about this painting since we have no idea if it involved purely and simply a profane theme, a mythological subject, or, in fact, an Adam and Eve. Nor do we know how the couple were presented, though it was probably frontally. But most of all, having no idea whatsoever of when it was done, we cannot even form any notion as to the level of skill it attained in the treatment of anatomy, the more so because in the course of time there seems to have been considerable change in Masaccio's approach to the nude. In the *Baptism of the Neophytes*, close in date to the *Expulsion from Paradise*, the male nude is always treated as a mass and robustly (large thorax, smooth belly, strong legs) but without the anatomical details which, at that very time, were being studied from classical statues. Thus, despite the admirable presence and physical vitality of his nudes, Masaccio's conception of man seems to have remained that of the Gothic, more concerned with spiritual factors than physical. However, soon his treatment of detail was to become much more thorough, in the *Trinity* in Santa Maria Novella (we know that he devoted an entire "day's work" to the thorax alone, and the accuracy of the skeleton in the same fresco is noteworthy) as well as in the leg of the Baptist in the side-panel in London.

69 - THE TRINITY (*detail:* architectonic elements) - *Basilica of Santa Maria Novella* - FLORENCE

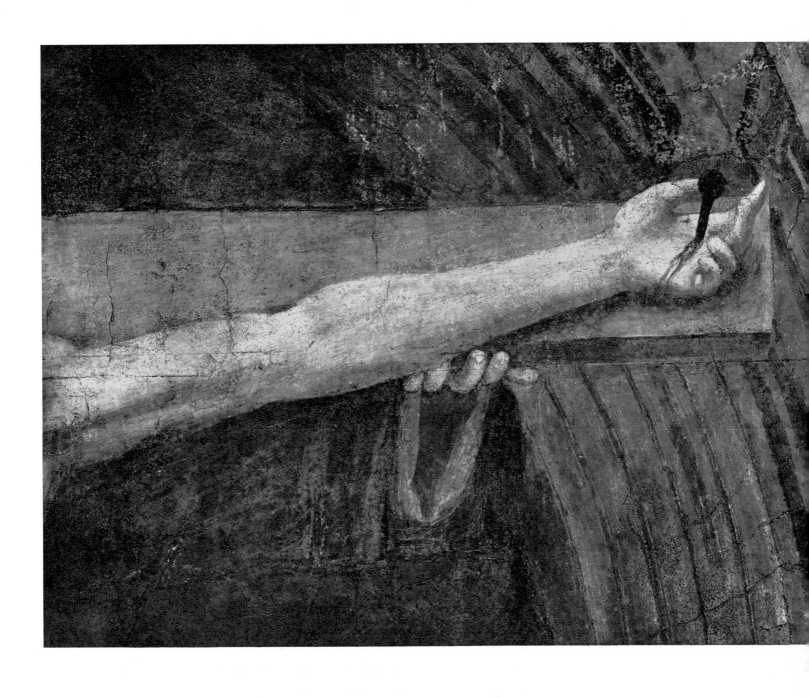

70 - THE TRINITY (*detail:* an arm of the Crucified Christ) - *Basilica of Santa Maria Novella* - FLORENCE

But already in the *Expulsion* light is used to model the nude figures with stupendous power in those areas where it is brightest, thereby creating contrasts between the very fine chiaroscuro modeling of the bellies (note how from the lower thorax of Adam the contour line must modulate subtly to correspond to the play of light on the volume) and the more summary treatment accorded to other parts which remain in shadow, such as the buttocks and the back of the legs. By such means, in the actual work of painting his fresco, Masaccio employed his consummate gifts as a painter to round out the energetic austerity of his initial design, an austerity in itself highly dramatic. But light too is a prime factor in this dramatic approach, the more so in that it is made to coincide with the real light, wan as it is, which comes through the window of the chapel: it deforms Eve, pours over her anguished mask down to the cry which spurts from her mouth still caught in shadow, and though Adam's shame-wracked remorseful face is buried in his hands, a fulvous shadow intensifies the drama, veiling the sinner's head. The light whips the two bodies like a symbol of the new earthly existence to which they are condemned, and behind their legs in criss-cross movement (a movement which suggests cinematography) their shadows stain the hard soil like a sign of the first steps on mankind's endless road.

The *Baptism of the Neophytes* [Plates 40-42] [246] obeys the requirements of symmetry evident in the entire cycle and balances Masolino's *Sermon of Saint Peter* on the other side of the window. Thus, the figure of the Apostle in both of these episodes is at the left, so in the two lower frescoes Masaccio places him to the right to achieve an equilibrium. It is likely that this equilibrium was planned from the outset and calculated for the two tiers in order to avoid excessive symmetry in the scenes at either side of the window, as we should have had if, in the *Baptism*, the Saint Peter had been placed at the right and facing the center. Moreover, it is reasonable to suppose that artists of such high caliber took into account, for their own advantage, every practical contingency: in this case, the position against the light at the side of the window was highly adapted to the somewhat hazy effect of aerial perspective which dominates in the *Baptism*, as if in the cold mountain valley the water of the stream were sending forth some sort of vapor. Is the impression due only to the present patina of the painting? The discovery behind a cornice of the adjacent altar, of a strip which had been protected from the fire in the church and was therefore unaltered [Plate 40] and which reveals in the last head to the left an unsuspected sharpness in a limpid light (as in a Castagno or even in the crystalline painting of Piero della Francesca) does not shake my conviction that the entire group in the middle ground in the center may well have been treated more sketchily and as if blurred by haze. Moreover, it can be shown that this entire group was painted in a single day. This shallowness in the "field of vision" (to borrow a term from optics), that is, in the scene in sharp focus—which is matched moreover in the fresco beneath it where the foreground scene is likewise out of focus and also in the scene with Theophilus—is, I think, one of the secrets of Masaccio's "measure," especially in relation to the Flemish who normally treat everything as a "far shot," that is, with a fixed focus. This corresponds to the concentration characteristic of Masaccio's art and, moreover, manifests a new concrete and positive sense of space, no longer a void and non-existent, as in the Gothic, but rather a *medium* which, like any other, has consistency and atmosphere.

On the basis of this solution in the Baptism, we may perhaps also find some clue as to what pictorial means were used to obtain the effect of distance in the lost *Consecration*. Here, in the *Baptism*, there are admirable details in the wedge of figures which advances as if to repeat in horizontal depth the wedge-shaped heights of the mountains in the background: behind the shivering nude an elderly man in red has a thoughtful and bitter expression intensified by the shadow; in the neophyte who is undressing, the flesh bathed in light appears an innocent and delicate natural material and its clarity is heightened by the whiteness of his shirt; behind him there appears a bit of the upraised face of a young man which rather resembles that of one of the grooms in the Berlin *Adoration of the Magi* (a self-portrait?); moving also, in his thoughtful absorption and his fists pressed together, is the bearded figure in green, a kind of Saint John the Baptist with his feet immersed in the greenish water. The various expressions, caught as in a flash, are skillfully pinned down; above all, the deep concentration of Saint Peter, officiating at the baptism, with his gesture rendered with utmost verisimilitude, from the right foot pressing forward to support the bending body to the extension of the arm as it pours the water of baptism from the small basin. This is the central point of the action, and the copper basin is, in fact, the central point of the fresco from which the various figures radiate outward, and it is emphasized by its foreshortening and by the chiaroscuro which delineates its concavity while the falling water drips from the drenched hair of the baptized convert [Plate 42]. In all, there is a simple but perfectly true rendering comparable to certain celebrated examples of literary realism, and the rhythmic architecture of the entire episode is likewise simple and perfect.

The *Tribute Money* [Plates 45-51] [247] remains the work considered most representative of Masaccio. This opinion apparently dates from far back and seems valid even if we take into

71 - THE TRINITY (*detail*: the female donor in prayer) - *Basilica of Santa Maria Novella* - FLORENCE

72 - THE TRINITY (*detail:* Death) - *Basilica of Santa Maria Novella* - FLORENCE

account the other masterpieces of the artist now lost to us, and even if we consider, as I do, that this fresco is not the farthest point reached by Masaccio (after which, as some hold, he did no more, or almost no more, than the lower tier in the chapel) but rather that it does demonstrate the formidable maturity of the painter, after which he pursued his explorations in other directions.

Whatever may be the case, we have the impression that Masaccio poured the maximum of his forces into the *Tribute Money*, in which he accepted all the challenge of narrative painting, the genre considered at that time the highest form of painting (" a colossal figure may be the greatest task of a painter, but narrative painting earns his genius greater esteem than any colossus," wrote Alberti). The centralized structure, the clear, sober but exceptional force in the figures make of this fresco the exemplar of a genuinely new classicism.

This unifying force should not lead us to overlook a certain complexity in the fresco's basic organization. The vast space of the scene is closed off by the mountains surrounding the valley and encircling the human group which is the picture's protagonist, but its amplitude is ideally stressed in the continuity of planes running from the buildings at the right to the area at the left we have identified as a lake [248] and to the great mountains thrusting up toward heaven. Although what is most impressive in the *Tribute Money* is its broad synthetic character, minute analysis of both space and environment is not neglected in the group of buildings at the right with the tiles and rafters of their roofs, in the repeated angles of their walls, in the half-open doors and windows. That odd bit of palisade placed between Saint Peter and the tax collector at the right (which seems authentic, whereas the steps at the far right are false) has been ignored by other commentators, but it is no more nor less than a playful touch in the manner of Paolo Uccello, being aligned with the front pilasters of the portico and traced by the perpendiculars (incised in the plaster) of the interior of the room concealed by the door behind the two figures. The space of the *Tribute Money* is entirely contained within a single, though not very obvious, network of perspective: there are the wire-thin bits of vegetation which interlace and thread off on the mountains; there are the streaks of shadow on the ground; there are the two rows of trees of which the one to the left leads down to the lake and aids in delineating the distance where Saint Peter kneels at grips with the large fish whereas the trees in the center tie together the group of figures with the shrubby slopes of the mountain. The group is backed by these two rows which function as its directional axes: thus the four apostles at the left, as well as Peter and John in front, are aligned with one row of trees, while the diagonal of the other, which comes up from the lake, passes through the group to terminate in Peter and the tax collector at the right. The central point of the perspective, for all that it is played down and, as it were, muted, thereby becomes the bare tree trunk behind the head of the apostle between Christ and the tax collector (it is this head, and not the figure of Christ, which is the exact center of the fresco, and it happens to be the only one which looks out at us and whose auxiliary function is thus to invite our participation).[249] But the perspective is then articulated on another vanishing-point towards the left, and the Saint Peter of the central group acquires additional prominence by being placed at the angle between the two different lines of convergence. What is the formula of the central group? The Christ may be considered a center of radiation, or an axis of equilibrium, or the gear that drives and transmits the action which begins at the left and concludes at the right. Or we may trace three sides of a quadrangle (see Plate 47) on which ten disciples are disposed, but then the central nucleus of Peter, John, Christ and the tax collector do not fit into this scheme. The right hand of the tax collector which points to the city gate to pass which the tax is required also indicates the final episode to the right, thereby balancing the gestures of Christ and Peter which point to the intervening episode (in time) at the left.

A special word of warning is in place here lest we consider the art of Masaccio from one aspect only. Earlier we mentioned the possibility that the *Tribute Money* may have to be understood on various symbolic levels (*libertas ecclesiae*, the special tax levy in Florence)[250] and to bear this out we must now call attention to the curious fact that the four apostles at the left lack haloes. It has been supposed that all the haloes may quite simply have disappeared and that those now present may have been added later, merely neglecting to provide these four with their usual appurtenances (but why should they have been neglected?). I am inclined to think the case is quite different, that the group to the right may be equivocal in significance: it may simply consist of the number of figures needed to bring the group up to its full strength of twelve apostles, or it may merely represent four bystanders (there is nothing to say that all twelve apostles took part in this episode) among whom the so-called Thomas (who is barefooted but dressed in more modern fashion than the others) may be the donor Felice Brancacci. The haloes are certainly indispensable to the four apostles to the left [Plate 49] since they serve to close off the profiles which are somewhat overly oriented towards the background. They do not seem to be necessary for the four figures to the right, and indeed would create a too mechanical symmetry with the others, would conceal the foliage behind their heads, might project shadows, could even enclose the head of the tax collector in something like (no offence intended!) a dish basin. Also, haloes would interfere with that admirable sort of herm with a Janus-head

73 - STORY OF SAINT JULIAN
(*detail*: the Saint with dog and demon) -
Horne Museum - FLORENCE

74 - BIRTH OF THE VIRGIN (*detail:* a nurse with the child) - *Museum* - BERLIN

made up of the vulgar snub-nosed tax collector and the noble cameo-profile of the blond young man (Plate 50) bathed by a warm and precious light like some antique marble. The fact is, all of this is avoided by simply leaving out the haloes, and for these reasons they were probably omitted right from the start in view of this ambiguity or—better—plurivalence of significance. Indeed, I am even inclined to wonder if the two heads next to that of the presumed Brancacci may not be portraits also.

Finally, I should like to emphasize that just as space is made concrete in the *Tribute Money*, so is time also, so that not only the place but also the time of the action is made clear. This is achieved by the streaks of clouds that wander through the sky, the movement of the round waves over the lake, the tree trunks rustling with foliage which alternate with others naked as skeletons. All of these are allusions to time, and the action itself is articulated in three successive episodes close to each other in time and place and clearly distinguished.

But all these minute and marginal remarks should not be allowed to obscure the one primary and fundamental fact of this fresco's unity, simplification, centrality. We must try to grasp and even, if possible, to mirror in words the fundamental poetic choice made by Masaccio. For Alberti,[251] writing at a stage of theoretical eclecticism, a pictorial narrative can provide, at one and the same time, "delight and emotion," and the delight comes "from the copiousness and variety of things, just as in food and music novelty and abundance are what please," but also "the narrative will move the soul when the men depicted therein display the emotions of their own souls." For his part, however, Masaccio does not aim at Alberti's first criterion, a kind of dynamics of sensation which is both external and in a certain sense quantitative but, rather, at the second which is more interior and more qualitative. In such a conception of narrative, the accent must therefore be placed on the *dramatic* element, on psychological and ethical factors, and these are translated—within the conditions and limitations of painting—into physical movements, attitudes and physiognomies, whereas the other elements, of importance merely to the stage setting, as it were, must become secondary and subordinate.

In this connection it is interesting to consider the diagram which has been furnished me of the "day's work" plan of the *Tribute Money* (see p. 103). From this analysis of how much of the actual painting of the fresco was done in each day of work it appears that the scrupulous care exercised by the painter in the course of the final painting was concentrated on the dramatically significant factors in the narrative much more than on those details of value only to the setting. A single day's work was devoted to the building at the right, although certainly this was based on a previously prepared, accurately detailed under-drawing, which

75 - BIRTH OF THE VIRGIN - *Museum* - BERLIN

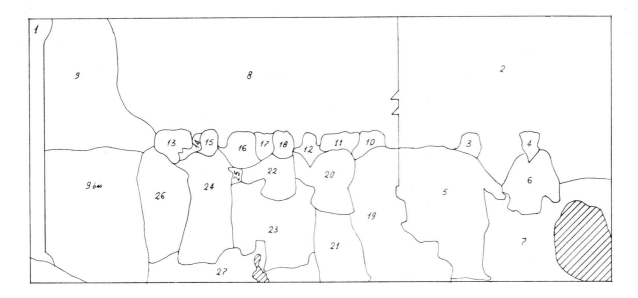

in itself gives some notion of how much time had to be spent in preparation for a single day of actual painting. For the upper portions with the landscape there was a similarly rapid procedure, again on the basis of an already prepared under-drawing. The case was quite different for the heads, of which never more than three were done at one time and often one only, as also for certain highly significant details such as the legs planted in an instable, dynamic pose [Plate 51] (a solution often used later by the Florentines beginning with Castagno) as well as the trunk of Christ's body which is conceived in torsion; there was even an entire day's work devoted to the intersection of Christ's right hand with Peter's left, the gesture which symbolizes the command transmitted and accepted. The partition into two days' work of the left-hand episode was certainly due to the presence of the small figure of Saint Peter with the fish which, it should be noted, was thought of from the outset as an integral part of its setting, the lake and shore. It is, however, a sound rule in dramaturgy to seek concentration in a quantitative sense also. Thus, Alberti tempers his appreciation of "copiousness" with that of "dignity":

And perhaps he who aims much at dignity in his narratives is most pleased himself by solitude. Parsimony in speaking confers majesty upon princes when they pronounce their decisions. In the same way, in narrative painting, the limitation to the small number of figures necessary lends no slight dignity to the work [in the Latin edition: "Meo quidem iudicio nulla erit usque adeo tanta rerum varietate referta historia quam novem aut decem homines non possint condigne agere."]

Here, one has the impression that, implicitly, Alberti is rejecting the crowded abundance of the late Gothic style and thinking of a sobriety like that of Masaccio's *Tribute Money*. With this in mind—Masaccio's deliberate choice of a dramatic approach of high dignity—we are better enabled to examine the question of the possible sources for the *Tribute Money*.

76 - BIRTH OF THE VIRGIN (*detail:* the visitors) - *Museum* - BERLIN

77 - SAINTS JEROME AND JOHN THE BAPTIST (*detail:* head of the Baptist) - *National Gallery* - LONDON

Greco-Roman prototypes, in whatever form they may have been known to Masaccio (statues, reliefs, portraits, gems, coins), and whatever their possible intermediary sources were (from Nicola Pisano to Donatello and Nanni di Banco), are evident for the Praxitelian profile of the fair-haired youth [Plate 50], sensual with his half-open mouth and characterized also by his small eye set far back from the broad base of his straight nose; also for the very similar but softer profile of the gentle Saint John; for the third head in the group to the left, with chestnut-colored hair, whose subtle and individualistic psychology resembles that of a Roman portrait bust; as well as for the next head with its haughty almost frontal presentation and for the down-to-earth greedy face of the tax collector at the far right "who looks at the money in his hand [more accurately, feels it] with the greatest delight" (Vasari). And yet the classical influence in this fresco is tempered and assimilated—so much so that it is neither dominant nor gives the impression of mere citation of another style— both by a simplifying and quite modern realism alien to the frigid and anachronistic pretensions of the Humanists as well as by an intensity of feeling which is still quite medieval (indeed, the energetic heads, Gothic as they may still be, of Saint Juvenal and Saint Anthony in the triptych of San Giovenale would not be too out of place among the bearded apostles of the *Tribute Money* if they were planted on the more ample, more monumental statuesque and Donatello-like bodies in that painting). And the laying-out of the action itself is related neither to the dense grouping of both protagonists and supernumeraries all in a single plane as in antique sarcophagi (method taken over in part from Nicola Pisano) nor to the free spatial articulation of antique painting. Rather, it conforms in the main to Giotto's approach to dramatic representation with the chief action clearly delineated in the foreground, except that here, with Masaccio, the group clusters at the center of an invisible but none the less real funnel of perspective.

Though Gamba and Offner [252] felt obliged to predicate acquaintance with antique painting in order to explain the entirely new importance Masaccio gave to light, it must also be kept in mind that the emphasis on light is closely related to the painter's dramatic approach. The problem of how light is received by objects was brought to a head in Florence simultaneously with that of perspective construction of which it was a logical, optical corollary. Shortly after the time we are considering, Alberti wrote:

They say that Zeuxis, a very ancient and very famous painter, virtually surpassed all others in understanding the power of light and shade, and to others such praise was rarely given. For my part, I almost never consider an adequate painter anyone who does not really understand the effect of light and shade on every surface. Indeed, both the learned and the unlearned praise those visages which seem sculpted and as if they stand out from the painting, and they condemn those in which perhaps no other art than drawing is perceptible.[253]

78 - SAINTS JEROME
AND JOHN THE BAPTIST
National Gallery - LONDON

One gets the impression that the writer may not have encountered this major quality in whatever ancient remains he may have known (and in fact he says that except for Zeuxis the ancients were not expert in chiaroscuro) and that he is in fact recommending it with a certain urgency as a consequence of the whole new modern theory of painting. It is certain that if any example already painted could have given support to his argument it would have been precisely the superb sense of light in Masaccio's work. It may well be that Masaccio's conquest of such an overt feeling for light and shade, certainly absent from the San Giovenale triptych of 1422, may have matured in the lost *Consecration* which, because it was monochromatic, must have depended much on strong contrasts in lighting.

It has already been indicated that the decisive precedent for the *Tribute Money* may probably have been the *Consecration* with its rows of figures in foreshortening, some of them in contrapposto, and all of them highly individualized. If the *Tribute Money* rises to a high level of centralized structure, it is perhaps not absolutely necessary to attribute this to a "mentality made grander by memories of Rome" [254] because there was already in Florence a prototype adequate to stimulate Masaccio's imagination, the sculptured hemicycle of the Four Crowned Saints by Nanni di Banco at Orsanmichele, and because here the subject itself must inevitably have led to this further step. What was concerned was, basically, the obligation to rise from a mere chronicle-picture of the contemporary event of the Consecration to a religious narrative on a more ideal plane, to represent, by formal means also and with the new earthly concreteness figurative art aimed at, the pre-eminence and focal importance of human values. Remote as the comparison may seem, we can liken the invention of the circular group in the center of the *Tribute Money* to the central cupola-crowned space in a basilica which functions as the dominating and unifying element for the convergence of the naves. Supposing that Brunelleschi's development was influenced by Masaccio's achievements, Argan has written:

It was Masaccio who transformed the abstract spatial values into concrete human values, and it is on the basis of these values that, in classical architecture, in the documents of its grandeur which survive, one begins to perceive no longer an ideal perfection but, rather, the living evidence of an exemplary humanity.[255]

The two scenes of the lower tier on either side of the window and altar converge towards it with their oblique perspectives. Moreover, the *Story of Ananias* [Plates 55-58] [256] and the *Saint Peter Healing by his Shadow* [Plates 52-54] [257] are two successive episodes in the Acts of the Apostles, so that tying them together symmetrically by means of converging perspectives seems justified also by the fact that they represent two aspects of life in the first fervid Christian community:

79 - SAINTS JEROME AND JOHN THE BAPTIST (*detail:* the Baptist's leg) - *National Gallery* - LONDON

And the multitude of them that believed were of one heart and of one soul: neither said any of them that aught of the things which he possessed was his own; but they had all things in common. Neither was there any among them that lacked: for as many as were possessors of lands or houses sold them, and brought the prices of the things that were sold, and laid them down at the apostles' feet: and distribution was made unto every man according to his need... And by the hands of the apostles were many signs and wonders wrought among the people... insomuch that they brought forth the sick into the streets, and laid them on beds and couches, that at the least the shadow of Peter passing by might overshadow some of them [*Acts*, IV, 5].

It is useful to recall directly this text from *Acts* since commonly the first scene is interpreted as mere alms-giving which, properly speaking, it is not, although it might be possible to suspect in it an allusion to the Florentine special tax levy as symbolized by an example of extremist early Christian communism and divine punishment for its infringement: Ananias made "a false declaration" to the Holy Ghost (*Acts* V, 1-5) by selling a possession and keeping back part of his gain from the common treasure and was first denounced by Saint Peter and then struck dead "and great fear came on all them that heard these things."

The vanishing point of the perspective is placed outside the picture in both of these scenes, and this is unique and is not done elsewhere, not even in the *Expulsion from Paradise*. This creates a dynamic force in the actions represented, so that even the settings give an impression of movement with their strongly oblique positioning. In the *Saint Peter Healing by his Shadow* [Plate 52] the figures are scaled along the city street following the direction of the buildings and are moreover underlined—indeed, overlined, so to speak— by them: Saint John and the old man who is last in line are projected against a house with a rose-colored jutting-out second storey which is the last of the houses just before the barely glimpsed tower. But the majestic and dominating figure of Saint Peter, unlike the two square-cut figures to his right, is not in any way overshadowed by the other projecting upper storey in white lime but instead stands out against a smooth vertical strip of building (here again Masaccio was perhaps forced to make certain changes in the original design in order to give Saint Peter this greater sense of free vertical space, since it is difficult to understand exactly what this section of the building is meant to be). Furthermore, to each one of the three men who plead for a miracle there corresponds exactly, as if to emphasize them, the opening of a door. The figure placed before the broken line of the base of the building does not give a vertical effect but rather one of descending movement leading down to the miserable creature sprawled on the ground. Saint Peter advances, with his healing shadow, along one of the perspective lines whose vanishing point is out of the field, to the right. And if he walks in a direction opposed to the convergence of the perspective lines, the result is to increase the strong-willed power of the figure. The three sick men, strung out along

106

a scale of height—and, one might say, of misery—acknowledge his passing in both their physical attitudes and their psychological reactions: the first one, standing with joined hands, seems already to have been healed by a miracle; the second, kneeling, concentrates all the resources of his faith in a single gesture; the third, with the face of a miserable brute [Plate 53], stretches forward awaiting the instant when the healing shadow will fall on him too. Such concentrated power of representation within a narrow street setting of such great verisimilitude with its various types of buildings is truly exceptional for what it accomplishes with so few elements, and I cannot think of any comparable work unless perhaps it be Caravaggio's *Seven Works of Mercy* in Naples.

In the *Story of Ananias* [Plate 56] the scene is shifted if not to a country place at least to the outskirts of the city where it shades off into the countryside: the glimpse we get of the open country [Plate 57] with its green hills and white castle is there, moreover, to allude to the precise text of the story—"for as many as were possessors of lands or houses sold them." One sees also a noble iron-gray tower with its rusticated lower level and its biforate window; the whitewashed parallelepiped of a new house which stands out against the mountain in the background; and on the left another dwelling with its overhanging storey, a little smoke-stained by the years and roughly built and poor. Masaccio's feeling for geometry finds full outlet in this scene: the rosy pyramid of the roof on the new building, the various dark rectangles of its windows and small openings on the side, the crowded row of tall windows on the second storey in front (seven, just as in Brunelleschi's Pitti Palace) to which, on the third storey, there correspond only three which are aligned on alternate windows of the seven below. To the left, the buttresses of the overhang are like hypotenuses of increasingly larger length on the same right angle, and these likewise are allusions to the pure volumetric and geometric forms on which all these buildings are based: indeed, the white house has neither windows nor doors at the ground level and is treated only as a compact cubic block.

But the function of the white house in the center, with its two faces clearly seen, is also that of a kind of hinge for the two groups of figures, that headed by Saint Peter which comes from the right (the chiefs, as it were, of the early Christians) and the group of commonfolk, led by the young mother, who hurry up from the left; at the fulcrum of hinge (or rather a bit to the left, at the exact center of the fresco) appears a kneeling figure in red, perhaps Cardinal Brancacci who inspired the fresco cycle,[258] and he is half hidden by the principal gesture of the action, that is, the hand of Saint Peter which, without ostentation, places in that of the woman her share of charity which she receives in both pride and gratitude [Plate 58].

At the feet of the saint lies the corpse of Ananias (which is most beautiful and impressive with his agonized face and his hands one on top of the other, an anticipation of Caravaggio much more than of the more rhetorical mannerists), and his cadaver pushes back the commonfolk at the left to the middle ground as if in a hierarchy of respect.

It has been pointed out that these two frescoes represent an advance over those of the upper tier, of progress in the use of tonal values and brush work (in the castle in the background). Certain solutions were, in fact, at this precise moment in Masaccio's career, being subjected to a simplification over and beyond his already extreme simplicity, with certain daring traits that have been taken up again only in recent times. Among these are a plastic form which tends to its own peculiar sort of overall unity, and also broad coarse brush strokes which build up forms in a free sketchy manner. In the *Saint Peter Healing by his Shadow*, the legs in dark knitted stockings of the personage presumed to be Masolino become deformed by enlargement, his clasped hands make a cluster of fingers which is equally crude, the body of the grovelling cripple is a poor construction of cylinders on which only the spiritual outpouring of light confers any human dignity, and the leg like half a bread roll is repellent. Here we have already reached the point of Rosai, the modern Florentine painter.

In the *Story of Ananias*, the expansive triumphal Roman magnificence of Saint John's red mantle is there for pictorial effect rather than for any objective reasons of verisimilitude (one need only compare it with the drapery in the *Tribute Money*); the profile of the old woman with a white veil, to the left, is built out of tonal values and not plastic form [Plate 55]. The light, no longer striking directly on objects but rather, one might say, softly stroking the colors, does not here give rise to effects of chiaroscuro, of quantitative definition of light and shade, as in the *Tribute Money*, but instead creates qualitative effects: there is an exquisite kindling of light in Saint Peter's green sleeve and yellow mantle (of a yellow which rivals that of the gold in his left hand), in the red mantle of the presumed cardinal in the background and in that of Saint John. The chromatic notes, in this tonal approach to construction and unification, are brought into contact with each other, repeat each other, are linked—all this with the greatest freedom and cohesion. Moreover, they determine even the basic schemes of the composition (chromatic-tonal architecture now rather than merely geometrical-volumetric): thus the green gowns of the two women are linked with the green sleeve of Saint Peter and all of them with the landscape in the background; the reds form a circular movement from the bald man at the left to Ananias and Saint John and finally to the kneeling cardinal, thereby re-creating the noble circular plan of the *Tribute Money;* the touches of white in veils, headgear, the child's shirt, hair and beards such as Saint Peter's are echoed in the little castle in the background, nor does Masaccio shrink even from juxtaposing the whites of the mother and child with the whitewashed building behind them. With such color variations, it seems that there was less need to vary the physical types: the two women resemble each other, the profile at the far right is much like Saint John's, the two large heads behind him differ mostly in the color of the hair and the one behind Saint Peter bears a close resemblance to the saint.

Masaccio's work in the Brancacci Chapel appears to have been interrupted with the *Story of Theophilus* [Plates 59-65].[259] It is really superfluous to linger over the question, settled for many years now except for a few questionable details, of how much of the fresco in its present state was done by Masaccio and how much was completed by Filippino Lippi in the ninth decade of the century.[260] The diagram [Figure 62], in any event, makes it all quite clear and simple: Filippino is responsible for the left-hand group, except for the fourth head from the left, an opinion held as far back as Cavalcaselle;[261] then Filippino's contribution resumes with the forearm of Saint Peter and continues beyond the saint's body with the resuscitated youth and the entire group to the right of the head looking down on the boy which, itself, belongs to Masaccio, and this goes on as far as the profile of the first Carmelite facing in the opposite direction and looking toward the throne of Saint Peter in the episode to the right. There may, however, remain some question as to which of the two painters did the panelled wall which links the line of heads with the cornice on which rest the round vases.[262] But such a wall crowned by vases was obviously already part of the conception, and it appears more than probable that Masaccio would have given it a rhythmic scansion by means of polychrome marble panels since this was common in the early Renaissance, as we know from, among others, Filippo Lippi's altarpiece for Santo Spirito of 1437 now in the Louvre and from Andrea del Castagno's *Last Supper* in Sant'Apollonia in Florence. Nevertheless, one problem remains unresolved concerning the interruption of work on the fresco. Was it left incomplete after Masaccio had conceived and laid out most of it (and probably with different and far more powerful plastic-spatial solutions in the groups and various figures than those realized by Filippino)? Or, according to the hypothesis of Brockhaus, was it really complete and a certain number of the figures later removed when the Brancaccis were condemned in 1434-36, because the figures depicted them and their supporters?

What lends support to this second hypothesis—over and beyond the question as to why a fresco should have been left half-finished for more than fifty years[263]—is the fact that the scene was completed in its lower areas in the figures beneath the throne of Theophilus and in the Saint Peter resuscitating (as in all the parts of the Saint Peter enthroned, but this may

80 - CRUCIFIXION (*detail* of the under-drawing showing Masaccio's contribution: the horsemen) - *Church of San Clemente* - ROME

have been executed as a separate episode) which means that Masaccio must have put off doing part of the left side and the whole right side of the center, including, it should be noted, the heads, whereas—as we know from the *Tribute Money* (see diagram Page 103)—Masaccio's usual practice was to paint all the heads one after the other. If we attribute the fourth head from the left to Masaccio, it becomes even more difficult to explain why he should have done this one head and no others in the group.[264]

If, however, parts of Masaccio's figures were later deliberately destroyed, especially the faces, all these incongruities become easy to explain, including even the head presumed to portray the powerful Cardinal Branda Castiglione. In that case, it may be objected, would it not have been enough to chisel away or repaint the heads alone? But perhaps the remaining bodies of the figures might have reminded contemporary viewers of the Brancaccis and their friends, probably gathered together in groups. The fury of the anti-Brancacci party against the exiles and the rebels as well as the prudent caution of the friars may well have been such as to make such a radical solution more to their liking.

Furthermore, even the resuscitated young son of Theophilus may have presented matter for contention. This is suggested by the way the fresco was cut, as we shall soon see, since in order to eliminate the youth's figure (supposing it to have been originally more to the left) it proved necessary to sacrifice also Saint Peter's forearm and the bodies of Saint Paul and of the last figure in the center, all of them by Masaccio. To justify the destruction of the figure of the youth it suffices to point out the hypothesis of Meller that he may have represented Giovanni Maria Visconti whose family soon thereafter renewed their war with Florence, a war instigated, it should be noted, by the exiled enemies of the Medici themselves.[265] If not, he may well have been one of the young members of the Brancacci family or of their party.

Whether we opt for one or the other hypothesis, that of a work unfinished or a work demolished, a question of extreme interest remains: how would Masaccio have conceived this figure of the resuscitated youth?

Salmo and Mariani maintain that it would have been substantially as it was finally rendered by Filippino, because in a fresco of 1458 by Niccolò Alunno at Santa Maria in Campis in Foligno there is a similar though more energetic figure of Gad resuscitated—in the act of raising himself from the ground he exerts considerable force on one bent leg—and Alunno, it is thought, may have copied this figure from the original fresco, either by tracing it from the under-drawing or by making a sketch or a painting of it some time before Filippino reworked it.[266]

But Luisa Becherucci has suggested to me a different and very acute possibility, that the son of Theophilus was originally depicted by Masaccio on a catafalque seen in foreshortening. This would be an extraordinary anticipation of what Piero della Francesca did later in San Francesco in Arezzo (where, however, the figure is seen from the back) and of Andrea del Castagno, working at the same time as Piero, who in the choir of Sant'Egidio in Florence "bestowed great diligence in foreshortening the bier on which the dead Virgin rests. It seems to be three braccia long, although it is no more than one and a half" (Vasari).

When one considers the remarkable foreshortening in the bed of Saint Julian's parents in the Horne Museum predella panel [Figure 66], it does not seem at all impossible that in the *Story of Theophilus* Masaccio may have ventured to foreshorten a catafalque and a body well before all the others, including Paolo Uccello and Mantegna. This would also justify the open space which acts like a wedge in depth in this portion of the scene but which is not very much exploited by Filippino who places the action of the miracle in the foreground. If, on the other hand, there were a foreshortened catafalque here which stretched as far as the wing constituted by Theophilus on his throne with the courtiers seated to either side, then Saint Peter would be like a rotating column in the center and front of the funnel of perspective, and this would make for a composition of great force. There would then be a contrast with the scene to the right where the saint occupies a throne set back in the center of a convex hemicycle of figures.

In short, the arguments in favor of this hypothesis should not be overlooked, even if it remains a mere supposition. Even if we accept it, it does not tell us with certainty that the foreshortened catafalque was painted as we propose. It may have been, in fact, quite differently disposed, on an oblique line towards the right, so that the head of the youth would be approximately beneath the last figure in the center which survives of Masaccio's work. Nor can we be certain how the boy was depicted, whether he was still fully stetched out or instead half raised up by the miraculous command. It should be noted that, in any event, the basic disposition would still have been related to a model from Giotto brought up to date by Masaccio in this episode, since the organization into a space bounded by two wings of buildings derives, as is known, from Giotto's *Burial of Saint Francis* in the Bardi Chapel, whereas for the actual incident of the resuscitation he would have reworked in modern terms, in perspective, the scene of the *Resurrection of Drusiana* in the Peruzzi Chapel from which certain elements in Masaccio's painting certainly derive, as for example the figure of Saint Peter and the man who raises his hands in amazement. And even though Filippino reorganized the scene in his own manner (succeeding in justifying the previous arrangement of the figures, heads and expressions as left by Masaccio), we can nevertheless conjecture that Masaccio's right-hand group may well have been different from the mechanical, thin row of figures we see now, strung out along an oblique and with dead space behind their backs; it may have included a bent-over figure carrying the catafalque (as in Giotto) and a wider variety and range of figures as in Masaccio's left-hand group, and perhaps even some female figure (again as in Giotto) to break the monotony of that miracle which today seems reserved for men only.

FROM THE CARMINE TO THE TRINITY I have deliberately limited myself, for the *Story of Theophilus*, to the problem of its original compositional structure, without singling out the many details which, in such a richly orchestrated picture, reveal an admirable variety of pictorial possibilities while remaining within the supremely coherent unity of the whole. The way in which Masaccio's self-portrait on the right stands out luminously from the shadowy background, the consequent penetrating psychological force of that visage looking out at us, as if both to tell us something and to pose a question—these seem to belong already to seventeenth-century art, to that century's feeling for both flesh and soul. The kneeling prelate in red a little more to the foreground, incisive in conception but limited to the most essential details, is painted with such intense and warm tonality as to remind us of the Venetians of, say, a century after the early paintings of Lotto. Saint Peter seated on the throne —with an even greater force in relief than the Madonnas of the Uffizi and the London National Gallery—is in every sense a personification of the Faith, so profound is the inspired meditation of that visage, all thoughts directed to Heaven [Plate 64], and its spiritual illumination realized in luminous pictorial touches. The prodigious group of four Carmelites [Plate 65], each one of a different personality, age, appearance, religious character—from the expert theologian acute and determined to the unself-conscious fanatic—contains within itself already all the possibilities of characterization of a Ghirlandaio and has no equal in realistic depiction of human temperaments, not even in Van Eyck. At the other side of the picture, there is Theophilus set in profile within his niche [Plate 62], impassive and subtle tyrant like certain high-placed personages of the Renaissance we know from the medals of Pisanello; and the bird-of-prey head of the swarthy Saint Paul [Plate 61] raised in anxious prayer as if to guarantee the miracle; and in the thicket of onlookers in the background there are certain faces like bloodless bald masks or like madly staring Pierrots...

But now, as we look back on the frescoes of the Carmine, I think that we are all equipped to take a stand on some of the principal questions, whether we proceed by gathering together our various observations and comparisons or, instead, by basing our decisions on overall impressions of the total structure.

Is it a work concentrated into less than a year, from the second half of 1427 to 1428, as Procacci and Brandi maintain today,[267] or did it take longer, from 1425 to 1428, something like three years, as is more generally believed and as the present writer continues to hold? And since our aim is to trace a development, a progress in Masaccio's work, how does this reveal itself in the Carmine? Does Masaccio move there definitely towards a greater objective apprehension of the Real, an apprehension which is both a sign of humility in the face of science and, at the same time, of a more open intellectual mastery, the full measure and superb discipline of Humanism? Or, on the contrary, as certain writers today deem it more penetrating, more certain, more up-to-date to suppose, is the case quite the opposite, and had Masaccio already painted the *Trinity* at Santa Maria Novella? Did his ultimate goal become, by a voluntary about-face, something not too remote from what was to become the characteristic of twentieth-century art, something between metaphysical art and expressionism, like that of a Carrà or a Rosai?

As a case in point, consider for example the variations in the figure of the protagonist Saint Peter. In the *Baptism of the Neophytes* [Plate 41], the saint has a massive and rugged power, with a plasticity which is rather compact and sparing; in the *Story of Theophilus* [Plates 60-61] his drapery is very much richer and more animated in folds and pleats, the line is more active, the pose more studied in its three-quarter view with the profile less obvious. We can trace the progressive steps between these two terminal points by reviewing the upper tier of frescoes. The Saint Peter who gives the coin to the tax collector [Plate 45] reflects classicizing influences but is more robust and proud, more lower-class, like a figure by Donatello, with his body which makes an unshakable support for his large frizzled broad-profiled head; and yet the right arm is still rigid in gesture as in the Baptism. Here, as also in the Saint Peter who receives the command from Christ in the same fresco, Masaccio achieved an eloquently majestic character which yet retains great simplicity. It was this which Masolino sought to imitate, for better or worse, in the *Resurrection of Drusiana* and which I believe may have had great importance in the ripening of Raphael's classicism, however extreme the form it took. In the stories in the lower tier of Saint Peter who heals with his shadow and of Ananias [Plates 52 and 56] the physical characterization is, however, changed. Saint Peter appears less square-built and more elongated, his head more emaciated and spiritualized, the whole approach less sculptural and more flowing and painterly, especially in the Ananias episode. I do not think that all of these very marked changes could possibly have come about in a single year of work. I do believe, however, that such a change in style appears very possible between, on the one hand, the Theophilus episode and especially the Saint Peter enthroned and, on the other, the personages of the *Trinity* in Santa Maria Novella [Plates 60-61, 67 and 71], but certainly not between the latter and the *Baptism* whose power is still rough and unpolished and which is still somewhat block-like in structure.

Even the compositional structures confirm this. Only in the lower tier of frescoes in the Carmine do the creation, scansion and perspective articulation of space become truly marked in relation to the figures it encloses. In the *Baptism* and the *Expulsion of Adam and Eve* the human figure is the protagonist, true, but the spatial conception is still very limited and merely intuitive. Space opens up in the *Tribute Money* to allow air to penetrate that solemn human "rotunda" and to give proper disposition to the two minor episodes, and that space is defined and articulated by elements disposed in depth. However, it is only in the *Saint Peter Healing with his Shadow* that space flows according to the convergence of perspective lines, and in the *Story of Ananias* it is treated as a hinge, using the central building as fulcrum. Finally, in the Theophilus scene Giotto's old box-like treatment of space opens beyond the background wall into an infinite potential—one having to do with the earth, not heaven, thanks to the round vases (which suggest volumetric continuity) and the full-leafed trees against a sky which is truly atmosphere, not paint; further, a massive structure at the left conceived according to Brunelleschi's canons stretches out in foreshortening to confirm this disposition of natural space. Metric rhythms scan and tie together the architectonic elements of the courtyard in an order which is both Humanistic and highly civilized, while the actors are grouped in various ways symbolic of a rational geometric-perspective order: static groups in symmetrical balance, semicircles, wings, wedges.

On the other hand, there are some who insist that the *Trinity* of Santa Maria Novella is anterior to the entire cycle in the Carmine. Instead of speaking (on the whole without much justification) of Flemish influence having been experimented with there and then quickly abandoned to go on to the greater "freedom" of the *Adam and Eve* or of the *Baptism of the Neophytes*, they ought first to try to justify their position by replying to certain questions, elementary questions indeed:

1) How is it conceivable that the same painter who did the rigorous perspective in full Renaissance style of the architecture in the *Trinity* (remember, the proponents of this argument exclude all direct collaboration of Brunelleschi in this fresco) could have gone on, in the Carmine, to paint the naive box which is the setting for the *Resurrection of Tabitha* (if they concede that the background of that fresco is really by Masaccio) [268] and only slowly,

step by step, could have made his way to an ever more progressive characterization in Renaissance manner of the architectural elements the Carmine frescoes include?

2) Why, after having for the figure of the Virgin in the *Trinity* experimented, well before Alberti, with the devices of *velo* and *quadrettatura* (squaring off a surface to aid in accurate transfer or enlargement of the preliminary cartoon, using charcoal-dusted plumb lines or optical instruments or proportionate squares) [269] should Masaccio have then abandoned completely in the Carmine this secret which was, in fact, of immeasurably revolutionary significance not only for technique but also for style since it resolves with scientific objectivity the problem of insertion into space of even irregular volumes such as human bodies?

3) How could it happen that from the indubitably great maturity in drawing in the figures in the *Trinity* there should be a regression (the adherents of this notion call it a transition!) immediately afterwards, in the Carmine, to the stage of the *Metterza Saint Anne*? It suffices to compare the massive bodies and stubby hands in the latter painting or in the first scenes of the Carmine such as the *Baptism* and *Expulsion* with the anatomy of the Crucified Christ and the admirable treatment of hands in Santa Maria Novella (Compare Plates 9 and 42 with 66 and 70).

4) As for the two portraits of the kneeling donors in Santa Maria Novella, with their objectivity which is nevertheless so softly modeled and so wise in all the painter's art, are they closer to the two youths in the *Baptism* who are excessively hook-like and rigid or, instead, do they not make more sense if they follow the Theophilus and the kneeling Carmelite in the last fresco Masaccio executed in the Brancacci?

THE TRINITY   Procacci has dated the *Trinity* around the first half of 1427 which, according to him, means that this work was done between the Pisa polyptych and the beginning of Masaccio's collaboration in the Brancacci Chapel with the return of Masolino (as he believes). But this chronology is far from being established with certainty and could very well be fixed at one year later.

That the altar of the Trinity may have been erected by Fra Lorenzo Cardoni—prior of Santa Maria Novella from 1423 to 1425 (and in fact until to the first half of 1426)—is information gleaned from later sources, one of which moreover declares that the altar was indeed erected by Cardoni, but in 1430. Furthermore, it is generally agreed on the basis of the other date—which we owe to Procacci himself—that the donor depicted in the fresco may be, instead, a member of the Lenzi family who was *gonfaloniere* that is, chief magistrate of the Republic (and his costume bears this out) towards the end of 1425, whereas a tombstone

115

of the Lenzi family close by the altar of the Trinity gives the date of 1426. According to this external evidence, then, the date can therefore be pushed forward to the end of 1425, as Borsook does, or to 1426, as in the recent lectures of Brandi, or to the beginning of 1427 as in Procacci's calculations. However, one can also suppose that the altar was planned during Cardoni's time, but was only realized some time later at the expense of the Lenzis, and in this case it could have been done in the first half of 1427 or the second half of the same year or the first half of 1428.

On the other hand, as Schlegel recently pointed out, Cardoni may very well have begun an altar properly speaking set forward from the wall and, later, under commission from the Lenzis, Masaccio may have undertaken to paint the wall. And this real altar of Cardoni, if we grant that it ever existed, may have had on it the wooden Crucifix attributed to Maso di Bartolomeo—who likewise was called Masaccio—which was later installed in the sacristy of Santa Maria Novella, the Crucifix to which, in fact, the sources which speak of Cardoni refer and which certainly, even if we do not understand exactly how, must have been at one time set up on the altar of the Trinity.

In short, I am willing to go so far as to doubt that there was any relationship whatsoever between the altar of the Trinity and Cardoni, because, if anyone seems likely to have summoned Brunelleschi and Masaccio to Santa Maria Novella and proposed them to the good magistrate Lenzi who was a man of humble extraction, it seems to me that it was probably another Dominican of the same years, Fra Alessio Strozzi who in 1426 was appointed to succeed Cardoni as prior but had himself excused. Contemporary sources describe him as a man of great and lively culture, a fine connoisseur of architecture and goldsmith work, friend and highly authoritative counsellor of, precisely, Brunelleschi and Ghiberti. [270]

Now, there is an overall consistency in the modes (and moments) of historical-critical thought. The dating of the *Trinity* before the Carmine frescoes is no more than a final episode in the purely idealistic approach to the visual art. In line with that approach the notion of a collaboration of Brunelleschi on the daring perspective in this fresco was rejected. Moreover, perspective was deprecated as "programmatic" and "intellectualistic" as against the (presumed) immediacy of true art which, according to the gospel of Croce, expresses only sentiments. Time itself, however, decants the alcohol of history: it seems to me that today we finally have a clear intuition as to the part Brunelleschi really played in the *Trinity* [Plates 66-67] and of just how Masaccio at last came to achieve a full-fledged orientation to the Renaissance in the period when he was in closest contact with Brunelleschi.

The ensemble of the *Trinity*, which can now be evaluated in its entirety as a result of the discovery by Procacci of the skeleton at the base—even if certain problems have not yet been definitively settled, and perhaps can never be, regarding the structure of the lower part[271]—appears to be constructed on the basis of such a deep and rigorous science of perspective that it is strictly logical to presume that such science, at that moment, could have been possessed only by the inventor of perspective himself, the architect Filippo Brunelleschi. Sanpaolesi has recently reconstructed [Figure on page 119] the perspective plan of the fresco, with the two lateral points as measures which determine the foreshortening in depth, the basic diagram and the cross-section of the figuration. While certain points may be open to discussion,[272] this completely scientific approach is certainly convincing. The same can be said of the diagram Tintori constructed on the basis of the charcoal-dust lines which can still be made out on the fresco [Figure 69]. One can see traces of the twisted drawn cord and the knots of the ball of string. Squaring-up to convey with absolute faithfulness the foreshortening of the relief of the grooving in the capitals [see Figure 69] was applied also to the figure in three-quarters rotation of the Virgin [see Figure 70], and it will be noticed that that squaring-up is reduced to smaller elements in the face in order to obtain more accurate definition. All this is another convincing proof of the presence of Brunelleschi in Santa Maria Novella with that very new technique for achieving perspective which Alberti was later to boast of as his own discovery.

The opposing arguments do not carry much weight. It is claimed, for example, that the compartments painted in the barrel-vault are of an even number rather than uneven as in antique architecture, so that the bisecting beam acts like a frame, and this makes the convergence of the orthogonal lines stand out rather than the vaulting, whereas, it is said, Brunelleschi would have designed an odd number of compartments. Also that the pilasters depicted are thinner and longer than those used by Brunelleschi, but in the transept of San Lorenzo, for example, we find pilasters of very great length; moreover we do not know where the base of those in the *Trinity* fall since they are concealed by the two praying figures, and the base could very well be aligned on the same plane as the base of the Ionian columns.[273] As for the principle which determined the use of an even number of compartments with consequent accentuation of the median beam, this is characteristic also of the highly classicizing Alberti in the portal of the same church of Santa Maria Novella and in the vault of Sant'Andrea in Mantua, of Desiderio in his tabernacle for San Lorenzo in Florence, of Mantegna in the *Saint James Healing the Cripple*, of Giovanni Bellini in the altarpiece for San Giobbe, and of many others, so that it is anything but an exceptional case. There is an analogy in the fact that "Brunelleschi in designing his edifices, and in particular in certain of them such as the Pazzi Chapel, but above all in San Lorenzo and then in Santo Spirito, though the latter was actually carried out by his successors, imagined the church or the room generally as if divided by an axial plane indicated on the paving by a longitudinal strip, and in Santo Spirito also by the central column at the back of the arm of the crossing" (Sanpaolesi).

In the case of the *Trinity*, since the plane of the base is not visible, the axial line is relegated to the vault where it exercises its centripetal attraction on the observer and accentuates the symmetrical partition which is also rigorously respected in the disposition of the figures. On the other hand, contrary to what has been claimed, there is really substantially little in common between the more monumental, more tightly linked and more powerful architectonic structure of the *Trinity* fresco and the Tabernacle of the Merchants' Guild of 1423 by Donatello and Michelozzo with its slender members closely juxtaposed and its prevailingly ornamental character. The *Trinity*, for its part, as concerns the chapel architecture depicted therein, is clearly conceived according to Brunelleschi's scale (one need only think of the apse of the Old Sacristy in San Lorenzo), and despite the impressive arguments of Schlegel, it is related, especially as regards the treatment of the facade, to the Barbadori Chapel in Santa Felicita.[274]

The principal *trompe l'oeil* architectural elements are painted in reddish terra cotta color, the caissons of the vault are alternately red and greenish-blue, the interior of the illusionary chapel is gray, and the exterior elements are white, marble or limestone. All of these are chosen to give a sober polychrome relief indispensable to create the chromatic accents which make it appear that the painted projections really do project, that the painted background really does recede. In any event, classicizing elements in terra cotta were already present in the Florentine Romanesque style, for example in San Piero Scheraggio. However, is the architecture in the *Trinity* really strongly plastic in its projections and indentations in the manner typical of Masaccio, as we know it from the throne of the Pisa Madonna? Certainly, in the course of collaboration, Brunelleschi could himself very well have come under the influence of Masaccio, just as the Crucifix painted by Masaccio shows the influence of Brunelleschi's sublime wooden Crucifix in the same church [Figure 71] in the position of the head, in the very sensitive treatment of the hands and arms [Plate 70], and in a certain ascetic spiritualization of the face, even though Masaccio remains true to himself, his figure having much less tension than Brunelleschi's which is still very Gothic; also, he gives to his crucified Christ a simple clinging white drape around the loins which are marked with a touch of dark color.

118

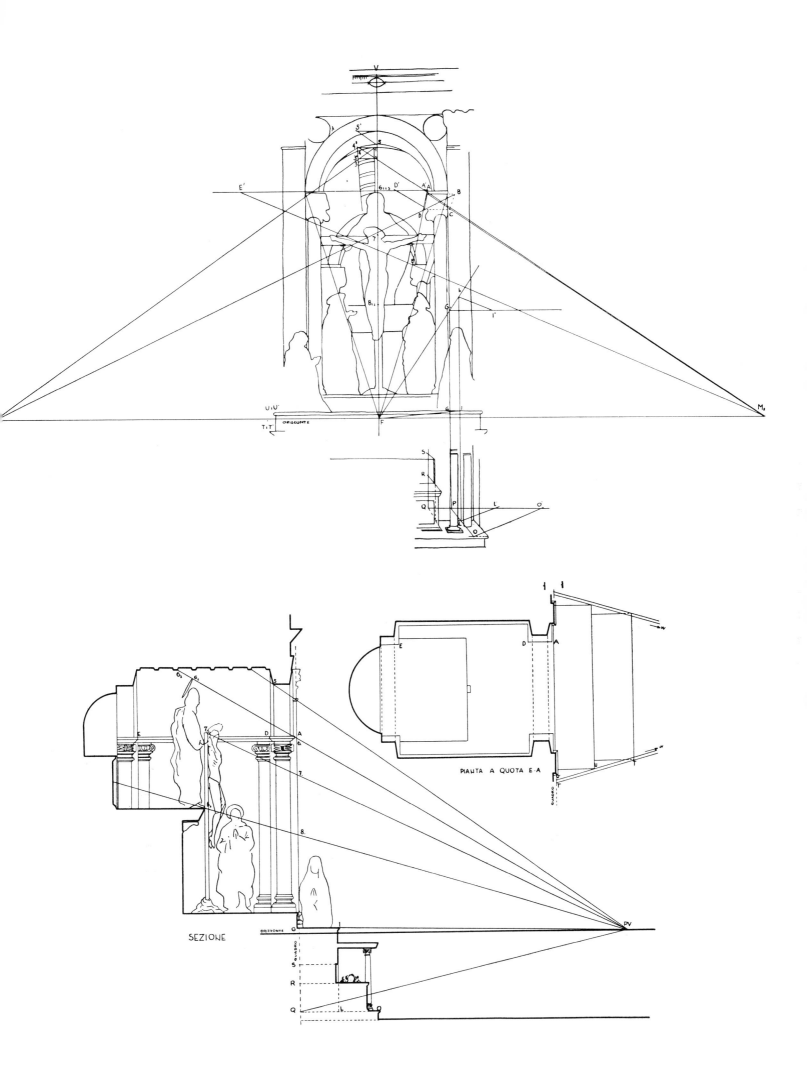

PIANTA A QUOTA E-A

SEZIONE

ORIZZONTE

The fresco of the *Trinity*, according to Sanpaolesi, "was constructed with all the elements that later Alberti was to describe in his *Della Pittura*, including the measuring points, and therefore it is an unassailable cornerstone, the milestone in Brunelleschi's construction of perspective... From it derives the Donatello of the round panels in San Lorenzo... and Andrea del Castagno, Mantegna." But Masaccio's own trend converged on and intersected Brunelleschi's in this fundamental point. Whatever may have been the practical conditions of the commission as concerns a collaboration of the painter with Brunelleschi, and whatever may have been the precise underlying theme (since over and beyond the Trinity itself, according to the very learned thesis proposed at the same time by both Schlegel and Tolnay, there may be an allusion to the double chapel which medieval tradition claimed stood on Golgotha, one at the mountain-top, the other below said to be the tomb of Adam and which is represented here by the skeleton at the base of the fresco) [275]—what is certainly obvious is that the result was a resounding manifesto for the Renaissance set up within the Gothic walls of Santa Maria Novella, a manifesto so decisive and so rich in implications that I know no other comparable among all the outstanding achievements of the first quarter of the fifteenth century in Florence, not even Brunelleschi's own cupola so much more gigantic, so much more concrete.

The Trinity is situated within a well-defined, perfectly visible but wholly imaginary painted chapel whose *trompe-l'oeil* reproduces architecture of classicizing style.[276] The two praying donors are portrayed in natural dimensions and, for the first time, on the same scale as those of the sacred figures, thereby setting up a completely human yardstick for both the architecture and the conception of the Divine. The entire construction is illusory, a *trompe-l'oeil* realized by remarkable intellectual science. The horizon line is placed, both in reality and symbolically, at the level of the step on which kneel the two praying donors, a level which coincides with the eye-level of the viewer (as Alberti was later to recommend in his theory), so that the skeleton of the "unknown warrior" at the base of the chapel, symbolic of the lower and transitory aspect of natural life,[277] is seen from above in its admirable foreshortened profile [Plate 72] and the eye is led to ascend slowly, step by step, until it reaches the divine figures.

The *Trinity* may appear simple, and to some has appeared so: merely a Crucifix-Trinity placed in an illusory architectural setting with the pair of donors in prayer at the sides. But the simplicity itself is the evidence of a revolutionary change in an entire system. If we let our imagination play over and beyond this painting, in a way like its own foreshortened forms, we can conclude that here perspective becomes symbolic of the graduality and of the unity of an absolute Humanism; here at last Brunelleschi's conception of architecture reveals that it is conceived on the scale of man, while man himself seems to take his place in an intellectual, contemplative, geometrical, hierarchic order manifested here in an architectonic organization of profound calm which is static and symmetrical but ascends in the form of a triangle, an order which embraces every grade and of which, however, man himself is the fundamental element. Schlegel has pointed out that depictions of the Trinity should have, logically, moved on directly from the gold backgrounds of the Trecento to the landscape or open sky of the later Quattrocento, but here, however, *everything is human*, because the setting is reduced to pure architecture, to a human creation and, indeed, is conceived (see Sanpaolesi's diagram on page 119) according to the measure of man—the width of a skeleton or a kneeling body, the height of a person, and the like—and the human figure may stand for multiple meanings, from the skeleton to the mortal man to the Eternal portrayed here as the Ancient of Days. This is what Nicholas of Cusa means, in his *De coniecturis*, when he speaks of an illimitable and, at the same time, by the nature of its being, absolute "human dimension":

Humanitatis unitas cum humaniter contracta existat, omnia secundum hanc contractionis naturam complicare videtur. Ambit enim virtus unitatis ejus universa atque ipsa intra suae regionis terminos adeo coercet, ut nihil omnium ejus aufugiat potentiam... Est igitur Homo microcosmos aut humanus quidem mundus. Regio igitur ipsa humanitatis *Deum atque universum mundum* humanali *sua potentia ambit. Potest igitur home esse humanus Deus atque Deus humaniter*, potest esse humanus angelus, humana bestia... Intra enim humanitatis potentiam *omnia suo existunt modo. In humanitate igitur omnia humaniter uti in ipso universo universaliter, explicata sunt, quoniam humanus existit mundus...* Non ergo activae creationis humanitatis alius extat finis quam humanitas.[278]

Far then from falling under Flemish influence, or from letting himself be hemmed in by the norms of the day or seduced by mere illusionistic and theatrical virtuosity—as has too often been claimed—in the *Trinity* Masaccio penetrates to the very heart of the Renaissance where there pulses the idea of perfect, integral human value, to that unique juncture of science and art, of ancient and modern, of the individually concrete and the geometrically ideal, of the highly complex and the extremely simple, to that paradigm of a Humanism which was the most radically and the most proportionally human it has ever been given the world to know.

It suffices to recall how Paolo Uccello exploited the extraordinary virtuosity revealed in Masaccio's *Trinity* (his *Sir John Hawkwood* was the first fruit of that fresco) as well as Masaccio's capacity for metaphysical penetration in perspective, but also how he lost sight of the full, all-dominant human measure of Masaccio; or how Andrea del Castagno, for his part, exaggerated the physical force of the human figure; or how Fra Angelico limited himself to giving a metrical scansion to his mystical visions; or how Piero della Francesca was content to contemplate the sublime formal beauty of the new system of proportions and of the new idealism. If nothing else, these all prove what a daring equilibrium was achieved in the *Trinity*. From it there stemmed a long and many-branched ideal line to which belong not only those masters of the early Renaissance mentioned above but also Buggiano in his work at Pescia and Desiderio in his tabernacle for San Lorenzo as well as Alberti and Mantegna among many others, as Schlegel has very well and very thoroughly indicated. Essentially, in fact, there derives from the *Trinity* also the relationship between the framework itself and the figuration which is typical of so much Renaissance art and which leads even to those altar-pieces of Giovanni Bellini which are said to be in the style of Antonello da Messina. And yet it is true also that the possibilities of Humanism in the visual arts, so completely revealed for the first time in the *Trinity*, were perhaps never again demonstrated in such a rigorous and pure manner and without the slightest deviation.

Perhaps also we must admit that this fresco constitutes a unique point in the line of development of Masaccio, a line which we must now review and reconsider.

Those who claim to find Flemish influence in the portrait of the donor Lenzi [279] are probably thinking of Van Eyck's portrait of 1433 of the man with a turban, and there is no doubt some analogy, for all the more insistent and microscopic analytical approach of Van Eyck. On this basis, we must admit that, precisely in the *Trinity*, Masaccio's style reached a turning-point. In the Carmine frescoes, what dominates is a plastic and synthesizing feeling created by the lighting with its strong contrasts in chiaroscuro which, as it were, thrusts all the volumes into projection; line itself collaborates in giving force and body to the figures by emphasizing their contours; an ever more painterly approach brings about, in the pictures of the lower tier, something we can call "modern." But in the *Trinity* it is drawing which predominates and austere, reposeful objectivity with tranquil illumination which lights up the fresco from the front and diminishes as the perspective deepens. It is evident from this that here the influence of Brunelleschi is accentuated as against that, previously dominant, of Donatello. The organization of the forms in a rigorous order of symmetry and perspective, the preponderant intellectuality and objectivity expressed in the precision of the drawing aided by scientific procedures, the tranquil measure in the conception of light in the *Trinity*, these are all elements typical of Brunelleschi's attitude, however they may be transformed by Masaccio's particular temperament.

In the *Trinity*, Masaccio returned to the tendencies already marked in the triptych of San Giovenale: order based on symmetry and perspective, contemplative character, limpidity of light, a hierarchical symbolism carried even into the humanizing treatment of figures, whereas the *Metterza Saint Anne* is characterized by a plastic-luminous concentration and a tendency towards dramatic power. Thus, to repeat what has been said, but from another standpoint, the *Saint Anne* was, if I am not mistaken, already approaching if not already at the point of the first tier of the Brancacci frescoes (it must be kept in mind that painting on wood may very well be somewhat more conservative than the rather more free technique of fresco). But also the polyptych of Pisa is not far behind the upper tier of frescoes in the chapel: the Madonna, though richer in treatment, has the imposing power of the apostles in the *Tribute Money*; the head of the angel musician to the right is quite similar to that of the tax collector demanding his payment or to that of Saint John in the same scene, just as the bearded Carmelite saint in the Berlin panel resembles the apostle to the right of the figure generally said to be Saint Thomas.

However, in Masaccio's work for Pisa, Brunelleschi's influence is evident in the throne of the Virgin as well as in the highly intellectual ordering of the scale of the figures both in the panel with the Madonna and in that with the Crucifixion. But Masaccio also absorbed, perhaps from the Pisanos themselves, a certain neo-Gothic tension [280] which is not, in any event, in contradiction with his Brunelleschian tendencies. Moreover, something of that tension even passes over into the two episodes of the lower tier of the Carmine frescoes to either side of the altar and modifies in part the sense of the form. At the same time there is an almost nonchalant flexibility that we found even in the two small panels in Altenburg. But in the last episode, that of Theophilus, for all that much is carried over from his various experiences, there occurs the turn towards Brunelleschi's approach which was to culminate in the *Trinity*: space is now something no longer in question, is fully domesticated, and the Carmelite kneeling before Saint Peter enthroned has much in common with Van Eyck's figures.

And in the *Trinity* finally there is established as primary element the Florentine kind of drawing, in which forms are not set down as in a flash nor affected by sentiment or fleeting impressions but, instead, as the result of a synthetic process in which what is observed is elaborated conceptually and stylistically. The use of the pricked transfer, the *velo*, for the figure of the Madonna is conclusive evidence that the definition of a figure in foreshortening was a deliberately scientific procedure and no longer merely intuitive (though Masaccio himself certainly did not need this aid). Already in the contours of the two donors [Plate 71] one can observe that liberty is held in check, that there is a classic mastery in the final solution and supreme wisdom in the use of the brush to avoid rigidity in the contour lines which themselves are now free of every excessive plastic materiality and of all exaggeratedly violent illumination of the form.

We must therefore conclude that, even in this respect if in no other, the experience of the *Trinity* was indispensable to the foundation of painting in Quattrocento Italy, above all as regards the Florentine approach to drawing which it was able to dominate. And it was the total equilibrium of this fresco—from the noble creation of its perspective to the application of the pricked transfer and to the harmonic correlative measure, in the creation of the forms, of "circumscription," "composition," "effect of light"—which, perhaps more than in any other work of art, inspired Alberti in his epoch-making book on the art of painting.[281]

THE BIRTH SALVER AND OTHER WORKS   Having traced the principal steps taken by Masaccio in the five or six years which separate the triptych of San Giovenale from the *Trinity*, we can now attempt to place in their proper order certain lost works not as yet mentioned or, like the *Annunciation* for San Niccolò, discussed elsewhere, as well as two surviving minor paintings. These latter are the fragment in the Horne Museum of Florence with the story of Saint Julian [Plate 73 and Figure 66] and the birth salver—the *desco da parte*—in Berlin. Of the former[282] however I can say little more than to agree with the opinion that, damaged as it is, peeled off and scratched, it retains sufficient power to make attribution to Masaccio convincing. The skinny dog in foreshortening (it can be left to more romantic imaginations to see it as starved) which stands by the saint conversing with the crafty demon disguised as a sturdy youth; the steep foreshortening of the bed where lie the saint's parents with its heap of white bedclothes at the head; the dialogue between the saint and his wife, she rigidly erect pointing to the scene of the murder while clasping her gown with her left hand, he with his head thrown back imploring pardon from heaven to which he displays his guilty hands—in every single detail there is a power which simply could not have come from any of the assistants in Masaccio's workshop. As for its date, it must certainly be around that of the Pisa polyptych, but we cannot accept the ingenious notion that it might have been a first version, later discarded, for part of the predella because, among other reasons, the Horne panel bears evidence of having been exposed to the public, as shown by the scratching out of the face of the demon done by pious fanatics. Nor is it possible to go along with the other suggestion, that it was done for the triptych at Santa Maria Maggiore, because, for that work, there already exists a far more plausible depiction of the story of Saint Julian, that by Masolino now in Montauban. But certainly Masaccio might very well, at some time in his life, have chosen to present the same story, and it is my personal impression that the Horne panel may have been done around 1427, sometime close to the fresco of Ananias for example [compare Plate 56] because of the space which fans out from the center, the lines which separate two figures but at the same time throw into relief the relationship between their gestures as in the scene between the saint and his wife, the women with proud bearing, the forms which are spare but dramatically expressive in their linear energy.

As for the birth salver in Berlin [Plates 74-76],[283] it is considered suspect only by those who hold that Masaccio's workshop lived only on great commissions and always thought and worked only in grandiose heroic and dramatic terms. The fact that this painting comes from San Giovanni Valdarno is in itself obviously not without importance. Further, it is quite possible that the picture contains an ingenious allegorical allusion to the Republic likely to appeal to our painter: the birth of Saint Anne attended by the homage of the Florentine Republic, and on the reverse side the Amor with a marten as a reference to the Duke of Athens who attempted to win Florence over by his blandishments. Moreover, the types depicted are characteristic of Masaccio: it suffices to compare the trumpeter in profile with the young king with clasped hands in the *Adoration of the Magi* in the same museum [Plates 24-25], or the solemn march of the two nuns [Plate 76] with the fresco of *Saint Peter Healing with his Shadow* [Plate 52], and finally the brilliant reds, blues and blacks of both the salver and the *Adoration*.

Of a certainty Masaccio took pleasure in mere description in this wooden circular panel whose frame has a festoon which anticipates the Della Robbias, and it should not be overlooked that, in all probability, this is the first example of a birth salver in circular rather than polygonal shape. Everything is closely observed: the grassy ground in front of the courtyard; the serenely graceful rhythms of the courtyard itself realized—perhaps in this painting even before in some private dwelling in Florence—in the very new style of Brunelleschi, with its flight of columns set on rectangular low walls supporting the shallow azure vaults with their florid brackets and iron cross-bars; the red brick blocks of the flooring and the Romanesque-like inlays of the front of the edifice; the room still Trecento in decoration with its upholstered hanging beneath the lunette looking out on an orchard, and the big high bed constructed like a great chest; nuns and ladies who come to pay their respect, though the most richly dressed among them is distracted at the sight of the men who enter from the left making music and bearing gifts; and in the chamber the women busying themselves with the mother and newborn child but certainly quite ready to drop all to take part in the visitors' gossip (the only sour note in all this graciousness is the scowling high-foreheaded face of the second trumpeter half-hidden by his partner—another of Masaccio's self-portraits?). But from this birth salver, or from other paintings like it but now lost, derive not only Pesellino and the painters of *cassoni*, of marriage chests, but also Fra Angelico whose fascinating predellas begin to appear around 1432-33 as well as Domenico Veneziano beginning with his *Adoration of the Magi* now in Berlin. So great was the worth of Masaccio that even this smiling, relaxed little painting, executed late in 1427 or early 1428, with its perspective and its Brunelleschi-like character, was able to point yet another direction for later developments. From it were to come countless enchanting scenes of myth and fable in the Renaissance.

The fact remains that what Masaccio sowed in his brief existence has yet to be properly evaluated. Quite rightly Salmi has raised the question of the influence on Paolo Uccello's battle scenes that may have come from the "birth salver from the hand of Masaccio" depicting a skirmish which figured in 1492 in the inventory of Lorenzo the Magnificent's possessions.[284] Or, similarly, we may wonder about the lost fresco in the Badia which showed Saint Ives in a niche viewed from below and beneath him widows, schoolboys and poor people. This was most likely the precedent for the foreshortened saints in niches by Paolo Uccello in the chapel of the cathedral in Prato and for his lost Giants in the Vitaliani house in Padua (which must have been a model for Mantegna) as well as for the heroic Great Men Castagno painted for the Villa Carducci.[285]

What has been said of the Saint Ives holds true also for the lost Saint Paul of the Carmine which likewise was foreshortened from a low viewing point and was a portrait of Bartolo Angiolini (thus inspired from life, like certain statues of Donatello) possessing "a great and terrible force."[286] We have already discussed above what a marvelous work the *Annunciation* for San Niccolò must have been, the probable precedent for both Fra Angelico and Piero della Francesca.[287]

No one who has read thus far in this portrait of Masaccio—which seeks to explain his art and not to praise it all as a miracle—will be surprised at our contention that Masaccio constitutes the center from which start or through which pass all the strands of the early Florentine Renaissance: the sensual sensitivity of Filippo Lippi and the candid but highly knowledgeable moderation of Fra Angelico; the lyrical gift of description of Domenico Veneziano and the harsh and heroic realism of Andrea del Castagno; even Paolo Uccello's fanatical preoccupation with perspective and Piero della Francesca's solemnly harmonious rhythms. This was true also of Giotto with his great—though perhaps less great—successors up to the middle of the fourteenth century: a doctrine gives the measure of its truly revolutionary contribution in the extent and greatness of the school it creates, in its impact on the greatest personalities of its time and later. For all our appreciation of the formidable gifts of those masters who were in contact with Masaccio and heeded his words, it was nevertheless Masaccio himself who threw open the way to the art of Renaissance Italy. There is no doubt that sooner or later the way would have been found, if only because of the fatal necessity of cultural circumstances and needs, but in order to occur history needs particular acts and particular individuals and, in this case, took the course prepared by Masaccio.

LAST WORKS For some years now yet another and final achievement has been ascribed to Masaccio, and with a certain amount of evidence, even if it seems to be something of a problem to criticism and even if the work in question remained unfinished, perhaps no more than a sketch to be completed by others.

We refer, as must be clear, to what Masaccio did in Rome. The external facts, already touched on above, are simplicity itself. In 1428 Masaccio moved to Rome where, soon after, he died. In the fresco of the *Crucifixion* in San Clemente in Rome there is evidence, now definitively proved by the under-drawing, of another hand than Masolino's. Meanwhile, in 1951, there was discovered a side-panel of Masolino's triptych for Santa Maria Maggiore in Rome, and this too is incontestably by another hand. In both cases, as is now generally conceded, the traits of this collaborator of Masolino are of the highest quality and decidely like those of Masaccio. Thus, elementary logic tells us that, in all likelihood, these are the final works of Masaccio.

Critics however have not been content to draw this obvious conclusion. Longhi (seconded by Clark for the panel in London) remains attached to his hypothesis of an earlier visit of Masaccio to Rome, in 1425, and has insisted on this dating with the result that he has encouraged the debatable claim that the style of what Masaccio was doing in Florence in 1428 is impossible to relate to these two Roman fragments. Brandi and Gioseffi, on the other hand, have both proposed to replace the name of Masaccio with that of the young Domenico Veneziano, thereby giving comfort to the doubting Thomases of art history who are always reluctant to accept anything new and who claim to discern in the panel in London characteristics of a later date (and thereby contradict the previous argument that the two panels are obviously earlier than the Pisa polyptych and the Carmine frescoes). Only Salmi has been willing to accept quite simply the date of 1428 and the possibility that Masaccio, in the Rome of Martin V, may have been affected by that environment which was still late-Gothic,

127

but even Salmi's acceptance, at least in what he has written up to now, is limited to the new side-panel for Santa Maria Maggiore.

I do not know if that panel with Saint Jerome and Saint John the Baptist [Plates 77-79] [288] in the National Gallery in London still carries, as it did some years ago, the name-plate "Ascribed to Masolino," which is one more proof of British conservatism and is perhaps not lacking in an implied and highly skeptical note of humor. Certainly the well-known difference between Masaccio and Masolino is obvious there, since in the same room there hangs the other side-panel with Saints Liberius and Matthew which is certainly by Masolino. It is evident even in minor details: in the haloes, for example [Plate 78], which, as usual, are so beautiful that Masaccio must have designed them himself and which here, in his panel, have energetic motifs of vine twigs with lance-shaped leaves like those of the Madonna in the Naples *Crucifixion* [Plate 21], whereas in the other panel their decorative motif is trite and conventional; or in the ground which makes a flowery carpet for the two saints but which only in Masaccio's panel acquires true life-like relief, again very much like that in the Naples picture. There is no point in going further, since immediately we come to those few but marvelous inches of the foot and leg of the Baptist [Plate 79] which contain already all the anatomical knowledge and power of the Quattrocento, and this was beyond the capacity of Masolino. It is precisely these correspondences, even in minor details, to the Masaccio of the Pisa polyptych which should suffice to prove that they are from the same hand and to invalidate the attribution to Domenico Veneziano, a hypothesis which, if not gratuitous, is, to say the least, indifferent to its own implications.

But does it date from before or after the Pisa polyptych? Not only because the technique of painting on board makes it difficult to compare it with other major works such as the Carmine frescoes, but also, in any event, it is far from easy to distinguish between a Masaccio of 1425 or 1426 or 1428, all of which have the same high achievement. Moreover, the Pisa polyptych lacks its two side-panels with the pairs of saints which would give us a point of reference. Perhaps all we have to go on is no more than a personal sentiment: the Pisa work is more vibrant, the side-panel calmer, more skillful as if the artist were now able to rely on his own gifts and had no hesitation in deploying his virtuosity even in the most minute details such as the twisted scroll and cross-capped staff of the Baptist, the tiny church and the book held by Saint Jerome, the multicolored flowers in the grass. The London side-panel seems to sum up all of Masaccio's achievements beginning with the triptych of San Giovenale [Plate 2] in whose right side-panel there is also the motif of the book which here is viewed almost from the front as in the very much foreshortened hand holding it. The aged wrinkled face of Saint Anthony in the earlier work [Plate 4] is echoed in the later Saint Jerome, but in the latter the brim of his cardinal's hat—this too in skilled foreshortening—casts a veil of shadow over the face as if to emphasize his more subtly meditative character. And shadow touches with melancholy the gloved left hand of the saint, veils the flank of the little church and the pages of the book, though in the figure of the Baptist it is less dominant. The lessons learned in painting intent expressions such as that of the Saint Paul for Pisa carried over to these two later heads, even to the Baptist's; the latter's features—especially the nose and the eyes dug into the cheekbones—are patently of the same type as the portrait of Masolino wearing a red headpiece which Masaccio inserted into the Carmine fresco of Saint Peter healing the sick [Plate 52], one of the later frescoes in date in which should be observed likewise the head to the left of Masolino's, so very similar to that of Saint Jerome in the London panel; further, the shadow between the Baptist's half-open lips lends a note of pathos which had already been present, though much more ferociously sorrowful, in the Eve of the Carmine. But the air of inward-turning self-knowledge of Saint Jerome can be found only in the last frescoes of the Carmine, in the Theophilus (where there is similarly the motif of a circular headpiece) or in the Saint Peter giving alms. In the panel the color, with its daring juxtaposition of cardinal red in the Jerome and purplish rose in the Baptist (like that of the donors in the *Trinity*), is spread decisively and broadly over a wide field and scarcely modeled by chiaroscuro except in the mantle of the Baptist.

Can it really be presumed that Domenico Veneziano could have so fully assimilated the style of Masaccio in the early 1430's?

As for Masaccio's activity at San Clemente in Rome, it remains more problematical, despite Vasari's assertions in the 1550 edition of the *Lives*. And yet, a sentimental intuition, if nothing more, impels us to seek his presence in that modest chapel where Florentine painting of the early Renaissance (and who, at this late date, would still presume to call it late-Gothic?) made its first bow in the Rome of Pope Martin V, likewise at the dawn of a new era in its policy of patronage by the Curia which was to lead to a far-flung diffusion of the many currents of Italian art and which was to culminate in the Sistine Chapel and Raphael's Stanze in the course of the coming century (and in fact in exactly a century, since the Sack of Rome in 1527 was to put a dramatic end to this policy and drive many artists into exile with further tremendous consequences for art and culture). But in Masolino's admirable fresco cycle in San Clemente there was something like a concentration of the memories of a thousand years within a new expressive system still crude but wonderfully fresh: ancient Roman

Christian stories, colonnaded basilicas, cupolas capping rotundas, inlaid panels of porphyry and serpentine, draperies around the base, physiognomies borrowed from ancient coins, high blind Roman arches, interiors like cubes, deep-plunging streets or open landscapes in perspective, foreshortened polyhedrons of altars and lecterns... Here, however, we must limit ourselves to what may reveal Masaccio's direct participation in these frescoes, and that means the *Crucifixion* in the back of the chapel.[289] The question of Masaccio's share, of which the most staunch and influential champion has been Longhi, recently took on new importance when the fresco, so badly ruined and altered by restoration as to render any judgment difficult, was removed from the wall and the under-drawing exposed [Plate 80 and Figure 80]. Badly damaged as it is, the under-drawing revealed two different styles in the initial laying-out of the painting. Up above, the Crucified Christ and the Good Thief to the right (though little remains) are drawn with a delicate and thread-like touch, as are also, below and in the center, the mourning Saint John, the beautiful profile of one of the Holy Women as well as some minor fragments. The under-drawing of the *Beheading of Saint Catherine* [Figure 81], another fresco which has been detached, reveals the same hand, that of an artist who draws with a light thread-like line most apt to catch the flexibility of the image *in fieri*; in fact, in the under-drawing the body of the martyr was first planned in another position, and the variants between the final fresco and the under-drawing, close as they remain to the initial idea, are as a result quite numerous, including the saint herself who, in the final version, awaits the executioner's blow more logically, with body erect and not already prostrate. If all this is by Masolino, as seems entirely likely, someone else must have been the author of the under-drawing of the landscape in the *Crucifixion* with its chain of heights firmly outlined and with their masses strongly marked by chiaroscuro. This is unlike the landscape in the drawing for the *Beheading of Saint Catherine*, and what remains of the horsemen at the left shows strength and sureness. Beginning with the left-hand margin [Plate 80], the first horseman (who in the under-drawing holds a long lance and not a club as in the fresco now) raises his head to gaze intently and with animation at the crucified figures. He is entirely worthy of the Masaccio who painted the cripple in the scene of Saint Peter healing or the Saint Paul in the story of Theophilus [Plate 61]. Even the muzzle of his horse, seen almost directly from the front, has great beauty. With the same feeling for close-knit mosaic already noted in the group of horses in the Pisa predella, the neck of another horse (obviously contrasted in color with the first horse) plunges across and conceals the lower half of the muzzle of the first horse and is in turn cut off by the next figure, the armored knight on horseback seen from behind, a figure which, even in this back view and faceless, likewise

130

has certain traits typical of Masaccio (typical from as far back as the small angels in the San Giovenale triptych all the way to the figure kneeling before Saint Peter's throne) and, what is more, anticipates in its de-humanized volume the art of Piero della Francesca. There follows, but much farther in the background, a young horseman with a tall hat seen squarely from the front, but even here it is possible to discern a resemblance to certain heads in front view in the background of the Theophilus fresco. Then, though much less remains of it, there is the figure shading his eyes with his left hand as he gazes up (a genuine invention, this pose) followed by the badly mutilated Good Centurion with hands joined in prayer, another of Masaccio's formulas summed up especially in the Carmelite praying before the throne of Saint Peter. Finally, beyond the first cross, can be seen a head in profile with a tall headpiece very much like a figure by Pisanello (and it may be that Pisanello noted this detail here at San Clemente) but, for all that, certainly not inconceivable in the artist who painted the two bourgeois in profile in the *Adoration of the Magi* or the portrait of Theophilus.

I have limited myself to what can still be clearly made out in the under-drawing—currently exposed in San Clemente but against the light and not very visible—without taking into account the fresco itself which is badly ruined and repainted and which, in any event, may well have been executed entirely by Masolino (there are, in fact, certain weaknesses in the fresco as compared with the under-drawing, such as the head of the first horse treated in strict front view and the disappearance of the foreshortened neck of the horse seen from behind beyond the second horseman). Nor shall I insist on the rugged power of invention, so well stressed by Longhi, which created those horsemen like rough-hewn rocks scattered here and there across the jagged height of Golgotha, and not against a conventional background of sky but rather (here again one thinks of Masaccio's *Tribute Money* or *Adoration of the Magi* with their depths closed in by mountains) a vast and melancholy vista of mountain heights (surely the body of water at the left is rather misplaced in Golgotha and was not foreseen in the under-drawing, though it is typical of the taste of Masolino)—a vista certainly inspired by the hills of the Roman countryside and, like the figures of the horsemen, austere, sharply defined, sculpturesque and modeled in chiaroscuro.

I have already expressed elsewhere my opinion that, in the face of what the under-drawing has revealed, the most prudent, most considered and most objective conclusion is simply to admit Masaccio's collaboration in it. I can understand the reasons of those who, before the under-drawing had been exposed, preferred to concentrate on Masolino alone as well as of those who, in the same circumstances, were led to think of the Domenico Veneziano of the round panel in Berlin. But, as regards Masolino, it is a fact that such a difference in

131

drawing technique within a single under-drawing is most strange and nowhere else did Masolino express himself with such truly powerful and decisive accents in figures and landscape: indeed, his conception of landscape was quite different, more abstract, often with emphasis on the vertical, and still Gothic. As for Domenico Veneziano, it is certain that the heroic and severe character of the insertion into the San Clemente fresco has little in common with the highly detailed and analytical narrative style of his Berlin *Adoration*. Furthermore, there are valid external arguments: why did Masolino call Masaccio to Rome as a collaborator, and why did the latter disappear from the scene so quickly, leaving no traces of his presence in the lower part of the under-drawing and certainly not in the other frescoes in San Clemente? And finally, who in 1428 or even up to 1431 could have had similar capacity?

It has been necessary to insist on the convincing evidence for including these two works, the side-panel in London and the insertion into the *Crucifixion* of Masolino, in the canon of Masaccio, and precisely at the end of his production. Here, his path is lost, his career finished. The quality of the two works is very high, but we must concede that they betray a certain initial shock in the artist new to Rome.

Without indulging in generalizations or literary fantasies, one does not wish to go so far as to say that perhaps Masaccio, like so many other Italians up to 1870 and beyond, once he had arrived at his ideal goal, Rome, found himself instead before an abyss. Yet it needs little imagination to contrast the Florentine environment from which Masaccio came, with its complete and well-rounded character and its density and coherence, with the Rome of Martin V where, around a still vital nucleus, there spread for miles ruins beyond measure in the vast emptiness of a depopulated countryside, unhealthy and infested by bandits. And then, for an artist what an impact must have been made by the first direct contact not only with the innumerable remains of a mythical antiquity but also with the entire Christian tradition in art back to the most ancient times. In short then he must have experienced a certain bewildered insecurity at finding himself out of his familiar environment, confounded further by the need to face up to the eclectic and ill-defined tastes of the papal court.

The reaction of a Masolino can be seen in the frescoes in San Clemente or in his *Foundation of Santa Maria Maggiore* from the Colonna triptych. In the latter, the timid and gentle painter seems to regress to the late Gothic or even earlier, alluding synthetically by means of two abstract theatre-wings in the manner of Maso di Banco to the archaeological character of Rome, disposing in regular rhythm little clouds across a melancholy sky above a distant landscape, in the lower half of the picture setting up a kind of conversation-piece with little figurines taking their places as in some courteous council and, above, something like a medallion with Christ and the Virgin. Masaccio's reaction, however, was that of the two works indicated, and in the London panel one can see how he tried as never before to harmonize with the other sections by Masolino or to assume a para-naturalism, temperate and decorative like that of Gentile da Fabriano who shortly before had imposed his style on Rome, whereas in the *Crucifixion* he seems to become conscious, as if for the first time, of how his figures, horsemen half-antique half-modern, feel themselves gone astray in the sad vastness of a landscape seen from a great height, in some way analogous to an infinite perspective of time which cries *Vanity*! upon even the great historical moment below.

Here too, at this moment, the line of Masaccio approaches that of the late Gothic but also that of the early Flemish Renaissance, in the quest for decorative intensity and in the virtuoso treatment of details which is characteristic of the London panel and also in the more relaxed cohesion of the component elements within a cosmic infinity as in the *Crucifixion*. This explains the justifiable difficulty historians feel in admitting in these works the presence of Masaccio or at least of the Masaccio of 1428. But anyone who considers it highly likely that Masaccio would sooner or later have overcome in his own way this incipient crisis cannot help indulging in the fascinating and exciting hypothesis that if Masaccio had not died prematurely in 1428 he would have assimilated into his own knowledge of form and perspective, and into his own deliberately ethical position, both the Roman world and the first stirrings of the new Flemish art just as he had already done on the walls of the Carmine for the Florentine Renaissance. Then, with the broader grasp acquired through these experiences, he would have gone on to endow his painting—the only truly modern painting in those days in Italy—with the power to impose itself immediately and triumphantly as a model not only for Florence but for the entire peninsula... The road painting had to take in his century would have been thereby greatly shortened: it would have sufficed to follow Masaccio's indications towards the ideal goal.

But this did not occur. What for a brief moment was so miraculously united in a single artist splintered up into a multitude of facets. Thus, from the Roman works, the London panel led to Fra Angelico or Castagno, the insertion into the *Crucifixion* to Domenico Veneziano or Piero della Francesca, to limit ourselves to the closest offshoots. Be that as it may, there did come about, in any event, the marvelous flowering of the early Renaissance. And yet —and this is the proof of the value of individual genius in relation to the overall historical struggle and progress—that renaissance was no longer Masaccio's. It took other paths than his great synthesis, his affirmation of humanity so simple but also so profound and so noble,

133

his wide-embracing solution whose import transcended the artist's own limits in space and time. In so few years Masaccio created a new classical archetype for modern man and, for painting, a moral example still unsurpassed.

NOTES

For those works cited here with no more than the name of the author and the date of publication, complete information will be found in the general bibliography.

1) In support of this can be mentioned the thesis of Count GAMBA (1934), dubious as it is, that the painting of Masaccio —"sketchy in style with coarse effects of brushwork and light"—may have been influenced at a certain moment by examples of antique art.

2) Likewise for a Madonna of the youthful Pontormo (published by the present author in the *Catalogo della Mostra di Pontormo*, 1956, 2nd ed., No. 14, Pl. VI) I now find a previously unsuspected ancestry in the mother of the *Distribution of Alms* in the Carmine. See also SRICCHIA-SANTORO in *Paragone*, 163, 1963, p. 12, concerning the Masaccio-like character of a predella panel by Franciabigio at Oxford. A drawing (Naples, Capodimonte 763) of the trembling nude in the *Baptism of the Neophytes* is attributed to Rosso.

3) The episode is recounted in Vasari's biography of Perino.

4) Although open to discussion, and treated here in our third chapter, it may be worthwhile to recall, with reference to the first manifestations of the influence of Masaccio, the lineage proposed by LONGHI (1940, pp. 172 ff.) and also SALMI, 1948, pp. 133-34.

5) It is well known that Ghiberti is peculiarly reticent when it comes to mentioning artists in Florence after Orcagna, except for himself: "There were in our city many other painters some might consider excellent, but for my part I do not consider them so."

6) The hypothesis of Janitschek (1877)—that the Masaccio mentioned along with Filippo (Brunelleschi), Donato, Nencio (Ghiberti), and Luca (Della Robbia) in the prologue to the Italian edition of Alberti's *Della Pittura* may have been, instead, the sculptor Maso di Bartolomeo who was likewise called Masaccio—is no longer taken seriously. Alberti's personal tastes were quite different, both richer and more erudite; at his arrival in the city in 1428 (the time to which the prologue refers and while Masaccio was still alive, as MALLÉ noted in his critical edition, 1950, p. 8) and, moreover even as late as 1436, he must have found in the frescoes in the Carmine the unique exemplification (MALLÉ, p. 8, n. 3, ably refutes Longhi's comments on Alberti's very limited catalogue) of a painting perfectly in line with the innovations, the science and the "truth" of Brunelleschi and Donatello and based on the same *Weltanschauung*. One can well imagine him speechless before the *Trinity* in Santa Maria Novella in which, through the wizardry of perspective, he saw for the first time a classical coffered barrel vault of the type which he himself would one day realize on a grandiose scale in Sant'Andrea in Mantua. In short, Masaccio was an indispensable god in the pantheon of the dawning Renaissance which converted into enthusiastic faith the former melancholy doctrine of the young exile Alberti. Indeed, if one can even imagine him lacking the sensitivity to understand Masaccio, he would have been set straight, and in no uncertain terms, by the same Filippo Brunelleschi to whom he dedicated his *Della Pittura*.

7) The critical fortune of Masaccio from Alberti on is surveyed in SALMI, 1948, pp. 141 ff.; numerous direct quotations can be found in SOMARÉ, 1924, pp. 166 ff. (sources) and pp. 183 ff. (criticism). The general bibliography on Masaccio by O. H. GIGLIOLI (1929) is useful although incomplete and often with inadequate references. Also see U. PROCACCI, "Il Vasari e la conservazione degli affreschi della Cappella Brancacci al Carmine e della Trinità in Santa Maria Novella," in *Scritti in onore di L. Venturi*, 1956, pp. 211 ff. in which it is amusing, in light of the loving and provident protection which Vasari, even after his death, guaranteed for the work of Masaccio, to contrast this with the ignorant common opinion such as that of the friars who, at the end of the seventeenth century, said that, if the Marquis Feroni had completely re-done the Brancacci chapel and destroyed everything in it, "Nothing would be lost by no longer having to look at those ugly fat figures dressed in antique cassocks and heavy mantles." For Gabburri's defence of Masaccio as an example of morality as opposed to modernism (especially that of the eighteenth-century Florentine Sagrestani), see PROCACCI, in *Rivista dell'Arte*, 1955, pp. 235 ff., n. 10. As for Manetti, it will be recalled that he insisted on the "marvelous" quality of Masaccio, who "even in his own time, to the best of our knowledge, was reputed the greatest master." Manetti obtained his information from Masaccio's brother Scheggia and is therefore important for what he can tell us of works in Rome and elsewhere, including Pisa, even if they are not specifically described.

8) Dated by some 1488, by others as late as 1493. Cf. P. BAROCCHI, *Commento* to the *Vita di Michelangelo*, 1962, II, n. 101.

9) For the positive identification of the Albertina drawing Sc. R. 150 with the *Consecration* and for other evidence of Michelangelo's studies after Masaccio (the drawing in the Teyler Museum, Haarlem which has been linked, unjustifiably, with the lost *Resurrection of the Dead* in the Carmine; drawing 2191 of the Graphische Sammlung, Munich which is a copy of the detail of Saint Peter paying the tax-collector in the *Tribute Money*), see SALMI, 1948, pp. 231-32, commentary on Plate 221 (with bibliography); BERENSON, *I disegni dei pittori fiorentini (Drawings of the Florentine Painters)*, 1961, nos. 1474, 1544, 1602; BAROCCHI, *loc. cit.* (see note 8 above) and BAROCCHI, 1964, nos. 2-3.
Very recently Tolnay has announced the attribution to Michelangelo, from around 1504, of Louvre drawing 3897, a copy of the Adam and Eve driven from Paradise of the Carmine; this drawing was formerly catalogued as Raphael's.

135

10) In the second edition of the *Vite*, 1568 (all quotations from Vasari's second edition in the present book are taken from the standard translation, *The Lives of the Painters, Sculptors and Architects*, London [Everyman's Library], 1927, 4 vols.).

11) This appears even in the first edition of Vasari's *Lives*. The adjective "modern" appears to have been generally applied to Masaccio, and is more than a personal impression of Vasari's: "And the most excellent artists... universally affirm that from Giotto on, of all the old masters, Masaccio was the most modern ever seen." Similarly also in the passage quoted from the biography of Perino.

12) G. BRIGANTI, *Il Manierismo e Pellegrino Tibaldi*, 1945, p. 102, n. 29.

13) Rumohr says that the error consists in concentrating the maximum of light in the center rather than on the periphery of the forms.

14) As, for example, the present writer in a recent article on Fra Angelico in *Acropoli*, 1962-63, whose conclusion is that Fra Angelico, the most important successor of Masaccio in the decade 1430-40, introduced into his religious version of the Renaissance the tradition of medieval idealism, both in working out the chromatic problem and in form, and thereby facilitated the transition from the Trecento to the new century. Cosimo dei Medici, who was the decisive personality in the social background of Florentine art, included the two moderates, Fra Angelico and Michelozzo, among his favorite artists.

15) As a curiosity, it can be mentioned that Passavant found that the Expulsion of Adam and Eve in the Loggias of the Vatican was an exact imitation of Masaccio's and this is true except for minor differences in the figures. But the Vatican painting is already in the flowing, lively, haphazard style of a mannerist like Beccafumi.

16) PITTALUGA, 1930. However, it should be obvious that the present study is not in agreement with the evaluations of Pittaluga.

17) C. MALTESE, *Storia dell'arte in Italia*, 1960, p. 371.

18) LONGHI, 1940, pp. 155-56.

19) PITTALUGA, 1935, p. 64.

20) P. P. PASOLINI in *Espresso*, 1962, no. 22, and also nos. 23 and 26. Naturally Longhi placed the dialogue between Masolino and Masaccio in the Carmine, but the reference here is to the rest of his study in which he maintained that their dialectical collaboration continued also in San Clemente. With what he has to say about "points" and about their collaboration in the *Crucifixion* of San Clemente, although our chronologies differ, I am in agreement.

21) P. FRANCASTEL, *Lo spazio figurativo dal Rinascimento al Cubismo*, 1960 (Italian edition), pp. 32-36.

22) A. CHASTEL, *L'Art italien*, 1956, I, p. 209 (translated as *Italian Art*).

23) For the diffusion in art works of the early Florentine Renaissance of humanist printing (antique letters) replacing Gothic characters, cf. L. BERTI, 1962, pp. 161-62, no. 2 (with bibliography), also D. A. COVI, in *Art Bulletin*, March 1963, and G. MARDERSTEIG, *Alphabetum Romanorum*.

24) Cf. the richly thought-out appendix by R. KLEIN to the recent French edition (1958) of *The Civilization of the Renaissance in Italy* (1860).

25) It was in a penetrating lecture on modern architecture given by the architect Lando Bartoli that I was struck by this sociological fact about the general character of crafts and arts in Florence of the past.

26) E. CASSIRER, *Individuo e cosmo nella filosofia del Rinascimento* (1927), Italian edition, 1950, p. 95.

27) The various quotations which follow are from the critical synthesis of KLEIN (see note 24 above).

28) *Della Pittura*.

29) This was already noted by a competent scholar like E. MÜNTZ, *Precursori e propugnatori del Rinascimento*, Florence, 1902, pp. 34 ff.: of the Roman edifices few remained, the most important pieces of sculpture comprised only the few sarcophagi in the Baptistery plus some odd bits that could be found in Fiesole (cf. also KRAUTHEIMER, *Lorenzo Ghiberti*, 1956). In this regard, in A. CHASTEL, *Art et Humanisme à Florence au temps de Laurent le Magnifique*, the chapter-heading "Les incertitudes du Musée florentin," pp. 31 ff., is in itself significant: the "natural museum" (vestiges *in situ*) was quite poor; the "private museums" (collections) consisted of a few cabinets of curiosities put together by Humanists like Niccoli and in a few statues owned by artists like Donatello and Ghiberti; the Medici collection was not begun by Cosimo until around 1440. The collections in northern Italy were much richer, and commerce in antiquities flourished there (towards the end of the fourteenth century, a statue which was turned up in Florence in an excavation in the houses of the Brunelleschi in Via Teatina quickly found a purchaser in Padua, as Ghiberti recalls). As for the "ideal museum," that is, a cultural conception of Antiquity, Florence had certain quite peculiar notions about it: it considered as Roman or Roman-influenced certain of its edifices, among them the Baptistery and the Carolingian church of Santi Apostoli, but also, envious of Rome, it also had a certain intuition of its autonomy dating back to its Etruscan origins; it cultivated its own "Hellenistic" vein (CHASTEL, pp. 184-86; Ghiberti, for one, acquired pieces from Greece); and to the literal, fanatical and alchemistic interpretation of Antiquity given in the Paduan regions, Florence opposed a calmer sentiment, a general image of the Antique which was less concrete and all-dominating and therefore more open to imaginative and intellectual development. The transition, within a half-century, from Cennini's treatise with its single reference to the Ancients to Ghiberti's *Commentary* with all its talk of the Olympiads and the like came about through an intellectual process rather than because of any increase in archaeological discoveries or any abundance of already existing material.

30) F. ANTAL, *La pittura fiorentina e il suo ambiente sociale nel Trecento e nel primo Quattrocento* (original edition, London, 1947, cf. Bibliography), 1960, pp. 82 ff. It may be mentioned that if Antal, as a good Marxist, tends to be skeptical, suspecting in the case of Bruni secret designs towards an oligarchical hegemony, there is certainly no more validity in the superficial optimism of writers who do not go beyond the letter of certain declarations of principle and of certain acts of a Salutati or a Bruni and therefore conclude that everything in those times was noble.

31) G. TOFFANIN, *Che cosa fu l'Umanesimo*, 1929.

32) "...whence sprang the notion, as they were renewing this type of wall-building, which was said to be *alla Romana* and *all'antica*... that first they were all by 'Germans' (Goths) who today are called modern" (MANETTI, *Vita di Brunelleschi*, ed. R. TOESCA, 1927, p. 2). There is a recent authoritative monograph on Brunelleschi by P. SANPAOLESI, 1963, in which see especially pp. 38-40.

136

Overall considerations on the construction of the cupola can be found in P. FRANCASTEL, *Op. cit.*, n. 21, pp. 203 ff.

33) "...he saw the manner of building walls of the ancients and their symmetries; and it seemed to him that he recognized therein a certain order in the members and parts which was clearly similar to that which God had infused into greater things... And having seen what great and difficult things had been achieved therein, he could not help but try to figure them out and to grasp the way in which they had been done and with what tools" (MANETTI, *Op. cit.*, pp. 18-19).

34) *Della Pittura*, 1436.

35) E. PANOFSKY, *La prospettiva come "forma simbolica"* (*Die Perspektive als symbolische Form*, 1927), 1961 (with appendix by DALAI with bibliography to date, with reference also to Brunelleschi), pp. 72 ff.: "Thus history of perspective can be conceived at one and the same time as a triumph of the sense of reality which places things at a certain distance and objectifies them, or as a triumph of man's will to power which tends to cancel out all distances: either, then, a consolidation and systematization of the external world, or an extension of the realm of the I."

36) Such is the title of a study by Brandi, 1960, in which the question is considered with great breadth of vision: he holds that this is the case up to Brueghel (who is considered in relation to Michelangelo!), Rubens and Caravaggio, after which the positions of the two great schools seem to have been inverted. One may however doubt the thesis that Van Eyck's knowledge of perspective was the result of contemporary discoveries in Florence, and that the Flemish artist limited himself to "quotations of perspective". Quite acceptable is his claim that for Van Eyck the norm consisted in including in the image nothing less than already existed in the phenomenon itself, as are also the fundamental antitheses he lays down for Masaccio and Van Eyck: respectively, space (perspective and primary) as against atmosphere (secondary to things themselves); light against lighting; tint against timbre ("in the sense that while in Masaccio the subordination of color, as local color, to the plastic structure is a basic requirement, in Jan Van Eyck just as basic are the purity, transparency, differentiation of the individual chromatic timbre"). The author likewise points out very well that painting as conceived by Van Eyck, by the fact of its absolute completeness in itself, could not permit further progress, and in this was quite unlike the multiple possibilities of development offered by the nucleus of Masaccio. He traces out the Flemish influences in Italy (proposing a particularly fruitful effect on Giambellino) and the Italian influences in the North (with effects as early as Memling): active and indeed finally dominant in the sixteenth century but with particular effects (due to the initial contradictory roots) among the so-called Romanists.

37) The study by G. C. ARGAN (1955) treats this aspect with considerable penetration and density: the conception of history as an experience which casts light on individual responsibility became the ideal of the man of the Renaissance, leading him to an objective study of Antiquity as a rationalistic aspect of Nature; Masaccio's role in the formative process of the Renaissance was above all to create "une nouvelle structure morale. Son objectif est donc d'éclairer la valeur de la personnalité humaine, de trouver les sources morales de cette conscience de l'histoire."

38) Salvini, whose overall study *Pittura fiamminga*, 1958, should be consulted, has also treated in parallel the question of Masaccio and Van Eyck in a recent course

at the University of Trieste, but I know of this only at second-hand.

39) ARGAN, in the study cited above, remarks that Masaccio employed a gold background for the Pisa polyptych without concerning himself with creating a broad spatial environment for his figures, wishing instead perhaps to counterpoise the "non-being" of that background to the massive, absolute, almost brutal "being" of the figures. Further, he points out, in connection with Masaccio's lack of enthusiam for archaeology, that he was, instead, "attaché à la découverte de la valeur primordiale, originelle de la vie, aux sources les plus archaiques de l'humanité."

40) For the older comparisons of Masaccio and Van Eyck by K. MORITZ-EICHBORN (1899), G. BERGER (1903) and MESNIL (1911), cf. GIGLIOLI, 1929, p. 89, and also H. BEENKEN, in *Belvedere*, 1932, fasc. 7-8, who, believing there was collaboration between Masaccio and Masolino at San Clemente, places the former in relation with Jan, the latter with Hubert van Eyck.

41) L. VENTURI, "Arte e pensiero nel Rinascimento" (a review of the history of Renaissance philosophy by De Ruggiero), in *L'Arte*, 1930, fasc. vi, pp. 519 ff. The author places emphasis on the religiosity of Masaccio which he considers immanent and not transcendental, on the anthropomorphism he conferred upon Nature, on his stoicism which express itself artistically in "synthetic rigor," "Dante-like disdain of exterior beauty to the advantage of interior beauty," "psychological expression without any need of movement," "in short, pure art rather than the ornate rhetoric of the literary men." On a more general level, he points out the "mystical transvaluation," that is, the sense of religion and magic conferred also on the science of geometry-perspective, and consequently the deep-rooted folk strength of the art of the Renaissance, however refined its form may be. Another interesting remark about the quality of "popularity" —of roots in the people —of a Donatello or a Masaccio concerns the basis (found by De Ruggiero in Petrarch) of the double-aspiration "of humanism and of the Reformation... of classical perfection and Christian purity, in which the ideal of the *orator* is corrected by that of the *idiot* (the simple in heart) which is a concept derived from the romantic ideality of a primitive, simple and uncorrupted nature." Further, cf. PITTALUGA, 1935, especially pp. 23 ff. (the "stoic" of the Quattrocento, unlike the stoic of Antiquity, is not subject to fate; instead, "a true dominator, he has in himself, as a Christian, control of his own destiny, because his choice is free"); cf. also BERTI, 1962, p. 158.

42) ANTAL, *Op. cit.*, 1960. For a deliberate attempt to apply Antal's principles, but on a rather broader cultural basis, cf. my article, 1962.

43) Cf. MELLER, 1961, for other details of his thesis. The Brancacci Chapel, in which was kept the venerated image of the *Madonna del Popolo* (thirteenth-century), was a public rather than private place of worship: the greatest victories of the Florentine Republic were celebrated in the Carmine, and in 1406, for example, the trophies won from the Pisans were hung in front of the *Madonna del Popolo*. The *Tribute Money* would not refer to the famous passage in St. Matthew, "Render unto Caesar...," because the tax to be paid to enter into Capharnaum was a tax for the Temple; nor does it have anything to do with the ecclesiastical impositions demanded by Pope Martin V; instead, it must be interpreted in accord with the Gospel passage as explained by Saint Antonino in terms of the *libertas ecclesiae*, which did not consider the money as tribute for its own property, but *ex esterioribus* concerned goods accepted from others. Moreover, there is an implied admonition of humility (like

that of Christ in the episode) directed to Filippo Maria Visconti, reminding him of the Pope's efforts to mediate the war in progress. Furthermore, even the order in which the scenes are presented—beginning with those on the wall with the window, then the *Healing of the Cripple* and the *Resurrection of Tabitha* (Meller shows that the two youths in the middle of the scene are not arbitrary additions by Masolino but play an integral part in the story), then the scene of *Theophilus and Saint Peter Enthroned*, finally the *Liberation of Saint Peter* (executed by Filippino Lippi)—all this refers to Saint Peter as the founder of the churches of Jerusalem, Antioch and Rome. The reference to Jerusalem recalls also the Holy Land from which came the Carmelites. Meller singles out various portraits of political significance in the cycle: Cardinal Branda Castiglione, one of the pontifical mediators in the conflict between Florence and Milan, in the only head by Masaccio in the group of five figures at the left in Filippino's fresco of *Theophilus*; Coluccio Salutati, the chancellor who wrote the sonnet of invective against Gian Galeazzo Visconti, in the figure seated below the Theophilus who stands for Gian Galeazzo; while Felice Brancacci may perhaps be the Saint Thomas in the *Tribute Money* formerly thought to be a portrait of Masaccio himself; and a figure dressed in purple, half-hidden between Saint Peter and the populace in the *Distribution of Alms* may be either Cardinal Rinaldo Brancacci, famous for his charity, or Cardinal Tommaso Brancacci, mediator within the Curia for the Florentines but a person of rather dubious morals. Note finally that the chronological deductions of Meller do not conflict with my dating of the second tier of the frescoes in 1425 and their continuation in 1426-28 by Masaccio alone.

44) W. WELLIVER, *L'Impero Fiorentino*, Florence, 1957, cites Lorenzo the Magnificent: "and by adding some fortunate success and increase to the Florentine empire, as we not only hope to but shall, with all our mind and strength, aid the good citizens to achieve." The book, which treats of Lorenzo's period, is audaciously imaginative in its various interpretations of literary and art works, but has many suggestions of interest and is not without value.

45) A. CHASTEL, *Op. cit.*, 1959, p. 4, pp. 181 ff.

46) The documentary evidence is in WELLIVER, *Op. cit.*, p. 27.

47) See note 37.

48) H. BARON, *The Crisis of the Early Italian Renaissance*, Princeton, 1955.

49) H. BROCKHAUS, 1930; ANTAL, *Op. cit.*, p. 436.

50) The liquid assets in circulation in Florence at that time were evaluated at two million gold florins, equivalent to thirty-five billion lire of today, or roughly 60,000,000 dollars. But even more "incredible was the value of the merchandise, possessions and loan credits" (Ammirato).

51) PROCACCI, 1953, especially pp. 12 ff.

52) For the tax rolls, the best recent source is PROCACCI, 1953, pp. 17 ff.

53) E. SANTINI, *Firenze e i suoi "oratori" nel Quattrocento*, 1922, p. 89.

54) In connection with the "Romanism" of the early Florentine Renaissance, I believe attention should be paid to the nuances which came to characterize the binomial linkage Florence-Rome. Already the beginning of Bruni's *Historia florentina* (whose first book completed in 1416 aroused much enthusiasm among the citizenry) is significant in that it sets forth a new rela-

tionship, no longer so much a veneration of the Roman tradition (as in Petrarch) or a boasting of descent (as in the elder Villani) but rather a discreet and at the same time audaciously ambitious emulation based on a healthy and essential realism. Brushing aside all mythology, the historian explains the founding of Florence as a colony of Sulla's troops. At first the new colony had a certain splendor echoing that of the capital, but later, after the failure of the Catiline conspiracy, there was no longer the possibility for the colonists to maintain themselves by further profitable adventures and they settled down to a more austere provincial routine of work and daily living. Bruni also remarks that as long as Rome dominated, the shade of that great tree suffocated the vitality of minor growths, and that the collapse of Rome restored healthy vigor to the local forces. In short, heir to the tradition of autonomy of the medieval commune, and with an attitude of stoic impassibility and impartiality, Bruni justifies the Italian multi-state pluralism characteristic of the Renaissance quite differently from the passionate fantasies of a Dante or, later, of a Machiavelli. The myth of Rome was therefore far from absolute (in Masaccio we do not find the kind of nostalgia for Rome we see in Mantegna) but the initiative had passed to the Rome which at that time was once again burgeoning. The motive force of political ethics could not reside in great ideals of unity and tradition; it became instead the patriotism of the City-State and concentrated itself in the virtue of the individual citizens, the puritanical middle-class figures we meet in Masaccio's paintings.

55) As communicated by U. PROCACCI to E. BORSOOK, *The Mural Painters of Tuscany*, 1960, p. 143.

56) The reference is to the course on Masaccio given in 1961-62 at the University of Palermo, of which I have been able to consult the lecture-notes.

57) See the beginning of the third chapter of this book and note 230 to the fourth chapter.

58) Here I must thank for their assistance and advice (and without fixing on them any responsibility for what is contained in this book) my friends Umberto Baldini, Luisa Becherucci, Alessandro Parronchi, Ugo Procacci, Enio Sindona, and Leonetto Tintori.

59) ALBERTI, *Della Pittura*.

60) The non-prejudicial hypothesis others are currently proposing, according to which the diminutives Masaccio and Masolino suggest a homosexual relationship, is not entirely improbable, but if true it would be no more than an adventitious and highly personal factor with no effect on Masaccio's personality, at least on the social and not intimate level. It may also be that the two diminutives merely refer to the two artists' physical build, one large, the other small.

61) P. MELLER, 1961, pp. 300-301. I differ, however, from Meller in believing that Donatello's portrait is to be found in the elderly man to the rear of the group (as Masaccio is portrayed blond, so Donatello is shown more aged than his forty years at that time would justify) rather than in the standing supplicant. The fact that Donatello is given this position of greater dignity in the company of the Apostle seems to me to confirm this. Meller supposes (pp. 216 ff., in which he follows Pope-Hennessy) that the original marble tabernacle for the *Madonna del Popolo*, on the altar of the Cappella Brancacci, may have been assigned to Donatello and that to it may belong his relief of the *Ascension of Christ and the Consignment of the Keys to Saint Peter* now in the Victoria and Albert Museum. In that case, Donatello would have been portrayed in the fresco as the third of the artists responsible for the Brancacci Chapel.

138

62) Giovanni di Paolo Morelli (1371-1444), *Ricordi*, ed. V. Branca, 1956, pp. 87 ff. Morelli's description of his ancestral Mugello proceeds, it will be noted, in three orders of consideration: "the first is of beauty, the second of goodness, the third of grandeur." The primary aspect is, therefore, aesthetic, even though the beautiful and the good are shown to be in perfect correspondence: for example, the men are handsome peasants but also God-fearing, honest and patriotic; the lands are picturesque and at the same time fertile and rich; the beautiful castles are also strong, healthy in climate and well organized. This is an example of coincidence of the aesthetic, moral and practical-economic sense typical of the Florentines and is not without some affinity to the Greek *kalòs kagatòs*.

63) With reference to the high level of Florentine agriculture of the time, we can cite L. B. Alberti, *Della Famiglia* (1437-38) in which great praise is lavished on the "villa" (Book III: "The villa is of very great, very honest and very positive utility... In springtime the villa offers you infinite pleasures, gardens, flowers, odors, songs... What a happy life is yours there! It provides your house with now one, now another fruit, and never leaves your dwelling bare of some of its gifts."). Niccolò Algerti acquires plants from all over the world to improve the production of his property. Morelli speaks of groves of oak-trees near the dwellings, "and many were laid out for pleasure-parties, the ground cleared off so that it was like a meadow where one could stroll barefoot with no fear of anything that might offend one's feet."

64) Cf. L. Gori Montanelli, *Architectura e Paesaggio nella Pittura toscana*, 1959, on the subject of Giotto: "His is a landscape which still does not have and could not have an existence in itself. Man is always the chief focus and, above man, God. Beyond this, there is only what is strictly necessary, that which in fact is the concern of either God or man." On the other hand, it is well known that the Sienese Gothic attained considerable verisimilitude and autonomous vitality in the urban and country landscapes of Ambrogio Lorenzetti's *Good Government* fresco; cf. also C. Gnudi, in *La peinture gothique*, Skira, 1954, pp. 104-5. Gori-Montanelli, pp. 111 ff., analyzes with many excellent observations the stylistic constitution of the environment in the painting of Masaccio.

65) K. Clark, *Landscape into Art*, 1956.

66) This information was given to Manetti in 1472 by Masaccio's brother Scheggia.

67) For San Giovanni Valdarno, cf. E. Repetti, *Dizionario geografico fisico storico della Toscana*, V, 1843; G. Magherini-Graziani, in *Masaccio, Onoranze nel V centenario della nascita*, Florence, 1904, pp. 73 ff. (with bibliography); and L. Berti, *Il Museo della Basilica a San Giovanni Valdarno*, Florence, 1959.

68) For Masaccio's family, cf. especially U. Procacci, 1932 and 1935: one of those exemplary documentary contributions (unfortunately without commentary) typical of that author but for which, in those years of "idealism," he virtually had to apologize. Mone, Masaccio's grandfather, must have lived to the age of eighty-six at least, since a document of 1435 shows him alive and of that age.

69) The surname Cassai appears in a document of 1426. Guidi, the other surname often attributed to Masaccio, was however assumed only later by his brother Giovanni, called Scheggia, at the time when the middle and lower classes began to acquire surnames (Procacci, 1951, p. 8). Procacci thinks that Giovanni may have taken it from the family name of one of his two wives. The "*cassai*" fabricated the various types of chests which

were at that time fundamental features of household furnishing, from the humble *cassapancha salvaticha*—the rustic bench—on up, including travel cases, wedding chests for linen (*cassoni*), chests used as seats, bed-benches, coffers, beds; cf. A. Schiapparelli, *La Casa Fiorentina e i suoi arredi nei secoli XIV e XV*, 1908, pp. 231 ff.

70) This was the composition of the family in 1393:

Mone Andreucci, head .... aged 46
    Monna Chaterina, his wife .... » 42
    Andreuccio, his son .... » 15
    Nanni, his son .... » 13
    Agnolo, his son .... » 9
    Sandra, his daughter .... » 7
Lorenzo, his brother .... » 36
    Monna Mea, his wife .... » 25
    Lucia, his daughter .... » 12
    Jacopa, his daughter .... » 6
    Antonia, his daughter .... » 1
Monna Francescha, their mother .... » 70

An old woman, two married couples, their youngsters and babies—one can imagine them gathered at table, perhaps in one of the rooms still existing in the house in San Giovanni Valdarno—this was the nucleus of a family group still growing and which was soon to produce Masaccio.

71) Monna Jacopa was the daughter of one Martinozzo, innkeeper at Barberino di Mugello; her dowry, it appears, was 100 florins. Born around 1382-85, Masaccio's mother was still alive in 1433.

72) This is the list of property in 1401: "Item One piece of arable land planted with vines, located in Campo Donicho, on side I Checco d'Agnolo, on side II a gully; five staioras in area.
Item One piece of arable land planted with vines located in Acqua salsa, on side I a gully, on side II Valdo Carlini; area three staioras, ten panori.
Item A piece of arable land located in Canpo Donicho, on I Piero Ciuffardi, on II a gully; six staioras.
Item A house in Castello San Giovanni, on I the street, on II Masso del maestro Fecie.
Worth CC pounds."
Tedesco di maestro Feo, who would marry the widowed mother of Masaccio a few years later, had a very small family but in 1401 was not much better off than the Cassai: 278 pounds.

73) This was doubted by G. Magherini-Graziani, *Op. cit.*, 1904, pp. 83-84, n. 1, who suggested that the house, or indeed half of the house, might have gone to Giovanni by inheritance from his mother, from the property of her second husband Tedesco. From the documents brought to light by Procacci, 1935, pp. 91-92, and n. 1 *et seq.*, it appears however that the house which in 1427 belonged to Mone, grandfather of Masaccio and Giovanni, was later listed as belonging half to Agnolo, their uncle, and half to Giovanni (Scheggia); this occurred after 1435, and it appears also that the house was acquired by Giovanni in compensation for part of the dowry of Masaccio's mother which was still owed to her sons by the Cassai. Thus, if Mone still owned in 1427 the same house he had in 1401, which is quite likely, then it was there that Masaccio was born, and it was the house which in part went to his brother. Procacci in a personal communication has advised me that he has found the complete documentation which proves that it was the same house.

74) Masaccio's brother Giovanni wrote: "My father died at the time I was born, and he left nothing, so my mother remarried and brought me up until I went off as a soldier at 17." So Giovanni was for a while a soldier of fortune, as Mesnil, 1927, p. 20 has noted, but probably not so much out of need as for the adventure of it. However, see our next chapter and Note 145.

In an article in the weekly magazine *Epoca*, Procacci mentioned that Masaccio and Giovanni also had a sister, Alessandra.

75) Tedesco was born around 1347 and in 1406 was therefore over sixty. He appears to have died between 1414-16 and 1426 (more precisely, August 18, 1417, according to a personal communication from Procacci).

76) W. Cohn, in *Bollettino d'Arte*, 1958, I, pp. 64 ff. Mariotto's works include: the two panels, which once formed a double-faced altarpiece, with the *Resurrection* and the *Marriage of Saint Catherine with Saints* (1447) in the Accademia, Florence; the *Assumption and Scenes from the Life of the Virgin* in the Accademia, which shows influence from Fra Angelico; a fresco with the *Redeemer* wounded by workmen's tools (an admonition to respect the Sabbath) in San Miniato al Monte, Florence; a *Pietà* in Santa Lucia, San Giovanni Valdarno. The latter two paintings, especially the first of them, are iconographically quite unusual for Italy and show Northern traits. Mariotto died in 1457.

77) The more so since Masaccio's stepfather, Tedesco, had from his previous marriage only the two daughters, Nanna who was probably already married in 1406 and Caterina born between 1401 and 1406.

78) Cf. the biographical repertory in Somaré, 1924, p. 161. On October 6, 1422, the artist paid two lire to the chamberlain of the Guild of Physicians and Chemists (Procacci, 1951, p. 25). The lost *Annunciation* for San Niccolò, in view of the extreme stylistic maturity that can be deduced from Vasari's description of it, was certainly executed for the parish church before 1422, nor need it necessarily date from the time the artist lived in that parish; in fact, it is likely that it may have been done around 1427 when Masaccio was living in the parish of San Michele Visdomini.

79) U. Baldini, 1962, reports information from U. Procacci according to which, very probably, Masaccio had already come to Florence as early as 1417. Perhaps Monna Jacopa and her sons found themselves more free to move about after the death in that year of Tedesco.

80) The estimate of the value of the florin as around 17,500 lire of today (but probably even more) can be found in U. Procacci, "Di Jacopo di Antonio e delle compagnie di pittori del corso degli Adimari nel XV secolo," in *Rivista d'Arte*, 1961, p. 45, n. 66.

81) The Tabernacle of the Linen-Weavers' Guild, a very large and elaborate work, was commissioned from Fra Angelico for 190 florins; for frescoing the Chapel of Saint Helena in Santo Stefano, Empoli, Masolino was paid seventy-four florins; Lorenzo di Bicci in 1399 received fifty-two florins and three lire for a polyptych at Empoli (cf. *Rivista d'Arte*, 1950, p. 201). From the *Ricordanze* of Neri di Bicci (ed. Poggi, in *Il Vasari*, 1928, pp. 326, 329-30, 334) we can gather these examples of tariffs current in 1454: for an altarpiece for the Benizi in Santa Felicita, including wood, gold, azure, etc., 560 lire (= 140 florins); for an altarpiece for Poggibonsi, complete with frame, predella with five scenes, gold backgrounds and silver friezes, 100 lire (= twenty-five florins); for a small portable altarpiece with a Madonna and two Saints, about one meter high, everything included, five lire and ten soldi; for a fresco with Saint James and a figured frieze around it, fifty-two lire (= thirteen florins). The eighty florins Masaccio received for the Pisa polyptych were therefore not inclusive of the expense of the wood, which was another eighteen florins.

82) The thesis of a voyage to Rome with Masolino in 1425 and of the execution there of certain works is

maintained, on the basis of Vasari's vague indication, by Longhi (1940, pp. 163-66) who supposes that Masaccio at that time worked on the chapel in San Clemente. The notion was taken up again by Clark (1951) when the side-panel by Masaccio for the triptych of Santa Maria Maggiore in Rome was discovered. Procacci has not yet presented all the historical and documentary evidence against this thesis (1953, pp. 3 ff. and particularly pp. 41 ff.), and there is now some indication that documents show the Jubilee did not in fact take place, although in itself this would not rule out a journey to Rome by Masolino and Masaccio in 1425, but other circumstances make it unlikely (see Chapter III, note 178, this book).

83) The text of the document was published by Tanfani-Centofanti in *Miscellanea d'Arte*, 1903, p. 189. The documents for the successive payments to Masaccio are in L. Tanfani-Centofanti, *Notizie d'artisti tratte dai documenti pisani*, 1897, pp. 177 ff.

84) Salmi, 1947, p. 139 noted with much reason that the commission to the artist was probably due to the same Fra Bartolomeo da Firenze, at that time vice-prior of the Carmelites in Pisa, who appears as witness for one of the payments for the polyptych and who must have already appreciated Masaccio's work in Florence enough to recommend him to the Pisan notary.

85) "*Victorio vocato Johanni suo fratello*," from which we learn that Scheggia's name may have been originally Vittore, and that it may have been changed to take that of his deceased father.

86) 1961.

87) Eve Borsook has very effectively compared the London Madonna and the Madonna in the Berlin *Adoration* with the *Madonna and Child* of Giovanni formerly over the door and now inside the Baptistery; she has also done this for a Prophet by Nicola and one by Giovanni, both in the Baptistery, comparing them with, respectively, the *Saint Paul* of Pisa and the Lanckoronski *Saint Andrew*. Schmarsow had already suggested certain similarities between the horses in the *Adoration* by Masaccio and that of Nicola's pulpit, as well as between Masaccio's Eve in the Carmine and the *Prudence* (or *Modesty*) by Giovanni on the pulpit in Pisa. The latter comparison, however, does not justify dating the Carmine fresco later than Masaccio's work in Pisa because, aside from the fact that Masaccio could very well have visited Pisa many times before 1426, there is proof that a *Venus pudica* like the one which inspired Pisano is known to have existed in Florence at the end of the fourteenth century (cf. J. Mesnil, "Masaccio and the Antique," in *Burlington Magazine*, 1926, 2, p. 91 and n. 5).

88) As Longhi (1950) noted, it is "a Holy Family most daringly de-centered in the composition, seeming almost to move and pass by," that is, the image belongs to the type of depiction of the Madonna and Child in movement characteristic of the Flight into Egypt. For this reason, I suggest comparison with Giovanni Pisano's *Flight into Egypt* on the pulpit of the Pisa Cathedral: the same hand toying with the serene Child, the same circular movement in the outer contours, mantle and cape.

89) Likewise for the wave-pattern on the step of the throne of the London *Madonna*, with its design flowing in from each side to form a mandorla in the center, Masaccio may have been inspired by something seen in Pisa, for instance, the antique sarcophagi in the Camposanto (cf. R. Papini, *Pisa*, 1914, II, for example the figure on p. 69).

90) PROCACCI, 1932, p. 495; in the *Libra* of 1426, "*Maso e Giovanni di ser Giovanni di Mone Chassai in Firenze*" are taxed for six soldi.

91) PROCACCI, 1935, pp. 97 ff. compares the original entry for Masaccio in the *Catasto*—the tax roll—and the "*Campione*," an extract from it copied by a scribe (in a volume erroneously marked as the Catasto of 1429) and provides copious annotation for them. The statement given in our text is taken from Procacci. The beginning of the document as reproduced in our text is from the photograph in PINI-MILANESI, *Scrittura di artisti italiani*, I, 1876, n. 14.

92) The house was in Via dei Servi where later was built the Niccolini-Montauto Palace (personal communication from Procacci). However, see also F. FANTOZZI, *Pianta geometrica di Firenze*, 1843, p. 149, n. 342.

93) The workshop was in Piazza Sant'Apollinare, that is, the part of the present Piazza San Firenze closest to the Bargello: "*una botegha e uno androne in sulla piazza di San Pulinari.*"

94) Niccolò di ser Lapo, born around 1375, had his workshop and probably his dwelling in the same Piazza Sant'Apollinare. He is documented up to 1447, but completely unknown as an artist. For the sum owed to him (about 437,000 in today's lire), which he hoped to collect even after Masaccio's death in Rome, see the documents in PROCACCI, 1935, p. 101, n. 4.

95) Among the various debtors of this well-to-do goldbeater, in 1427 besides Masaccio there were Bicci di Lorenzo, Mariotto di Cristofano, Arcangelo di Cola da Camerino, Ambrogio di Baldese, Piero Chellini as well as other totally unknown painters such as Michele di Benedetto, Andrea di Stagio, Lippo d'Andrea, Donino di Giovanni, Giuliano di Jacopo, Franco, and Iscolaio. Masaccio's unpaid debt was carried in the books of the gold-beater until 1433. Cf. PROCACCI, 1935, p. 108 ff.

96) This was, it seems, a company of clothing merchants who sold garments retail.

97) The lending agency of the Lioni is not otherwise known; that of Vacca, also in private hands, was the most important in Masaccio's time and was located on the present Via dei Pecori near Via Brunelleschi in the center of the city.

98) We have found documentary evidence of the collaboration of Andrea di Giusto with Masaccio on the Pisa polyptych where many authorities think they can make out his contribution in the part of the predella with the stories of Saint Julian and Saint Nicholas.

99) The money owed from her dowry to Masaccio's mother from both families was later partly paid off with half of the house of the Cassai in San Giovanni Valdarno (see note 73 above); while on the part of the family of Tedesco it was objected in 1427 that "we have not aided her because she has to turn over to us certain edifices which have approximately the same value," and the affair was settled only after 1433. On the other hand, the heirs of Tedesco did not see fit to concern themselves with what he left to Monna Jacopa.

100) All of Masaccio's debts together total forty florins (700,000 lire of today, roughly 1130 dollars or 396 pounds sterling) while the credit for his mother's dowry came to 1,750,000 lire of today. The tax was fixed at about 1,000 lire in present value.

101) Cf. the article already cited in *Rivista d'Arte*, 1953, pp. 17 ff.

102) The first special tax levy, collected June 30, 1428, brought in around 25,000 florins from the city and 18,000 from the countryside, for a total of around 750 million lire in present value (about 1,290,000 dollars). But during the war with Visconti, Florence spent 70,000 florins a month! (in 1426, as we know from the chronicle of Morelli; cf. PROCACCI, p. 16, n. 29). Expenditures dropped after the victorious battle of Maclodio in October, 1427 and the peace that followed, but increased again with the revolt of Volterra in 1429 and the war against Lucca in 1430 and once more against Visconti until 1433.

103) PROCACCI, 1953, pp. 30 ff. reports the complaint of Mariotto di Cristofano, the artist related to Masaccio: "My art is not bringing in anything these days—it needs peace, not war, and I have six mouths to feed, and I am at the end of my tether: I am ruined" (appeal to the tax board, 1430-31); but this is an isolated case from which one cannot draw general conclusions. It can be objected that, what with taxes and wars, the situation was already serious in 1425, when there were a great many bankruptcies, and nevertheless no one stinted on lavish expenditures for art works.
In fact, among the many paintings of the period which are not dated, there are a few which do bear dates, and they are precisely from the moment of greatest financial difficulty (Francesco d'Antonio 1429; Bicci di Lorenzo 1427, 1429, 1430, 1433; Fra Angelico 1429). If it is objected that it may have been the more expensive works done under private commission, such as the entire decoration of a chapel, that could no longer be afforded between 1427 and 1434, there is an example which contradicts this: in July 1427, precisely during the special tax levy, Masolino was asked to decorate a chapel of the Franzesi dalla Foresta family in San Francesco in Figline at an estimated cost of 1000 florins. I think, however, that the question can only be settled by checking on every art work commissioned by private individuals or public bodies during this period and then seeing if there were variations in the financial conditions of artists between the tax declarations of 1427 and those of 1430-31 and if many of them were condemned for unpaid debts. This sort of data is indispensable to any evaluation of the effects, positive or negative, of the financial situation.

104) MELLER, 1961, p. 225, n. 62 proposes that the setting up of the special tax levy was responsible for the interruption which took place in the decoration of the Brancacci Chapel.

105) As Vasari put it: "Not feeling at ease in Florence, and being urged by his love and devotion to art, he determined to go to Rome in order to study and surpass his rivals."

106) LAVAGNINO, 1943, supposed that, when Gentile died in August, 1427 leaving unfinished the fresco cycle in San Giovanni in Laterano, Martin V sought a substitute in Florence, first fixing on Masolino (who according to Lavagnino was absent at that time in Hungary, although we now know that he returned in July of that year) and then settling for Masolino's collaborator Masaccio. The latter would then have dropped his work on the Brancacci Chapel, since an invitation from the Pontiff was both highly attractive and tantamount to an order, and —because in the second edition of the *Lives* Vasari speaks of part of the decoration in San Giovanni in Laterano having been assigned to Masaccio—he would then have undertaken the difficult task of trying to conform to the highly Gothic style of the fresco cycle as laid down by Gentile, from which only his premature death saved him.
Lavagnino further maintains that the chapel in San Clemente (on which Masaccio collaborated) and the tryptych of Santa Maria Maggiore both date from as far back as around 1423, and that after this initial sojourn in Rome in 1424 Masolino and Masaccio returned to

Florence. This hypothesis, however, crumbles not only in the face of all the historical evidence collected by PROCACCI (in *art. cit.*, 1954) but also when set against the very evident stylistic chronology. All that can be conceded is that the side-panel in London with Saint Jerome and Saint John Baptist from the altarpiece of Santa Maria Maggiore was executed by Masaccio and may have been done soon after the San Giovenale tryptych of 1422.

107) PROCACCI (1951) however thinks that Masaccio remained in Florence until autumn of 1428, but this does not allow time for his activity in Rome.

108) There exists no other information about Masaccio beyond his death in Rome. In the research into the documents of Del Migliore it was thought that one indicated that Masaccio had married (cf. MAGHERINI-GRAZIANI, *Op. cit.*, 1904, p. 81 note) but very probably the documents were ambiguous on this point (or this was a jest on the part of the distinguished scholar) because the name of this supposed wife is unknown and there is no trace of her, as there ought to be, in the tax records of 1427-29. MESNIL, in *Rivista d'Arte*, 1912, pp. 31 ff., shows that Magherini-Graziani (*Op. cit.*, pp. 82-83 note) mistook as referring to Masaccio a document of December 21, 1428.

109) *Della Pittura.*

110) Nor does Landino. However the rumor appears in the so-called Billi (codices Strozziano and Petrei, which give it as certain) and in the Anonimo Maglianechiano (cf. SOMARÉ, 1924, pp. 167-68) and is repeated by Vasari.

111) The notice of the death of Masaccio is recorded already in November 1429 in the Extract from the tax roll of 1427: the name of the artist is crossed out and another hand has written beside it, "said to have died at Rome." His brother Giovanni did not officially declare himself the heir, as is indicated in 1431 by their creditor Niccolò di ser Lupo (see note 94 above): "The heirs of Tommaso di ser Giovanni, the painter, should give me sixty-eight lire; the said Tommaso died in Rome, and I do not know if I shall ever be repaid since his brother claims not to be his heir."

112) In the *Saint Peter Enthroned* in the Carmine, the figure in profile at the far right with black habit and hood, as Meller pointed out (1961, pp. 304 ff.).

113) This is affirmed in the Billi and Magliabechiano manuscripts, from which we learn also that Masaccio "was well loved by Filippo di ser Brunellesco, the great architect, because he found him of penetrating intellect and he taught him many things about their art" (SOMARÉ, 1924, pp. 167-68).

114) Cf. PANOFSKY, *Meaning in the Visual Arts*, 1957, pp. 209-10.

115) This is hinted at also by Vasari: "Masaccio was a native of Castello S. Giovanni of Valdarno, and it is said that some figures made by him in early childhood may be seen there." Astute as always, Vasari thus shunted the problem of the *Frühwerke* onto the good citizens of San Giovanni, leaving them the responsibility of proudly proclaiming as the young Masaccio's whatever bits of art they had, as so often happens when native sons achieve glory. Except for a *Sainted Bishop* in fresco in San Lorenzo, in a condition to make judgment almost impossible (figure 8; cf. Attributed Works), nothing has remained in the town which, at least today, can be presumed to be by Masaccio, certainly not the large *Madonna* with Angels and Saints in the side-panels, now in the Museum, which is by the well-known Master of the Adimari Cassone and Paolo Schiavo; the badly deteriorated chapel in San Lorenzo frescoed with *Saint Anthony and Scenes from his Life* with the Evangelists in the vault may more likely be a youthful work by the Master of the Adimari Cassone or something by Masaccio's brother Scheggia. Cf. BERTI, *Il Museo della Basilica a San Giovanni Valdarno*, Florence, 1959.

116) For the relevant bibliography, see SALMI, 1948, pp. 171-72. In order to give some further notion of the relationship of Francesco d'Antonio in the decade 1430-40 with traits typical of Masolino or hypothetically of early Masaccio, see Figure 5 for a hitherto unpublished fresco in the Collegiata of Bibbiena (which also has a *Madonna* by Arcangelo di Cola) with at the top the Trinity and two angels, below an imitation in fresco of a triptych with the Madonna and Child between Saints Nicholas and Julian (two saints highly venerated at the time, to judge by the numerous images of them). Although the attribution may seem problematical at first sight, a comparison with the tabernacle in Piazza Santa Maria Novella removes all doubts.

117) R. LONGHI, 1940, pp. 152 and 172. It is surprising however that in these same pages (p. 181, and again in 1947) he continued to insist, admittedly with some caution, that the *Holy Family with Donor* in Altenburg is "worthy of the youth of the great Tuscan." The work, even in its conception, is as remote as possible from Masaccio's (a montage of building blocks with classical symmetries, a children's playground with insipid little angels); very probably it is not even Florentine. Cf. R. OERTEL, *Frühe italienische Malerei in Altenburg*, 1961, no. 156, where it is attributed to a Paduan painter of around 1460.

118) On board. Side-panels $34\frac{5}{8} \times 17\frac{3}{8}''$; central panel $42\frac{1}{2} \times 26''$. BERTI, in *Catalogo della Mostra di Arte Sacra Antica*, Florence, 1961, p. 281, no. 287 and then discussed at greater length in 1961 and 1962. See as significant and authoritative support for the attribution, S. BOTTARI in *Arte Antica e Moderna*, 18, 1962, "Notiziario."

119) To my knowledge, meanwhile only M. CHIARINI, 1962, p. 55 and C. VOLPE in *Arte Antica e Moderna*, 18, 1962, p. 165, have expressed doubts *en passant*. But the "Manes" of Masaccio have proved themselves vengeful spirits.

120) This fact, I believe, has never before been published. SALMI (1948, p. 36) however has already criticized the comparison of the throne of the London *Madonna* with the sacristy door in Santa Trinita (from around 1420) which was proposed by MESNIL (1927, p. 50, Pl. 20). The comparison is really too vague, and the door itself is of a graceful, florid and verticalistic classicism and at the same time still somewhat Gothic.

121) In this connection, see also BERTI, 1962, p. 164, n. 12.

122) 1961 and 1962.

123) For a more documented and detailed analysis of what is said in this paragraph, see my articles of 1961 and 1962.

124) See the discussion of Gentile da Fabriano later in this book and also Note 163.

125) This is a detail typical of the Madonnas by Masaccio (the Sant'Ambrogio panel, the London panel). To say, as Brandi does, that it is common in the contemporary fashions but in Masaccio is due simply to the stylistic intention of rendering continuous the passage from one plane to another of the face is to define as an aim what is, instead, no more than a formal consequence. Is it true that the eyebrows would interrupt

the continuity? They are present, nevertheless, in female figures by painters like Ucello, Angelico and Piero della Francesca who are concerned with ideal volumetric rendering. And why should such an attempt to avoid interrupting the plane be applied only to Madonnas? The fact is, the principal reason for this is obviously to make that particular figure less human, more noble. Although Masaccio's Madonnas are strongly energetic, he avoids insisting on too common naturalistic details such as the hairs of the eyebrows; moreover, despite his interest in plastic modeling, he scarcely puts any emphasis on the Virgin's breasts, unlike Castagno, for example.

126) 1962.

127) Further explanations of this "temporal" element in Masaccio, in association with the rendering of movement, are in the article indicated.

128) In the same article. See also P. SANPAOLESI, *Brunelleschi*, 1962, p. 43: "On a high level of analogy, Brunelleschi henceforth felt space was like time: each of them required a means of measurement."

129) Brandi in a personal communication.

130) Compare the figure at the extreme right of the *Resurrection of Drusiana* with the Saint Juvenal.

131) *The Italian Painters of the Renaissance*, London and New York, 1954, pp. 49-51. LONGHI (in *Paragone*, 9, 1950, p. 5) in this connection considers it necessary to insist on the unbridgeable gap which divides Masaccio from the painting of the Trecento, a sublime century but with a "pedal-point of transcendence upon which lean even the factitious building-blocks of Giotto." Berenson however had in mind a Giotto born again but equipped with "all that had been gained during his absence... The medieval skies had been torn asunder... new interests and new values prevailed," etc.

132) "Giotto nel Trecento," a chapter in his book *Rinascimento e Barocco*, 1960, pp. 50 ff.

133) There is a *novella* by Sacchetti from around 1360 in which Florentine painters of the time discuss the state of painting and Taddeo Gaddi complains that "our art has grown and continues to grow worse with every day that passes."

134) The painting in the Louvre, from the house of Giuliano da Sangallo, was ascribed by Vasari in the first edition of the *Lives* to Masaccio himself and not until the edition of 1568 to Doni. For the bibliography, cf. POPE-HENNESSY, *Paolo Uccello*, 1950, pp. 154 ff. Beencken was the last to believe the work was really by Masaccio. Lányi however noted the striking resemblance between that portrait which the inscription (added later) identifies as Giotto and the self-portrait of Masaccio in the Carmine as singled out by Salmi; he supposed that the other portraits must therefore derive from those of the lost *Consecration* in which Brunelleschi, Donatello and others appeared. However, the work is really a pastiche of Masaccio done in the late Quattrocento, an opinion with which Longhi agrees.
The whole question of this painting in the Louvre is complicated. Some have even thought it to be from the sixteenth century and yet today they agree with those who fail to find in it close ties with the art of Paolo Uccello. It might even be thought that the Giotto who resembles Masaccio and is posed as in a self-portrait may derive from an original by Masaccio with similar portraits in which Masaccio, out of modesty (sublime modesty!) may have portrayed himself in the guise of Giotto. Certainly the number of *five* for the *renewers of art* appears shortly after Masaccio's time in Alberti's *Della Pittura* where they are given as Filippo, Donato, Nencio, Luca and Masaccio; they reappear in Vasari's life of Masaccio as Filippo, Donato, Lorenzo (= Nencio), Uccello and Masaccio; the painting in the Fitzwilliam Museum, Cambridge done after the one in the Louvre has the same number of figures but substitutes Raphael and Michelangelo for Uccello and Manetti.

135) In the *Codice Atlantico* (cf. SOMARÉ, 1924, pp. 184-85) where he says that after the medieval decadence (with painters who learned from one another rather than from Nature) Giotto was not willing merely to imitate Cimabue but instead turned to Nature for his inspiration, following which there was a new period of decadence "until Tommaso of Florence showed in his *perfect* works how those who seek aid elsewhere than in Nature, mistress of all mistresses, exert themselves in vain." Note that implied in what Leonardo says is another concept: the *perfection* of Masaccio which managed to set up a fundamental naturalism as guide and which helped the art of the Quattrocento to avoid the kind of mannerisms which had led Gothic art to its decline after Giotto.

136) For the attitudes toward Dante in the early Florentine Renaissance, cf. CHASTEL, *Art et humanisme à Florence*, 1961, pp. 106 ff.

137) LONGHI, "Gli affreschi del Carmine, Masaccio e Dante," in *Paragone*, 9, 1960, p. 6: "But to give the same conviction of vital existence to painting, which exists on a single plane, something else was needed: and perhaps there came to his aid here an invention of Dante wilfully misunderstood by Trecento artists. After the visit to the dark depths of Hell, where no light shines and therefore no shadows can be made, Dante upon his emergence into the Southern light of the Mountain of Purgatory is repeatedly recognized as a living being by the shadow he casts. Masaccio perhaps meditated over this point, and with this basic premise came to understand that space as conceived by Brunelleschi could now be made habitable and alive."

138) For the first two, cf. the important contribution of A. SCHMITT in *Münchener Jahrbuch der bildenden Kunst*, 1960 (with a catalogue of the antiques copied); for the antique sources of Ghiberti, cf. the splendid monograph of R. KRAUTHEIMER, 1956, pp. 337-52.

139) Cf. L. GRASSI, *Donatello*, 1958, p. 64: it is significant that, in its turn, the head by Donatello itself derives from that of the Centaur on the Roman sarcophagus at Cortona which Donatello and Brunelleschi admired.

140) For the early development of Donatello up to the *Saint Louis*, cf. the article by L. BECHERUCCI in the *Enciclopedia Universale dell'Arte* (= *Universal Encyclopedia of Art*), IV, 1961, and for the anti-classical complexity of this founder of the Renaissance, cf. L. GRASSI, *Donatello*, 1958.

141) Which has already been compared here with that of San Giovenale. Here I might add that the rosettes on the front of the lower part of the throne in the Pisa *Madonna*—a motif much used for decoration by the Romanesque also, for example precisely on the bronze door of Bonanno in the Duomo of Pisa—appear elsewhere with similar isolated prominence, among others on ambos such as that in San Miniato al Monte in Florence; it was a completely classical motif and was used by Masaccio for its plastic quality, in line with his architectonic taste.

142) This excellent suggestion of Bicci comes from BRANDI in the notes of the course already mentioned, p. 19. Brandi interprets Bicci as the representative of "the most conservative strand, more Giottesque in a rustic way, and almost folk-like in style."

143) It is to be hoped that Procacci will devote to this workshop an analytic study like the magnificent one he published in *Rivista dell'Arte*, 1961, "Di Jacopo di Antonio e delle compagnie di pittori del corso degli Adimari nel XV secolo."

144) The two pieces by Bicci in the Museum at Empoli come from the Collegiata where the triptych decorated a chapel of Simone Guiducci da Spicchio (depicted at the feet of the Madonna) which was dedicated to Saint Leonard. The documents prove that it was executed in 1423 (cf. O. H. GIGLIOLI, *Empoli artistica*, 1906, pp. 66 ff. and VASARI-MILANESI, II, p. 66).
The workshop of the Biccis was often busy for Empoli, and as early as 1399 Lorenzo di Bicci painted a triptych (of which the Crucifixion remains: inventory number 6 in the Museum) for the same Chapel of the Company of the Holy Cross in Santo Stefano which, in 1424, would be frescoed by Masolino (here one may wonder if he was not proposed for the work by Bicci). Besides I believe that in the same year of 1423 Bicci was responsible for the other chapel with the *Life of the Magdalen* in fresco of which traces were discovered in 1943 (see Figure 25, an intent visage of an old man which I suggest should be compared with the Saint Anthony in the San Giovenale triptych); the sinopie were also uncovered at that time (cf. PROCACCI, *Sinopie e affreschi*, 1960, p. 227; he believes two artists worked on the chapel, one at the end of the fourteenth or beginning of the fifteenth century, the other around 1420; in that case the *Last Supper* may be by Stefano d'Antonio, an associate of Bicci's). On Bicci cf. especially the commentary by MILANESI to his edition of Vasari (1878) and SALMI in the *Enciclopedia Treccani*, VI, 1930, and among later literature F. ZERI in *Paragone*, 105, 1958. On Stefano d'Antonio, cf. W. COHN in *Bollettino d'Arte*, 1959, I, pp. 61 ff.

145) *Art. cit.*, 1959, p. 65 and document I on p. 66. He opposes the hypothesis that, afterwards, for a certain time Scheggia may have become a soldier of fortune.

146) The triptych by Bicci in Vertine has already been published by me in relation with that of San Giovenale in *Commentari*, 1961, p. 88, n. 6 and Figs. 9-10. The *Madonna and Child* of the Warsaw Museum (inv. 157819) transferred from panel to canvas, 26¼ × 18½", was acquired in 1949. Formerly attributed to the Master of the Bambino Vispo, Zeri made out influences of Agnolo Gaddi and Mariotto di Nardo, whereas the catalogue (*La peinture italienne des XIVe et XVe siècles*, exhibition, Cracow, 1961, no. 31) also calls attention to a work by Cenni di Francesco in the Thyssen Collection. However in the Child the painting reveals itself clearly as coming from Bicci's circle.

147) On Florentine painting of the end of the Gothic period in the international style still practiced during Masaccio's lifetime, there are the supplementary and critical notes in LONGHI, 1940 (on the Master of the Bambino Vispo, the Master of 1419, the Master of the Griggs Crucifixion, etc.) followed by specific studies (Zeri; also, in the miscellany in honor of W. Suida, 1959, Steinweg, Cohn, Baldini) and the overall sociological framework by ANTAL, 1948. This, however, is not the place to deal with personalities like Francesco d'Antonio, Schiavo, the Master of the Adimari Cassone and others who came after Masaccio in time. For Lorenzo Monaco, cf. the brief survey by R. AMERIO in the *Enciclopedia Universale dell'Arte*, VIII, 1958 (1961). E. CARLI (*San Gimignano*, Monte dei Paschi di Siena, 1961, p. 94) proposes the identification of Ventura di Moro, collaborator of Rossello Franchi, with the so-called Master of 1419.

148) P. TOESCA, *Il Trecento*, 1951, p. 669.

149) Cf. PROCACCI, the article cited in Note 152 below, specifically pp. 80-82 and n. 1.

150) *I Primitivi*, II, Novara, 1946, p. LXI.

151) From whose list, however, he has been removed in the most recent edition of *The Florentine School*.

152) Since the study by PROCACCI (in *G. Starnina*, Florence, 1936) the question of Starnina has made no further decisive progress. LONGHI (*op. cit.*, 1940), who as we have seen is determined to give the *Thebaid* to Fra Angelico around 1420, bases his argument on the one hand on Vasari who, he points out, places Starnina among the artists of the "first age," those who in no way go beyond the spirit of the Trecento; on the other hand, inasmuch as Vasari did indicate certain innovatory elements in Starnina's work, he insists that "nothing can be deduced from the elaborate embroideries in Vasari's biographies, obviously conceived on a merely ornamental basis and introduced here and there with the aim of making his text livelier and less ponderous." TOESCA (*Il Trecento*, 1951, a work written at a time when the author's position was close to Longhi's) simply dismissed Starnina as "until now little known" and the *Thebaid* as "of obvious Sienese derivation, the work of some miniaturist like Lorenzo Monaco and, in fact, a prelude to Angelico" (pp. 649-50). SALMI however ("Problemi dell'Angelico," in *Commentari*, 1950, pp. 78-79) opposes Longhi's attribution of the work to Angelico and again brings up the name of Starnina to whom he also attributes a series of small panels in the Cathedral of Toledo and a *Madonna* in the museum at Worcester whose style corresponds to that of the so-called Pseudo-Ambrogio di Baldese (but Starnina's style seems more decisive than that of the latter work). It is no more than hypothetical to identify the *Thebaid* with the panel in the Medici Palace ascribed to Angelico because we know that another anonymous work on the same subject and of dimensions even closer to those of our painting was at that time in the chapel of the villa of Careggi; in addition to the two Hungarian copies and the derivation in the Crawford Collection there is another copy in which various details are almost literally the same (and this is not a derivation from Paolo Uccello) in the fresco in the cloister of Cercina. One can conclude then that this was a work known and admired by the Quattrocento.
As for the youthful works of Fra Angelico, see below. With reference to the relationship between Starnina and Paolo Uccello, it will be recalled that a possibly early work of the latter is the altar-frontal from the Chapel of Saint Jerome in the Carmine with Saints Cosmas and Damian (nos. 1141 C/D in Berlin, with those saints, does not seem to me to be attributable to Uccello but rather to a foreigner, and it is entirely hypothetical therefore that they come from the Carmine). In regard to a possible connection between Starnina and Masolino and Masaccio, Starnina was a native of Gaville near Figline Valdarno and therefore a countryman of theirs, whence the probability of some contact with Masolino at least who was born in 1383; also, Vasari states perfectly clearly that Masolino was a disciple of Starnina. There might have been much to learn if we were still able to compare the two chapels in Santo Stefano in Empoli frescoed by Starnina and Masolino, even though there is a gap of fifteen years between them. Moreover, the few vestiges (U. BALDINI, *Itinerario del Museo della Collegiata di Empoli*, 1957, p. 14; PROCACCI, *Sinopie e Affreschi*, 1960, p. 227) of Starnina's frescoes (cf. Fig. 31-32) also raise the problem of relationships between Starnina and the Master of the Bambino Vispo, since his saints in Empoli lead naturally to works like the small detached fresco in the Museum of Santa Croce in Florence with the *Resurrection of Lazarus* (Fig. 33) which is assigned to the Master of the Bambino Vispo. In its

turn, a work like the latter is interesting because, for all the Gothic sickle-like curves of its modeling, it already reveals the clear and animated coloring, the softness of forms, the gentleness of lighting which we find, admittedly in more advanced fashion, in the works by Masolino in Empoli.

153) On Arcangelo di Cola, the fundamental material is still in L. SERRA, *L'Arte nelle Marche*, 2nd edition, 1934, pp. 284 ff.; cf. also F. ZERI in *Paragone*, 7, 1950, pp. 33 ff. There are two recent attributions by Longhi in the *Catalogo della IV Mostra di restauri*, Naples, 1960, p. 45 and Fig. 35, and in the catalogue of the *Mostra dei Tesori segreti delle case fiorentine*, 1960, no. 20 and Fig. 17.

154) SALMI, 1932 and 1948, pp. 11, 21 and commentary to Plates 212-14. Of the three points laid down by the author, I limit myself to discussing the second, the influence of Arcangelo on Masolino which, in my opinion, is based on much too fragile evidence. To say that in 1421 Arcangelo was supposed to paint a panel for Santo Stefano in Empoli (which he never carried out) and that in the lunette by Masolino in Empoli we find once again the standing Christ Child blessing very much like that in the Frick diptych by Arcangelo is an observation that can be simply turned around, since it is possible that the Frick diptych dates from after Masolino's lunette. In fact it is so much similar to and perhaps later than the *Madonna* in Bibbiena (Fig. 23) that Salmi agrees with Longhi (because of the motif of the Child who peels the grape He takes from the hand of the Virgin which also appears in Masaccio's Pisa panel) that it must date from after 1426. Besides, we have seen in Note 95 above that Arcangelo was in debt to a Florentine gold-beater which speaks for his presence in Florence at that time. However, it cannot be categorically excluded that the example of Arcangelo at the time of his first arrival in Florence may have had some influence on the soft but not cold chiaroscuro of Masolino, but for this we need more positive information about Arcangelo's art in that period. I must however state that the date of 1422 proposed by Longhi for a predella panel by Arcangelo with the *Martyrdom of Saint Lawrence* (1940, Fig. 53, n. 23) is merely hypothetical and, in my opinion, contradicted by the borrowings from the Carmine which can be made out in it (compare, for example, the raging executioner with the moustached cripple in Masaccio's *Saint Peter healing with his Shadow*).

155) L. GRASSI, *Gentile da Fabriano*, Milan, 1953; E. ARSLAN, "Gentile da Fabriano" in the *Enciclopedia Universale dell'Arte*, V, 1958; C. STERLING, "Un tableau inédit de Gentile da Fabriano," in *Paragone*, 101, 1958; B. SCHMITT, "Gentile da Fabriano in Rom und die Anfänge des Antikenstudiums," excerpted from the *Münchener Jahrbuch der bildenden Kunst*, 1960.

156) *Op. cit.*, 1960, in particular pp. 440 ff.

157) 1953, p. 31. We agree on this point, whereas the more extreme and generalized thesis of that author is discussed in our preceding chapter and in Note 103 above.

158) See our first chapter.

159) E. BATTISTI, *L'Antirinascimento*, Milan, 1962, pp. 19 ff.

160) Brandi in his course of lectures considers it on the contrary an invention by Masaccio taken up in the Quaratesi polyptych. But aside from the fact that a common source may be the Madonna of Casa Pazzi by Donatello (c. 1422?), it is not in fact true that the veil is an *apax legomenon* in Gentile: even if we set aside the *Incoronata* of Valle Romita, it returns (or appears

previously) in the Goldman Madonna in Washington, in that of Berenson, and that of Orvieto.

161) It will be recalled that Antal begins his celebrated work with the extremely significant comparison of the two Madonnas, Masaccio's from Pisa and Gentile's from the Quaratesi polyptych, both of them now in London.

162) Which dates from his period in Florence where the painting was acquired.

163) DEGENHART and SCHMITT, *art. cit.*, pp. 114-15 and Fig. 91. This drawing (Musée Bonnat, 1212) may well be from the Roman period of Pisanello but it may just as well have been done earlier and elsewhere. The murder episode in the background of the *Adoration* and the stupid-looking man wearing a hat with upturned brim may both derive—though this is a mere hypothesis—from the dionysiac figure. There remains the fact that Gentile is suspected of having utilized drawings by Pisanello for his *Adoration* and that the latter, in his turn, borrowed certain details from that work (cf. GRASSI, *Op. cit.*, pp. 24-25).

164) A. PARRONCHI, "Una Nunziatina di Paolo Uccello, Ricostruzione della Cappella Carnesecchi," in *Studi Urbinati*, 1962, 1, pp. 19-20 (with bibliography).

165) Bicci di Lorenzo had probably already imitated Gentile, turning designs scratched on gold into symbols of the Evangelists on the throne of the *Madonna* of Empoli of 1423 (cf. Fig. 18).
As for the enduring fame of Gentile in Florence, note the passage from the historian and chronicler Cavalcanti (c. 1440) given by PROCACCI (*art. cit.*, 1961, p. 20): "Numerous as are the stars in heaven, so are human creatures. And human wills differ as much as the influences of the natures of the stars; and there was a different will in Pippo di ser Brunellesco than in Lorenzo di Bartoluccio and another gift of imagination in Master Gentile than in Giuliano d'Arrigo (Pesello), and just as their wills differ, so also do the gifts of imagination and learning among men... and from such diversity of imagination derives such diversity of skills among men and likewise of their arts."

166) On Masolino, see the study by U. BALDINI in the *Enciclopedia Universale d'Arte*, VIII, 1962. There has been no progress in the definition of his personality for some time now, except for the excellent research of Procacci. Attention has been turned to him again with the discovery of the San Giovenale triptych and the course on Masaccio given by Brandi (cf. also the article by Brandi in *Studi in onore di M. Marangoni*, 1957, pp. 167-70).

167) LONGHI, 1940, p. 151. This observation as to Vasari's silence on this point in his life of Masolino is further supported by the fact that, when he added a lengthy appreciation to that biography in the second edition of the *Vite*, Vasari again did not speak of Masaccio as his disciple, although this would certainly have been the occasion to do so. Through misunderstanding what Vasari said in his biography of Masaccio, Borghini and Baldinucci both came to declare Masaccio a disciple of Masolino; but, as is known and as this proves, these two historians did no more than summarize Vasari for this material (though Baldinucci did make logical corrections in the chronology) and therefore they cannot be considered to have any independent value as sources in this matter.

168) PROCACCI, in a personal communication, has kindly advised me of his two chief arguments in this regard: (1) there does not exist any Panicale in the Valdelsa and it has never been mentioned by any geographer; (2) at

Panicale di Renacci the townspeople point out the house where according to tradition Masolino was born, and it is certainly highly unlikely that the tradition would have come into being only because of Repetti (cf. *Dizionario geografico della Toscana*, 5, 1843, p. 57) or of Magherini-Graziani.

169) For the sake of completeness only we can recall here the "pan-Masaccio" thesis of Schmarsow (1895-99 and again later although with changes of opinion in various cases) and of Oertel (1933). According to these writers, Masaccio was the author of the chapel in San Clemente in Rome (claimed to date from 1422-23), the triptych of Santa Maria Maggiore in Rome (dated before 1424), the Bremen *Madonna*, the Pietà of Empoli, the frescoes in the Carmine including the *Adam and Eve in the Earthly Paradise*, the *Sermon of Saint Peter*, the *Story of Tabitha* (these all dated as 1424-25), the *Madonna* of Novoli, and the *Saint Julian* and *Story of Saint Julian* in Montauban (also 1424-25).

170) The 1939 catalogue of the Kunsthalle, pp. 96-97, says the two coats-of-arms at the base of the small pilasters in the *Madonna* are those of the Carnesecchi and Boni families, thereby perhaps connecting the painting with a wedding.

171) As for the origins of Masolino—"the only artist in Berenson's lists for whom no genealogical tree is offered, in fact for whom no information is given" —it will be recalled that, at a time when others were content to class him in the International Gothic group, Longhi (1940, pp. 148-51) pointed out in Giovanni da Milano an ancester who was closer to home, older and more accessible to Masolino. Other than this fruitful notion, which perhaps has not as yet been widely accepted, it should be mentioned that Brandi (*Quattrocentisti senesi*, 1949, pp. 40-41) suggests minor artists such as the Master of the Straus Madonna and Pseudo-Ambrogio di Baldese. And in the present book, a possible ancestry has been traced, beginning with Starnina and going on to Antonio Veneziano (the delicate and luminous Antonio Veneziano of the tabernacle of the Agli) as well as a hypothetical period, along with Masaccio, in the workshop of Bicci di Lorenzo. What is lacking is a precise link to the first manifestations of Masolino.

172) The group of frescoes discovered by Procacci in 1943 and discussed by Salmi in 1947 and by Procacci himself in *Sinopie e Affreschi*, 1960 (illustrations plates 62-69, catalogued p. 227 and 13, 16-19; cf. also U. Baldini in *Catalogo della II Mostra di affreschi staccati*, Florence, 1958, nos. 50-53) has not as yet been as thoroughly studied as it deserves. In a passing mention (1961, p. 96) I recalled the painters of Casa Datini (1411) in connection with the style of the under-drawings, but I did not as yet grasp very well how much separated Masolino from the typical Florentine narrative painting, dry but still Gothic, which persisted as late as the frescoes in the Chiostro Verde.

173) Photograph 32344 of the Soprintendenza of Florence taken before the fresco was detached (Fig. 42) shows a section of fresco, the plinth with slender columns placed on parallelepiped bases, and a thin ring at the apex of the foot of the column which slopes upward (as in the *Annunciation* in San Clemente); there is a displacement to the right of the viewer as an optical illusion designed to make the point of view effective. At the right one can make out the lower part of the garment of a kneeling member of the confraternity.

174) "The circular forms typical of Trecento decoration are *re-formed* in the tondo, a specifically Renaissance format," according to Brandi. The tondo enclosing a head reappears in the frescoes of Paolo Uccello in Prato (cf. E. Sindona, *Paolo Uccello*, Plates 49-51), and there

is another instance, perhaps equally early, in the frame of an *Annunciation* by the Master of the Adimari Cassone, a fresco from the Badia of Soffena, now detached.

175) Brandi says of one of the two heads: "If we observe the shading of the hollow of the eye, we remark that the chiaroscuro there is not the counterfoil to a well-defined ray of light but serves to institute a soft and fluid rhythm without caesura: from this the entire image acquires a similar fluidity. What is the significance of the kind of nebulosity one notices? It is not there to underline an atmospheric element, but is the micrometric quality itself of chiaroscuro which has as secondary effect—but secondary only—the capacity to make the image stand out within a nebulosity." Here, in what Brandi says, we are at the extreme point of a sensitivity which is exclusively formalistic; after remarking on the general "fluidity" and the like, Brandi denies the "atmosphericity," that is, he does not feel it necessary to attempt to comprehend the intuitive values of which the form is the expression. Now, among these values no one will claim that there is only a *naturalness* understood strictly as an imitation of the immersion of the human figure in atmospheric nature; but there may also be a *naturalness inherent precisely in the form in which is contained* (or, *to which is reduced) sensory and intellectual perfection*. And precisely in these heads by Masolino —forms of perfect geometry traced as if within the circle itself (and indeed comprising the circle itself) with a flowing hand and gentle character —there is an imprecise atmospheric chiaroscuro, the historical and noble modulus of the cameo, in the figure, and it is carried over into fresco with the humble spontaneity of a popular technique. Indeed, such *naturalness understood also as a naive stylistic naturalness* seems to me a fundamental and constant trait of Masolino.

176) It is important to note that Vasari based himself principally on the activity of Masolino in the Carmine except for "the hall of the old Orsini house on Monte Giordano" (specified as an early work) which he himself could still have seen in Rome; he attributed to Masaccio various other works by Masolino. But is it not said that in his work in the Carmine Masolino is still Late Gothic? That it may have been "the pseudo-critical pressure of Michelangelo or even of other experts" which made Vasari in the second edition of the *Lives* lose sight of "the sense of basic difference between Masaccio and Masolino" (Longhi) and thereby re-evaluate the latter, is an argument that can easily be turned around: it may have been precisely Michelangelo—who was no fool—who urged Vasari to greater appreciation of Masolino.

Furthermore—and this is as good an opportunity as any to make it clear—Longhi's inference (1940, pp. 158-60) that in his biography of Masaccio of 1568 Vasari had lost the infallibility of the 1550 edition appears, admittedly, very suggestive and is often repeated. But precisely for this reason it must be pointed out that it is simply not true. The simple fact is that in the meantime Vasari had collected further information and re-examined in greater detail the works involved (for instance, the *Trinity* in Santa Maria Novella and the Pisa polyptych). Already in the edition of 1550 there were assigned to Masaccio the predella of the Carnesecchi triptych in Santa Maria Maggiore in Florence (and even the entire triptych, as in the biography of Uccello), the entire chapel in San Clemente in Rome, as well as many other works in Rome, although they are not specifically named but simply indicated as lost or disappeared. In the 1568 edition he added only: (1) the Santa Maria Maggiore triptych in Rome which he saw in the company of Michelangelo (and in which, moreover, as the side-panel in London proves, Masaccio did in fact have a hand), (2) the Sant'Ambrogio panel in Florence on which Masaccio certainly collaborated (and it is not true that it was previously cited by Albertini—who does not mention it—but that Vasari omitted it out of caution in the first edition), (3) the lost *Annunciation* from San Niccolò which Longhi has attempted to identify with the Masolino Goldman painting although this is in clear contradiction with a precise description by Vasari which must apply to a different work from Masaccio's own hand, (4) the lost *Saint Ives* from the Badia, done in foreshortening from below and in a niche, prototype for similar paintings by Uccello and Castagno, and which certainly could not have been by Masolino, so much the less so in view of Longhi's deprecation of its Renaissance character, (5) the portraits from the *Consecration* "which are also in the house of Simon Corsi." On the other hand, the Apostle frescoed in the Carmine of Pisa, assigned to Masaccio in the earlier text, is taken from him in the second edition and supposed to be by Filippo Lippi. It is obvious then that, rather than wishing to exaggerate indiscriminately the number of works, Vasari in fact reviewed them attentively.

177) Cf. 1961, pp. 98 ff.

178) It is useful here to recall certain now well-established facts (due especially to PROCACCI, 1954) and what may be inferred from them about Masolino's activities in this extremely important period of his contact with Masaccio:
January 18, 1423, Masolino enrolls in the Guild of Physicians and Chemists; the Bremen *Madonna* is dated 1423; November 2, 1424, payment of seventy-four florins to Masolino for the frescoes in the Chapel of the Holy Cross in Santo Stefano at Empoli; July 8, 1425, payment to Masolino of a small sum (a total of seven lire, three soldi, equal to around 32,000 lire today) by the Company of Saint Agnes which on May 17 of that year had presented a religious drama about the Ascension at the Carmine in Florence for which Masolino had "painted the cloud and used azure and fine gold" and also painted "the lambs which appear on the cloud"; September 1, 1425, Masolino leaves for Hungary; after the 7th and before the 20th of July 1427 Masolino has returned to Florence and has received 360 bank florins (= 180 ordinary florins, that is, 3,150,000 lire today) from the heirs of Pippo Spano; July 12, 1427 he is commissioned to decorate the Della Foresta Chapel in San Francesco in Figline. After that Masolino no longer appears in Florentine documents, although Procacci advises me that he has found documents on both Masolino's activities in Hungary and on his departure from Florence for Rome which *probably* did not occur until spring of 1428.
From these facts I drew the following conclusions (1961) and remain convinced of them, though I cannot presume to have fixed definitively such a controversial chronology. The group of frescoes in Santo Stefano at Empoli (including the Medici lunette) and the *Pietà* in the Collegiata were executed in 1424, a year in which, moreover, the plague which broke out in Florence in the spring made it wise to settle outside the city. Procacci quite rightly does not exclude the possibility that the work in Empoli may have continued even after the date of payment by the Confraternity of the Cross, but time must be allowed for Masolino to paint, before September 1425, at least part of the Brancacci Chapel plus the Carnesecchi triptych of Santa Maria Maggiore (on whose date of 1425, affirmed by various elements, Procacci agrees). On the basis of the later chronology suggested by Lindberg, Brandi supposes that the *Pietà* of the Empoli Collegiata may have been done in 1427, after Masolino's return from Hungary and (according to Brandi) at the same time as Masolino resumed work on the Brancacci Chapel; however, his grounds for supposing two sojourns of Masolino in Empoli are substantially that in 1424 Masolino was not as yet capable of thinking in terms of perspective (an opinion

shared by E. MICHELETTI, *Masolino da Panicale*, 1959, pp. 21 ff.). This, I believe, has been refuted in the present text.
If then during 1425 Masolino executed the Carnesecchi triptych (which proves in fact to have been done prior to his return from Hungary), *the logical conclusion is that by that time he must have already got as far as the second tier in the Brancacci Chapel*, that is, the story of Tabitha in which there are typological similarities with the triptych (compare the Carnesecchi Madonna and Child with the woman with a child in the background) and also of style in the somewhat sharp contours of the figures. SALMI (1948, pp. 200-201) observed these as well as the fact that the haloes in the Carnesecchi triptych are virtually identical with that of the angel below and to the right in the *Madonna* from Sant'Ambrogio and must therefore be due to the same gold-beater. *This confirms the general supposition that Masaccio was called on to collaborate with Masolino* (for the second tier at the Carmine and the Sant'Ambrogio painting) *in that period from the end of 1424 to 1425* when Masolino was faced with the problem of completing all of his commissions before leaving for Hungary; *and for the Carnesecchi altarpiece he also called in Paolo Uccello (as we shall see) who was to leave for Venice in the summer of 1425*.
Procacci has also quite rightly pointed out the unlikelihood, for a number of reasons, of a trip to Rome by Masolino and Masaccio in 1425—a notion favored by Longhi. Certainly if they had so much work on their hands at that time, and if Masolino had already fixed his departure for Hungary for September, then this is another reason to exclude the possibility of such a trip and, even more, of their having worked at Rome at that time since that would have meant several months away from their tasks in Florence. Further, as already mentioned, it has been suggested that 1425 was not celebrated as a jubilee year. For these reasons I cannot understand why PROCACCI himself (1951) should limit the work in the Brancacci Chapel in 1425 to the highest tier, now lost, and to Masolino alone who would have painted the *Evangelists* in the vault (and naturally the under-arch at the entrance), the two large lunettes with the *Calling of Peter and Andrew* and the *Shipwreck of the Apostles*, and the *Saint Peter Weeping for his Denial of Christ* to the side of the window. Procacci thinks that at the other side there may have been depicted Saint Peter cutting off Malchus' ear, but it is odd that Vasar makes no mention of it. I am likewise not convinced of the ideas of others, such as Meller who thinks that the scene of Saint Peter weeping may have occupied an entire large lunette, presuming that the original window was not as high as the present one. Similarly Procacci's deduction that a "calling forth the dead" by Masaccio could not have been included in that tier is not absolutely certain; MELLER, 1961, p. 224, n. 53 does not entirely exclude it.
Still following Procacci's chronology, the Brancacci Chapel frescoes were worked on again when Masolino returned in August 1427, this time in collaboration with Masaccio in the central portion, and work continued until Masolino left for Rome. Now, since here I can argue with Procacci on equal terms because, as far as I know, he has no documentary evidence for this point, I should like to appeal to his exemplary common sense as an historian to ask if he really believes it within the bounds of possibility that, within at the most a single year (August 1427 to, let us say, August 1428), Masaccio could have completed his part of the chapel which—as I am advised by the restorer, Prof. Tintori—involved at least some ninety distinct portions of work ("day's work" is the technical term) and counting the destroyed parts of the *Story of Theophilus*, a hundred. And would Masaccio not have needed a considerable time for planning and preparation before setting to work on those sublime compositions, on all those admirable and

thoroughly studied details, on the many portraits which, as Meller has shown, people the frescoes? It suffices to recall ALBERTI (*Della Pittura*, ed. *cit.*, p. 112): "And when we must paint stories, first among ourselves we think a long time about the ways and means to make them most beautiful, and we lay out our ideas and our models for the entire story and for each of its parts first, and then we call in our friends for advice, etc." *On the basis of an average of four days of preparation and execution for each "day's work", it is obvious that already the time estimated has been exceeded.* What is more, at the very same time *Masaccio very probably had to paint other works,* and these were works of considerable importance, like the *Annunciation* for San Niccolò (we know that the Pisa polyptych took him almost a year in 1426). And then it is presumed that he could have had the time to go to Rome and to turn out there at least the side-panel for the Santa Maria Maggiore painting! To believe this means to believe in miracles. Evidently some people imagine that Masaccio conceived his ideas and realized them with lightning speed, but I recall that Domenico Veneziano put in five or six years on a single wall or slightly more of the chancel of Sant'Egidio, and Castagno three for the other wall, and many other examples can be cited. Instead, I now suppose that Masolino, whose style should have permitted him to work more rapidly, may already in 1424 have begun the Brancacci Chapel (the upper tier) before going to Empoli, since for everything he did there the period between the end of 1424 and August 31, 1425 seems to me very short. Upon his return to Florence in 1427 Masolino could have taken on the commission from the Della Foresta family at Figline or, instead, soon after his return could have left for Rome where, following the lead of Martin V, eminent members of the Curia were engaged in beautifying the churches of the Holy City. Cardinal Branda da Castiglione was charged with the decoration of the Chapel of the Sacrament in San Clemente (and Masolino, with whom the Cardinal had perhaps become acquainted while he was legate in Hungary, may have been called to begin work in the second half of 1427), and the Colonna family, to which Martin V belonged, commissioned the triptych for Santa Maria Maggiore. What is more, early in the autumn of 1427 Gentile da Fabriano died in Rome, leaving the field more free to others. Even if Procacci's unpublished documents should prove beyond doubt that Masolino was in Florence until the spring of 1428, proof will still be needed of the thesis that he then resumed work on the Brancacci Chapel and that the Brancacci would have left their chapel unfinished ever since 1425, with nothing more done than the vault, while awaiting the return of the artist from Hungary, since there could have been no way of foreseeing that return, due only to the death of Pippo Spano in 1426. The reasons which lead me to consider this thesis improbable have already been discussed above.

179) MELLER, 1961, IV, pp. 291 ff. and cf. figs. 82-85, 76 a/b and 77, and 79-81.

180) Assigned to Masaccio by LONGHI (1940, pp. 155-56) because of the "calculated discrepancies of a persistently new spatial collocation" and "their melancholy and modern feeling."

181) The same "day's work" seems to be revealed by photograph 77997 of the Soprintendenza delle Belle Arti. Longhi considers as Masaccio's also the figure of Saint Peter except for the head and the extended arm, but it suffices to compare it with the Saint Peter by Masaccio in the *Baptism of the Neophytes* where the feet are foreshortened and not in profile, the drapery adhering to the lines of the body and not disposed vaguely, the energy such as to infuse the entire figure, the modeling round and not profiled. Now, for his part Masolino

proves his great capacities in the figure of Saint Peter preaching which he repeated almost identically in the Resurrection of Tabitha and even as Saint Matthew, though somewhat sketchily, in the triptych of Santa Maria Maggiore of Rome. Comparing these figures, one understands what is characteristic of Masaccio and what of Masolino, and if one underestimates the latter, one ends up by wronging the former, attributing to him things inferior to his true standard.

182) The two heads are reproduced in color in SALMI, 1956, p. XVII. Again in this case a critical presupposition—that Masaccio was brimming over with invention and was even a little "low-life"—has led Longhi to deprecate these two portraits of "nice young men (no longer wild youths)" because of their "ineffective repetition of an almost identical three-quarter view," and he has even had recourse to intellectual acrobatics in describing this as "a section which Masaccio may have, without thinking, left unfinished or merely sketched out in red ochre on the rough wall" (sic!). The fact is that the entire group of figures and heads to the right in the middle ground of the *Baptism* constitutes a single "day's work" overlapping (and therefore later than) the head of Saint Peter which has been somewhat repainted, and the latter in turn overlaps the two youths, each of whom required one "day's work" (cf. p. 155 for the diagram of the days' work on the Baptism). Although PROCACCI (1951, p. 31) dismisses Longhi's hypothesis about Filippino for these same technical reasons, nevertheless he too feels the need to consider Masaccio perfect (presupposing that whatever Masaccio did was, in fact, perfect) and so awards to Masolino the heads of the two youths and that of the Saint Peter, despite the fact that, beginning with the flat and perfectly foreshortened halo, the figure has nothing in common with that by Masolino. This is further contradicted by the formalism and the very different technique of the corresponding section—part of the face of a Carmelite—discovered in the *Preaching of Saint Peter* and untouched by the fire. Masaccio appears to be more incisive and precise in a Renaissance fashion, Masolino more generalized. I have insisted somewhat on these details in order to show how even the most refined criticism can go astray.

183) From the diagram of the days' work furnished me by Prof. Tintori (see p. 103), one should be able to make out that the first thing done was the part to the right of the viewer—Saint Peter paying the tax—and then the landscape above and Saint Peter fishing, and then the heads. Whether Masaccio began it from the right or the left, when he arrived at the head near that of Christ he began again at the end of the opposite row (no. 18 overlaps both 12 and 17). Last to be painted was the head of Christ. For the lower parts of the figures Masaccio proceeded from the right to the left.

184) 1940; as also for the head of Christ in the *Tribute Money*. SALMI (1948) with his usual objectivity accepted the proposal of Longhi for the background of the Tabitha episode. PROCACCI (1951) attributes to Masaccio only the perspective lines and the drawing of the houses and to Masolino the actual execution which he enriched by numerous details (once again a critical presupposition too rigidly applied, since in this case Masaccio would have had to design a deserted city).

185) Cf. the diagram of the day's work, Fig. 61.

186) Longhi has named them (from left to right) "the old man expostulating" in front of the house, the "bourgeois woman" returning home, the "child, followed by his lay-sister aunt, whining and resisting because he is being taken to Vespers," "the bilious man out of work." However, Salmi (1948, pl. 141) has

remarked on the relation to Masolino of the small central figures by analogy with the Madonna of Novoli.

187) See for example Jacopo's *Madonna* of Fonte Gaia finished in 1419, for the agitated sweep of the mantle from the knees down as in the *Madonna* in Munich.

188) In U. BALDINI, *Catalogo della Mostra di Quattro Maestri del Primo Rinascimento*, Florence, 1954, there is ample treatment of the various opinions on the Sant'Ambrogio painting. There seems to be general acceptance now of the divisions so ably determined by LONGHI (1940, pp. 152-54): to Masaccio belong the Madonna and Child, the base of the throne, the angel in green tunic holding the curtain at the right. Ragghianti however proposes to assign to Masaccio also the head of the angel above, but it is more likely by Masolino.

189) Cf. 1961. p. 101 and figs. 13-14.

190) The triptych with the *Assumption* (1437) in the Accademia, Florence which came from Cortona.

191) There are a few more things to be said about the work of Masolino contemporary with Masaccio. I now believe that the date of the *Madonna* in Munich can be pushed back to the beginning of 1424 instead of 1425, therefore a little prior to the simplification which set in with the lunette in Empoli which seems to be a closer precedent for the Sant'Ambrogio panel (compare the angels). On this basis the successive development of the Madonnas of Bremen, Munich, Empoli and finally Novoli seems to me more logical. Obviously this chronology does not exclude influence from Gentile as early as the Munich Madonna, an influence equally evident in the Kress and Goldman Annunciations which, in my opinion (cf. *Acropoli*, 1936, I, p. 36, n. 64), should be dated perhaps around 1423-25 rather than around 1430 (Parronchi, in his article on the Carnesecchi Chapel cited above, arrives at the same conclusion, although by different reasoning). In this connection, I wish to draw attention to the particular affinity between the Angel of Annunciation in the Kress painting, in its profile and in the treatment of the garment, with the two youths by Masolino in the Tabitha fresco. As for the two lost lunettes of the Carmine, I have reproduced here (Fig. 2) the *Calling of Andrew and Peter* from the predella of the triptych (1436) by Andrea di Giusto in Ripalta which is a copy of the missing painting (remarked already by SALMI, 1948, commentary to pl. 208) although it is much inferior to the Giovanelli copy published by LONGHI (1940, p. 105). In the same predella, the Saint Andrew baptizing derives from Masaccio's Saint Peter in the *Baptism of the Neophytes* (Fig. 1).

To finish with the Sant'Ambrogio panel, I venture to point out that, precious as is for us Masaccio's contribution to that painting, it was perhaps not entirely fortunate for the original equilibrium of the work as conceived by Masolino: consider the overly conspicuous sculpture-like block planted right in the foreground. If the initial conception had been Masaccio's, we should have expected from him a clearer and less compressed spatial solution, a half-bust treatment of the Saint Anne rising up from behind the throne, and the two censer-bearing angels brought into the foreground as at San Giovenale or even cut off by the frame as at Pisa. This I have tried to show by an elementary bit of photo-montage (Fig. 17): I have enlarged the Saint Anne somewhat, since I agree with LONGHI, 1940, p. 153 that she must have been initially conceived as dominant with the Madonna almost an adolescent seated between her knees, a conception altered when Masaccio took the lion's share of the painting and Masolino had to compress his figure; further, in place of the Masaccio Madonna I have substituted Masolino's from Bremen, although what would have been preferable would have been a Madonna like that of the Novoli panel, but it is

too emphatically vertical to fit well. The result, with the exclusion of Masaccio's collaboration (except for the base of the throne) and with the gentler flattening of the image, is an arrangement more closely related to that of Gentile's Quaratesi Madonna.

192) Cf. the excellent research of Padre S. ORLANDI (*Rivista d'Arte*, 1954, and elsewhere) and an attempt to reconsider the whole question of the youthful activity of Fra Angelico in BERTI, "Miniature dell'Angelico (e altro)," in *Acropoli*, IV, 1962 and I, 1963. Padre ORLANDI has recently published an important monograph on *Beato Angelico*, Florence, 1964.

193) ORLANDI, *Op. cit.*, p. 167.

194) Only one work by Angelico, a painted cross for Santa Maria Nuova, done in 1423, appears to be documented for this period.

195) BERTI, *art. cit.* in note 192 above. The first details decisively revealing Masaccio's influence do not appear until the *Annunciation* of Cortona from around 1433, in particular in the predella (the *Betrothal of the Virgin*); in a small tabernacle of the same time like that of the *Madonna della Stella*; and in the small panel of the *Naming of the Baptist* which POPE-HENNESSY (*Fra Angelico*, 1952) also does not date earlier than 1433-34 (when Andrea di Giusto copied it in 1435 he may well have been paying homage to a very recent painting). Similar conclusions as to chronology have been drawn by PROCACCI and BECHERUCCI in articles written in connection with the exhibition of Fra Angelico in 1955.

196) As to the limits of "ecclesiastical art" in Fra Angelico and his particular version of the pictorial *istoria*, "which, with Masaccio, analogously to humanistic historiography properly speaking, was oriented towards the *civitas terrena*, while with him [Fra Angelico] there remained intact the ancient vision of the *civitas caelestis*," cf. my article cited in note 192 above which develops further certain brilliant indications of G. C. ARGAN, *Fra Angelico*, 1955.

197) 1961, p. 101, n. 32.

198) Cf. M. PITTALUGA, *Filippo Lippi*, 1949, pp. 15 ff., for the development of Lippi at the Carmine through works of Masaccio, Masolino and Starnina but denying a strong influence from Lorenzo Monaco.

199) Cf. BERTI and BALDINI, *Filippino Lippi*, 1957, pp. 23-24 and 76-78 where, as in the present text, the date of Filippino's work at the Brancacci Chapel, given by Scharf as 1483-85, is advanced for various reasons. In his elegant lecture, "Incontro tra Filippino e Masaccio" in *Saggi su Filippino Lippi*, 1957, G. FIOCCO indulges in some polemic with me because—in the face of the general great enthusiasm for Filippino who completed Masaccio's unfinished work—I am guilty of underlining the difficulty of that task, above all for a temperament such as Filippino's, delicate and not oriented towards "prose" but instead towards fantasy. And I truly cannot convince myself that the work in the Carmine is among Filippino's best.

Since we are recalling the work of Filippino in the chapel, as is known it includes in the lower tier the completion of Masaccio's *Story of Theophilus* (later we shall discuss their respective contributions); the episodes on the two pilasters with *Saint Peter in Prison visited by Saint Paul* (Salmi, followed by Fiocco, thinks this was traced out by Masaccio) and *Saint Peter liberated by the Angel*; the *Story of Simon Magus and Crucifixion of Saint Peter*, a large scene forming a companion-piece to the Theophilus episode. Cf. F. GAMBA, *Filippino Lippi nella storia della critica*, 1958, especially pp. 86-87 for the bibliography on Filippino's work in the chapel; also

149

C. L. Ragghianti in *Critica d'Arte*, 37, 1960, pp. 28 ff. and n. 7 for information on Filippino at the chapel and for later interventions on Masaccio's work.

200) Attributions by, respectively, Ragghianti, Gioseffi (1962) and Brandi. Cf.—also for the relevant bibliography—L. Berti, "Domenico Veneziano" in the *Enciclopedia Universale dell'Arte*, IV, 1960, though I am bitterly contrite for having attributed therein the Berlin birth salver to Domenico di Bartolo as an alternative to Domenico Veneziano.

Not without interest is this little-known bit of information about a small problem which seems to relate Masaccio with Domenico and which—if the solution turned out to their advantage—would please very much those who find precocious traits of Masaccio in Domenico. There exists in a private collection in Florence a copy (cited by Schubring) cut down to make a dodecagon of Masaccio's Berlin birth salver and its back (Figs. 75 and 76) with as companion piece (Figs. 77 and 78) another dodecagon, also a copy, with a *Judgment of Paris* and on the reverse the same putti with a marten as on the other salver but facing in the opposite direction (Salmi referred to this dodecagon in a postscript, 1948, p. 232). It could therefore be supposed that the copyist imitated two originals formerly coupled which were contemporary and made for the same occasion, because the *Judgment of Paris* might very well be a flattering allusion to the choice made by the husband, and the reverse of the Berlin salver seems to call for a companion piece. Thus in the final analysis the *Judgment of Paris* which is stylistically close to Domenico Veneziano might prove to derive from a salver by the young Domenico around 1427 with the younger painter in contact with Masaccio (unless one insists on attributing to Domenico the Berlin salver also, as does Ragghianti). However, the two putti were made as mirror inversions of the same image (taken from Masaccio's salver); also the proportions of the figures on the front of the two salvers do not have the correspondance natural to companion pieces. So finally we are forced to conclude that the copyist created from two unrelated sources a couple of salvers which were not intended as such originally.

201) Cf. Berti, "Una nuova Madonna e degli appunti su un grande maestro," in *Pantheon*, VI, 1961, pp. 301-2 and n. 21.

202) Procacci, *Sinopie e affreschi*, pp. 234-35, Fig. V, and Cat. 7 (but for an example of how easily such problems were "solved" at the beginning of the century, cf. G. Carocci, *I dintorni di Firenze*, I, 1908, pp. 331-32) and U. Baldini, *Catalogo della Mostra di affreschi staccati*. The tabernacle, now reconstructed in the new church of Mater Dei near Novoli, has however been a little altered (sides at a wider angle, the segment of the little vault bent upwards in order to improve visibility from outside) with respect to the original which is still in place and has the sinopias. I think it would be superfluous to trace out this style which derives from Antonio Veneziano and Starnina. However, quite rightly Baldini has remarked that the image almost literally copies a widely diffused model (as in the museum of Santa Croce in Florence, the fragmentary fresco with the Madonna, Child and Donor from the circle of Bicci di Lorenzo), although this does not in itself suffice to exclude Paolo Uccello at the age of nineteen. Taking into account Uccello's later maturity, the style of the tabernacle is not too opposed to a vague idea which chance alone recently led me to: around 1420 Uccello might have painted like the artist who did the two splendid pinnacles with an Annunciation reproduced here in Figs. 37 and 38, although, it is true, they might possibly be ascribed to a "Master of the Sherman Predella" were they not more Sienese in character and harder in drawing. Similarities to the later Uccello and especially to the Uc-

cello-Master of Prato-Karlsruhe are not, however, lacking in the two small figures: note how the Virgin is quite exceptionally placed within the semicircular enclosure whose space is stressed by the lectern in perspective and also the flooring in which the bricks are patiently traced in connecting lines. But I repeat that this is only a remote supposition as to what Paolo Uccello might have been doing around 1420.

203) *Art. cit.*, 1961; p. 301 and nn. 17-19.

204) *Art. cit.*, 1962.

205) The *Annunciation* in fresco and very probably the related four Evangelists in the vault were assigned to Uccello by Vasari (after an indication of Albertini); the predella was ascribed to Uccello by Albertini, whereas Vasari attributes it to Masaccio (in reality, if the *Life of Saint Julian* in Montauban belongs to it, then Masolino must have worked on that panel at least). Vasari declares that the central panel of the predella was a *Nativity* like that in London.

206) For this, consult the many recent and basic contributions by Parronchi.

207) See Chapter I. Both Parronchi and Gioseffi in their studies have pointed out certain extremist tentatives of Uccello.

208) M. Chiarini, 1962, p. 55.

209) From Rosselli, *Sepoltuario*, manuscript of 1657, cited in Procacci, 1932 (see next note), p. 204.

210) Cf. U. Procacci, "L'incendio della Chiesa del Carmine del 1771," in *Rivista d'Arte*, 1932, pp. 202-12, and in *Bollettino d'Arte*, 1933-34, pp. 333-34. The total destruction of a work by Masaccio perpetrated at that date and in the Grand Duchy of Tuscany which was so respectful of its artistic patrimony is most surprising, but—alas—such wanton deeds are always possible when building interests become active. According to what Procacci has determined, the fresco was not on the side of the cloister adjacent to the church but on the following door at the angle of the side facing the piazza. Cf. also Procacci, 1956, pp. 214-15.

211) Procacci, *art. cit.*, 1932, pp. 200 ff., gives the various descriptions of the work from the early sources.

212) In the drawing in the Uffizi (Fig. 47) there is a balustrade at the top and rather close forward, but this is a detail so typically sixteenth-century in taste—as is the drawing itself—that it is likely not to derive from the fresco.

213) This movement was perhaps worked out after the rather crowded group on the left indicated in various drawings, and there was probably then a space followed by the sparser group on the right known from other drawings. It is, in fact, of note that the drawings copy substantially only these two groups: if the group in the center was seen from the rear, as I suppose, it would obviously have been of less interest to the copyists. However, one cannot exclude, as another secondary hypothesis, that the door of the monastery was depicted on the right side and that in the background there was the east side of the Piazza del Carmine.

214) The drawing in the Accademia of Venice was, in fact, connected by Lanzi with the *Consecration*, but on what basis? It might also depict, as Fiocco proposed, the Pope conferring the Rule of the Carmelites as seen in Lippi's fresco in the same cloister of the Carmine since—contrary to what has been objected—the Pontiff officiates with the mitre as well as the triple crown. Thus it seems to me clear that it is certainly a pontifical scene,

150

with its crowd of mitred bishops flanking the ceremony (there were only three at the consecration of the Carmine), but it is most likely connected with a study for some fresco of the early sixteenth century (Fischel points out that the celebrant resembles Julius II). For the relevant bibliography, cf. Salmi, 1948, p. 230.

215) For this also, cf. Salmi, 1948, pp. 29 ff.

216) The Uffizi drawing no. 76 has been correctly assigned to the sixteenth century because of its influences from Pontormo; indeed, it may well be from late in the century since in style it resembles the work of Empoli. Earlier, from the first half of the century, and correctly attributed to someone like Bachiacca or Puligo, is the drawing in private hands published by E. Berti Toesca, 1945. In the Folkestone Museum and Art Gallery there is a drawing from the end of the sixteenth century which was published by C. Clark (Burlington Magazine, 1958, p. 177 and Fig. 36) in which M. Chiarini (1962) has noticed that the group on the right, in reverse, is related to the group in Ghirlandaio's Saint Francis Resuscitating a Child in Santa Trinita. Chiarini thinks this may be a quite literal quotation of Masaccio on the part of Ghirlandaio, but this seems highly unlikely and it may well be that the copyist jotted down on the same sheet as his drawing of the Ghirlandaio a somewhat varied copy of Masaccio's Consecration. The absence from the drawing of the head supposed to be of Mainardi, which in the fresco appears before the figure at the extreme right which is a self-portrait by Ghirlandaio, does not prove the contrary, since that detail which Ghirlandaio squeezed in virtually by force may well have been deliberately omitted by the person who made the drawing. Moreover, the costumes of the personages wearing birettas (in the drawing also) are of the second and not the first half of the fifteenth century. Finally, the drawing in the Casa Buonarroti in Florence (36 F verso) is attributed to Antonio Mini (cf. P. Barocchi, Michelangelo e la sua scuola, Florence, 1962, p. 218), and we have already discussed in Chapter I the drawing by Michelangelo in the Albertina. Salmi (1948, p. 232) is probably correct in suggesting that the not hitherto located drawing by one Annibale Mancini seen by Cavalcaselle, with three figures of whom one wears wooden sandals, may be a copy of the same detail studied by Michelangelo. Other drawings of the Consecration owned by A. Scharf and U. Procacci are not known to me.

217) However, in view of his rope girdle, this is probably a friar.

218) The expression is used by both Manetti and A. Billi. Cf. Procacci, art. cit. in note 210, 1932, p. 200.

219) Parronchi dates them around 1424.

220) Mentioned by Vasari in the second edition of the Lives. Cf. Salmi, 1948, p. 157, though it is difficult to accept his opinion that there were two portraits and not a single picture. Were they copies by Masaccio himself or by someone else? Or simply a later and even partial copy from the Consecration? Borghini (1584, ed. 1730, p. 254) remarks on "a very beautiful portrait of Baccio Valori the elder" from the hand of Masaccio in the Valori house, but this certainly cannot be identified with Uffizi panel 1485 which has a portrait of an old man in the style of Ghirlandaio (or Filippino) which belonged to the Corboli family from the Val d'Arno (cf. Salmi, 1948, p. 162).

221) The Portrait of a Youth (no. 1937 in the Mellon Collection, panel, $16\frac{7}{8} \times 12\frac{5}{8}$", color reproduction in Cairns and Walker, Masterpieces of Painting from the National Gallery of Art, Washington, 1945, p. 21) is accepted for Masaccio in the second edition of the monograph by Salmi (1948, pp. 22-23, 155, and pl. 12) with

the date of around 1424, whereas the 1942 catalogue of the National Gallery suggests around 1425. Cf. also Pope-Hennessy, Paolo Uccello, 1950, p. 148 ("Florentine School"). It will be recalled that Schmarsow proposed either Masolino or Paolo Uccello. In 1843 it was in the Artaud de Montor Collection in Paris and already bore the attribution to Masaccio.

222) For the portrait in Boston (panel, $16\frac{1}{8} \times 11\frac{3}{4}$") cf. Salmi, 1948, whose bibliographical references are largely favorable to Masaccio and who dates it around 1425. Procacci, 1951, abstained from judging it without first-hand acquaintance but appears to agree, whereas Ragghianti (in Sele Arte, 2, 1952, p. 65) attributes it to the young Piero della Francesca who had been studying Masaccio.

223) For the Chambéry portrait (once again similar measurements, $18\frac{1}{2} \times 14\frac{1}{8}$") and Uffizi drawing 28 E ($11\frac{7}{8} \times 7\frac{3}{8}$") which is assigned to Paolo Uccello, cf. the exhaustive examination in Pope-Hennessy, Op. cit. 1950, pp. 147-50. Both are in the catalogue of the Mostra di Quattro Maestri del Primo Rinascimento, Florence, 1954, with catalogue entry by E. Micheletti. Berenson however thought the Chambéry portrait was by Masaccio, a hypothesis considered by M. Laclotte. Catalogue of the exhibition De Giotto à Bellini, Paris, 1956, no. 122, though loyal to Longhi, he still disputes it. Certain scholars have also attributed to Masaccio drawing 28 E of the, Uffizi, and I am told that this idea is gaining some ground.

224) See also the preceding chapter. In the lecture course already cited, it is stated that there must have been an interval between this painting and the Pisa polyptych of 1426: "In Masaccio was released an inner spring which permitted him, by means of the revelation of a new kind of painting, to achieve for himself a more marked plasticity. This was the first work by Masaccio after 1423." (Or 1422?).

225) $68\frac{7}{8} \times 40\frac{1}{2}$". Cited by Vasari (1568) as being then in the church of Sant'Ambrogio, then went into the gallery of the Accademia and, in 1919, into the Uffizi. It underwent a very delicate restoration which, in fact took from 1935 to 1954 (I find among my notes made during the examination for restoration that the eye of the angel by Masaccio had been repainted). I do not think one can state with certainty that it had ever been part of a triptych. For full information, see U. Baldini, 1954, already cited, and also our preceding chapter.

226) Longhi, 1940, pp. 153-54.

227) Cf. the fundamental study by A. Parronchi, "Le due tavole prospettiche del Brunelleschi," in Paragone, 1958, no. 107 and 1959, no. 109 (with all the preceding bibliography, including the recent studies by Gioseffi). Brandi, in the lecture course cited, 1961-62, pp. 47-48, observes that perspective with central vanishing-point was already applied in the relief under the Saint George by Donatello (which he dates as 1416, but whose chronology is uncertain) and that the Trinity by Masaccio in Santa Maria Novella has a perspective structure "of the greatest complexity and absolute perfection," to such an extent that it could not be "the end-point of a development worked out during no more than three or four years." Nevertheless he recalls that even before the little treatise Della Prospettiva attributed by Parronchi to Paolo del Pozzo Toscanelli, Biagio Pelacani of Parma, a physicist and mathematician who was in Florence in 1389 and died in 1416, had written his penetrating Questiones Perspectivae around 1390 in which he discussed the Perspectiva communis by Peckham (which was known at least from 1405 on) and, together with Pelacani, he may perhaps have had contact with Brunelleschi.

228) $45\frac{1}{4} \times 41\frac{3}{8}''$. It came from the Spence Collection in Fiesole. Besides the healing of the epileptic boy, on the left it shows the episode of "Render unto Caesar that which is Caesar's" and on the right once again Christ with the Apostles. For complete bibliography, cf. SALMI, 1948, pp. 227-28, particularly the attempt by SCHMARSOW (in *Belvedere*, 1928) to prove it an autograph painting by Masaccio with the date of 1426. Cf. also PARRONCHI *art. cit.* in *Paragone*, 109, 1959, pp. 8 ff. and fig. 3, in which he attributes it to the "Circle of Masolino." It seems to me that the aureoles which are curiously figured with the radiating monogram of Christ may well refer to the Florentine sojourn of Saint Bernardino of Siena in 1424-25.

229) Already in the first edition of the *Lives* where it is cited as a first work to demonstrate how Masaccio "diligently studied methods of work and perspective in which he displayed wonderful ingenuity."

230) The polyptych of Pisa was mentioned with praise in 1550 and described in more detail in the *Lives* of 1568. As is shown by the documents reported by TANFANI-CENTOFANTI, 1897, pp. 177 ff., the notary Giuliano da San Giusto had a chapel near the choir constructed by Pippo di Giovanni di Gante, the stonecutter: "a vault over two transepts with two and one-half columns of milk-white marble from Carrara... above an altar which I wish to have set up in the nave of said church over against the choir, that is with its back to the choir and extending from the portal which is the entrance of the choir to the lateral wall of the church towards the south." It involved, as we see, a twinned vault over an altar perhaps modeled remotely after that of the Dragomanni in San Domenico in Arezzo. The commission was settled on November 29, 1425, but the work was still unfinished in October 1426, though it must have been completed before January, 1427. Masaccio's painting was not commissioned until February 19, 1426, and was paid for on December 26 of the same year. The documents also state the height of the polyptych: "the painting with the altar shall have the height of eight and two-thirds *braccia* or thereabouts." The altar frontal, "of shadowed red and very beautiful, with friezes or real fringe around it, and a round picture with a bust of Saint Julian," was painted by a Master Cola d'Antonio of Florence who also appears as a witness for a payment to Pippo the stonecutter. The altar curtain was colored by Master Mariano di Piero della Valenzana. The panel was prepared and perhaps gilded by a Sienese artisan Antonio di Biagio for 18 florins (SALMI, 1948, p. 177, with the remainder of the bibliography).
Only relatively recently have the various dispersed sections of the polyptych been rediscovered. They were probably removed in a redecoration of the church in the late sixteenth century, not in the eighteenth as has been suggested. The *Saint Paul* ($20\frac{1}{8} \times 11\frac{1}{4}''$; original dimensions presumed to be, with the peaked arch, $20\frac{1}{2} \times 13\frac{1}{2}''$) came from the collection of a legate named Tucchetti in 1796 with an attribution to Masaccio written on the back in a seventeenth-century hand. For some time, in spite of SCHMARSOW (1895), it was obstinately claimed that there was collaboration by Andrea di Giusto. Another *Saint Paul*, formerly in the Bayersdorfer Collection in Munich, discussed by De Fabriczy in 1892, has disappeared, but it quite certainly was not related to this one. The *Adoration of the Magi* ($8\frac{1}{4} \times 24''$) and the *Crucifixion of Saint Peter* and *Decapitation of the Baptist* (a single panel $8\frac{1}{4} \times 24''$) were acquired by the Berlin Museum in 1880 from the collection of Gino Capponi in Florence (where they were listed in FANTOZZI, *Guida di Firenze*, 1864, pp. 398-99) and were already recognized as part of the Pisa polyptych by Cavalcaselle (1883). The Lanckoronski Collection *Saint Andrew* (likewise $20\frac{1}{2} \times 11\frac{1}{2}''$ but presumed to have been $20\frac{1}{8} \times 13\frac{3}{4}''$) was identified by Schmarsow as

early as 1896. The *Crucifixion* in the Museum of Capodimonte in Naples ($32\frac{5}{8} \times 25''$) was acquired in 1901 from a Sig. De Simone and was first labelled "Anonymous Florentine" despite the fact that it was immediately recognized as a Masaccio by Adolfo Venturi; in 1906 Suida connected it with the Pisa polyptych. The four small saints in Berlin—Saint Augustine, Saint Jerome, Saint Elijah the Prophet (?) and Saint Albert the Patriarch (?) (each $15 \times 5''$)—were formerly in the Bluter Collection and assigned to Masaccio. They were exhibited in London in 1893-94 and acquired by the Berlin Museum in 1905. The central panel with the Madonna now in London ($53\frac{3}{8} \times 28\frac{3}{4}''$) was discovered and recognized by Berenson in 1907 in the collection of Rev. G. F. Sutton and acquired by the museum in 1916. For it and for the entire polyptych, cf. the admirable, exemplary catalogue by M. DAVIES, *The Earlier Italian Schools*, 2nd ed., 1961. The *Story of Saint Julian and the Miracle of Saint Nicholas* ($8\frac{3}{4} \times 24\frac{3}{8}''$) was acquired by the Berlin Museum in 1908 and associated with the Pisa polyptych but held to be a collaboration with Andrea di Giusto. I share the hope of Brandi (in the lecture course cited) that the two main side-panels have also been preserved and will some day come to light.

As for the hypothetical reconstruction proposed by SALMI (Fig. 58), the following remarks can be made: (1) there is no reason to suppose that the two lateral predella scenes were wider: why should not the three small panels, all of identical size, have had those dimensions from the outset? (2) The same applies to the Naples *Crucifixion*, since its dimensions are sufficiently explained if we suppose it was placed in the trunk of a cusp slightly narrower than the picture below, as often happens, and any widening would destroy its admirable proportions. (3) Doubts can be raised for the same reasons about the proposed higher peaks of the cusps of the Saints Paul and Andrew. (4) On the left-hand slender pilaster, the Carmelite saint is painted in perspective from below and therefore it should be at the top and not the Saint Jerome which should be in the center, while the Saint Augustine should be at the bottom since his book is painted as if seen from above. (5) Analogously, the Carmelite saint on the right should be placed higher. Another plan of reconstruction can be found in STEINBART, 1947, p. 29.

While the appearance of the two side-panels of the Madonna remains highly hypothetical (cf. SALMI, 1948, pp. 182-83, and see below for the hypothesis of Shearman), it should be noted that PROCACCI (1951), utilizing Salmi's scheme, concluded for his part "that the polyptych must have had a height of around a meter more than indicated in the diagram; it is therefore probable that at the top, where Vasari recalled many saints around a Crucifix, the small panels were disposed in a double row." Evidently Procacci's deductions are based on the measurements furnished by the documents: height of the panel with the altar $8\frac{3}{4}$ *braccia*, that is around 16' 5"; thus, calculating as around 5' the height of the altar including the steps, the height of the polyptych would be 11' 5". Salmi's diagram, however, gives as maximum height in the center around 9' 2" (7' 10" which is the sum of the heights of the paintings plus 1' 4" for the frame): this leaves some $27\frac{1}{2}''$ to be accounted for, precisely what would be needed for a second row of saints in the cusps (or at least for a pair of panels with saints inserted between the Madonna and the Cruxifixion, as in the polyptych by Giovanni del Biondo in the Rinuccini Chapel in Santa Croce, Florence) and this might arrive at something like 20" without counting the frame. However, even more space might be gained, depending on the framing and pinnacles and even on the steps of the altar. Finally, I think one can exclude from the Pisa polyptych, in which it would seem to me pleonastic, the tondo in the National Gallery of London with the

Eternal Father blessing (Fig. 57) (diameter $4\frac{1}{8}''$; for the bibliography, cf. DAVIES, the catalogue cited, 1961, p. 189). I think this comes from Masaccio's workshop or from some follower, and it is certainly not Venetian.

231) John Shearman during a visit to Florence kindly discussed with me the content of a recent paper. If I can sum up his ideas in outline, he first observed that the panel of the *Madonna* in London was sawn through laterally and also must have been shortened below because otherwise the cross-piece on the back would have come too close to the base. Furthermore, above the arch of the cusp the gold appears to have been added where there must have been two half-brackets. Also, on the base of the throne, to the left beneath the praying angel, there is a knife-blade of shadow across its surface, whereas there appears to be another shadow lower down.
The conclusions Shearman draws are that the central panel was not separated from the two side-panels by thin columns but only by simple brackets and that it extended down farther than at present: that the paired saints at the sides were not disposed one next to the other but staggered obliquely (as in the Domenico Veneziano altarpiece in the Uffizi, and I would add the Piero della Francesca in Perugia), perhaps one of them, the outermost, on the step where the two foremost angels sit, and the other, the innermost, on the top step on which the throne rests (which would explain the shadow mentioned above). Or perhaps, better, that a third pair of angels appeared to either side of the throne on the last step, so that the Madonna would be encircled by angels (as in the small panel of Lippi at Empoli or the Fra Angelico of San Domenico), while the saints to the sides were staggered in position, the innermost on the next step down, the outermost on the plane on which the feet of the angel musicians would rest (the feet would then be visible). The figuration of each pair of saints was concentrated moreover in a side-panel with a single cusp (which would explain the rather narrow dimensions of the corresponding predella). Finally, in the central panel with the Madonna, the frame was rectangular as now, but revealed the original gilding in two pinnacles. Above it was the Naples *Crucifixion*, while on each side-panel there was, similarly, a single cusped panel (thus with the surviving Paul and Andrew we should have the second tier of the polyptych complete, although of this I have strong doubts). The small saints to the sides would have been placed on the slender pilasters as in Salmi's reconstruction.

232) On the subject of veils, though this time material, it should be noted how Masaccio carried the gold border over on to the Madonna's hood. This may be a bit illogical (and shows that he was not always austerely rationalistic) but gives a splendid effect of a luminous and motion-full spider-web.

233) See Chapter II.

234) The one remarked on by Vasari as "playing the lute and listening with his ear down to the harmony" is most probably the one on the viewer's right and not its companion to the left as some have said. In the Donatelloesque polychrome stucco in the Victoria and Albert Museum, the motif of the two angel musicians derived from this work by Masaccio is interpreted with more fluidity and liveliness but with less savory scansion: it is as if the "music" were different.

235) With reference to the spatial analysis to which this painting is subjected, Brandi (in the lecture course cited p. 61) remarks that "the foreshortenings of the lutes serve to 'gyrate' the orthogonals (which generally are realized by means of the flooring) to provide the fitting aperture for the perspective and to channel it in the focal point. Thus in the lute faces positioned on the

bias one feels the space which *declines* like the revolving beam from a lighthouse."

236) The restoration undertaken by the Soprintendenza of Naples was carried out by Tintori in 1953-58. Cf. B. MOLAJOLI, *Notizie su Capodimonte*, Naples, 1958, p. 22 and pl. 7, and R. CAUSA, *Catalogo della IV Mostra di Restauri*, Naples, 1960, pp. 40-41 (with bibliography) and pls. 20-29.

237) On the rendering in this scene of motion on pre-cinematographic principles, cf. BERTI, 1962, p. 162, n. 15.

238) Cf. P. N. FERRI in the commemorative volume of 1904, pp. 61 ff. and the relevant figures.

239) Cf. Note 230. Both SALMI (1948, pp. 49-50) and BRANDI (in his course) maintain that Masaccio's helper was not Andrea di Giusto. In disagreement with Brandi, one cannot even exclude the hypothesis that the collaborator on the polyptych may have been Filippo Lippi, then aged around twenty or perhaps even older.

240) LONGHI, 1950. Panel, $9\frac{5}{8} \times 7\frac{1}{8}''$, from a private collection, shown in the second exhibition of art work recovered from Germany, Florence, 1952 (R. SIVIERO, *Catalogo*, pp. 16-17). PROCACCI, 1951, p. 38, includes it among attributed works; it was not presented in the exhibition "Quattro Maestri del Primo Rinascimento" of 1954. On the back of the panel, surmounted by a cardinal's hat, is an escutcheon with a shield bearing six red stars on a yellow field divided in half by a black band with a gilded cross. The coat of arms belongs to Cardinal Antonio Casini of Sienese origin who was elevated to the purple on May 24, 1426 (which is therefore probably the *terminus post quem* of the painting) and who died in Florence on February, 4, 1439.

241) The elongated figure of the Virgin nevertheless has precedents in the Florentine and Sienese Trecento, from Taddeo Gaddi and Jacopo del Casentino to Barna; cf. D. C. SHORR, *The Christ Child in Devotional Images in Italy during the XIV Century*, New York, 1954. The type employed by Masaccio for the Madonna is Shorr's no. 27, essentially Florentine and already exemplified in Giovanni del Biondo (1377) and the School of Spinello. However, especially close to the form used by Masaccio is the relief on the door of the Campanile (c. 1335) with the Child who tries to push away the tickling hand of the Mother (Fig. 54), a relief attributed by Becherucci and others to A. Pisano and which must have been the prototype for the paintings.

242) The two small panels, no. 95 (92) of the Lindenau Museum, put together and the upper one cusped (probably thus from their origin as a painting for domestic devotions), have these measurements: the *Prayer in the Garden* $11\frac{3}{4} \times 13\frac{5}{8}''$, the *Saint Jerome* $7\frac{7}{8} \times 13\frac{5}{8}''$. They were acquired in 1844 from the collection of Dr. E. Braun in Rome. Complete bibliography in R. OERTEL, *Frühe italienische Malerei in Altenburg*, Berlin, 1961, pp. 140-42 and plates 54-57 including reproductions in color. While Schmarsow and Lindberg found in these paintings unmistakable evidence of Masaccio, Berenson suggested Andrea di Giusto, Longhi followed by Salmi proposed Paolo Schiavo between 1430 and 1440, Procacci and Brandi did not include them among the works discussed, but Oertel quite rightly pointed out the decisive inventive quality displayed in them and wondered if a certain slovenliness in execution was due to Masaccio himself or to an assistant, perhaps Andrea di Giusto. It should be remarked that the wings of the angel in the *Prayer in the Garden* were drawn in, but later their color, probably transparent, must have disappeared.

243) Panel, $40\frac{1}{8} \times 20\frac{1}{2}''$. Formerly in the Reserve of the Kunsthistoriches Museum of Vienna (?), then in a

153

Hungarian collection, then in Paris in the Duveen Collection, included in the 1935 Paris exhibition of Italian art, then from 1937 in the Mellon Collection, and finally after 1941 in the National Gallery of Washington (cf. *Preliminary Catalogue*, 1941, p. 125, which also mentions that it passed through the collection of Count Lonyay in Vienna; also *Paintings and Sculpture from the Mellon Collection*, Fig. p. 12). It was published for the first time by BERENSON in *Dedalo*, 1929, pp. 331-36 where he dated it around 1425. Further bibliography and the iconographical precedents in SALMI, 1948, p. 175 (the work is generally dated around 1424-25). PROCACCI, 1951, pp. 37-38, aside from the fact that it is largely repainted, denies that it could have been conceived by Masaccio, It was not discussed in my article of 1961. For BRANDI, 1961-62, pp. 75-76, it may be by Paolo Schiavo.

244) The Brancacci Chapel (Figs. 59-60): depth 22' 10"; breadth 17' 7¾"; first scenes at 5' 6½" from the floor; height of the double tier of frescoes 16' 5". The scenes are framed by angular half-pilasters in Renaissance style with reddish Corinthian capitals, foreshortened in thickness, and these are certainly due to Masaccio (SALMI, 1948, pp. 53-54); the two tiers are separated by notched borders. Ever since its foundation the chapel has been dedicated to the "Madonna del Popolo," a thirteenth-century image. As early as 1386 it belonged to the Brancacci family which lived on the left bank of the Arno in the Santo Spirito quarter. In our first chapter we reported the recent conjectures of Meller as to the significance of the fresco cycle commissioned by Felice Brancacci (not by Antonio, as Vasari says) first from Masolino and then from Masolino and Masaccio. For the completion of the cycle by Filippino Lippi, see our third chapter and Note 260; it is not certain who commissioned this work from Filippino, whether it was the friars or the Brancaccis who, however, at that time were impoverished although documents from 1473 and 1506 show that they were still connected with the church of the Carmine.

In 1674 the pavement was renewed and the marble facings around the lower walls plus the balustrade were executed. The altar was arranged as at present in the same century, and around 1670 someone had the "baroque" idea (which nevertheless reveals great consideration for the frescoes) of setting up "above the first tier a beautiful carved frame in wood and entirely gilded with four similar figures in the form of herms to hold it up." Around 1690 the very rich Marquis Ferroni wished to acquire the Brancacci Chapel and have it decorated like the Corsini Chapel which faces it, destroying the frescoes (cf. our Note 7), but this was vetoed by the Dowager Grand Duchess Vittoria della Rovere at the instigation, it seems, of certain connoisseurs including the Accademia del Disegno. Ferroni then offered to saw off the wall the first tier "where the best pictures are" in order to preserve them, but fortunately this too was refused and he was forced to settle for a chapel in Santissima Annunziata; cf. also PROCACCI, 1956, pp. 215 ff. In 1734 the frescoes were cleaned by the initiative of the friars. In 1746-48 Angiola Tempesti Masini, a widow, and her son Padre Lorenzo of the Carmelites were responsible for a general restoration which however involved redoing the vault and the large lunettes (in the vault V. Meucci painted the Virgin of Carmel giving the scapulary to the Blessed Simon Stock, and the lunettes were painted with architectonic motifs by C. Sacconi). They also had the large window built in place of the original two-light opening (whose base began at the height of a man from the floor; cf. GIGLIOLI, 1929, p. 78, from *Marzocco*, 1902). Soon after, Fra A. Spezzini took charge of setting up a new altar in marble. The pointed arch of the entry was transformed into a semicircular one by the architect Chaman. In all, a piece of unbridled foolishness certainly not compensated by the "delicate" restoration by Meucci of the

frescoes which were spared (those of the third tier which were destroyed were held to "have nothing worthwhile in them"). Cf. PROCACCI, 1956, *loc. cit.*

The famous fire of 1771 in the Carmine (perhaps of criminal origin, cf. PROCACCI in *Rivista d'Arte*, 1954) caused in the chapel damage to the facade, to the balustrades which were destroyed, to the flooring, the base and the altar, and burned the wooden framework between the two tiers and the window (which was promptly repaired to protect the pictures). Fortunately, the frescoes themselves were only smoked up with some lifting of paint and other damage, and there fell off only "two sections of plaster... on the side towards the sacristy," that is, to the left as one enters. Mengs who was in Florence at the time urged the authorities to take all necessary steps to save the paintings (cf. PROCACCI, 1956, pp. 221-22, n. 26). In order not to have to pay for the restoration, in 1780 the Brancaccis, who had many years earlier moved to France and become Marqueses of Brancas, renounced their patronage of the chapel. It was acquired by the Riccardi who re-opened it in 1782, equipping it with the present altar, flooring and balustrades, having the frescoes repaired and cleaned (perhaps by Romei), and decorating the entry in stucco to harmonize with the new decoration of the church by Ruggeri. In GIGLIOLI, 1929, p. 78, there is information about the various restorations (one in 1904, with dusting of the frescoes by Filippo Fiscali) and measures taken or planned for the chapel during the last century. Full bibliography, in addition to that of Giglioli, in SALMI (1948, pp. 183 ff.) who also introduced and published the entire cycle in color in 1948 and 1956 (in collaboration with UNESCO). See also E. BORSOOK, *Mural Painters of Tuscany*, 1960, pp. 144-46 (with bibliography). For the destroyed upper tier and Masolino's contribution, see our preceding chapter and especially Note 178, where will be found also Longhi's distinction between the three artists and, in the Note, the chronology.

245) *The Expulsion from Paradise*: 6' 9⅞" × 2' 10⅝". SALMI, 1948, pp. 187-88, with bibliography, shows that through restoration the sky has been changed from azure to leaden, and alterations have been made in the head, neck and red tunic of the angel and in the heads of Adam and Eve whose nude loins were covered, at some later stage, by the present ugly boughs. RAGGHIANTI (in *Critica d'Arte*, 37, 1960, p. 54, n. 7) expresses doubts about the angel's garment and the portion of it which extends over the two figures. BRANDI (in his *Corso*, 1961-62, pp. 96-97) considers this Masaccio's first painting in the chapel. This is doubtful, and it seems more likely that he began with the *Baptism of the Neophytes*, presuming that he would have started out on one of these two minor scenes. In fact, PROCACCI (1951) considers the *Baptism* as the earliest and dates the *Expulsion* even later than the *Tribute Money*. Finally, C. DE TOLNAY has kindly communicated to me his idea that for the pilasters at the entry of the chapel there may have been intended originally two other episodes from Genesis, the Ancestors at Work and the Murder of Abel, which were replaced by Filippino with the two episodes in the life of Saint Peter below. Other episodes from Genesis may have been planned to flank the exterior of the entrance arch. In these ways, the theme of the Fall of Man would have become more important than that of the Redemption limited to the interior of the chapel. There is a copy of the Adam in a Florentine drawing from around 1550 published by C. VIRCH in *Bulletin of the Metropolitan Museum*, New York, March 1961, pp. 191-92 and Fig. 8; see also our Note 9.

246) The *Baptism of the Neophytes*: 8' 4⅜" × 5' 3¾". The attribution to Filippino Lippi or to Masolino of the two portraits of bystanders on the left was refuted in our preceding chapter. However, one can accept Salmi's hypothesis that Filippino repainted the head of the Saint

154

Peter which, in fact, appears more hook-nosed (as in the two youths at his side) in Uffizi drawing 6 V (Fig. 63), a Renaissance and perhaps even fifteenth-century copy of the figure. Brandi attributes the "tubular" sleeve of the Saint to a late repainting (though it may be by Filippino) of the mantle, and in support of this one can compare it with the drawing where the posterior profile of the mantle is more abrupt and has vertical folds. SALMI (1948, p. 198) points out other evidences of damage and repainting, especially marked in the deformation of the head in profile on the far right. Brandi states that "the precarious state of conservation of the painting has given to the picture a vaporous quality it did not originally have." This can only be judged when the frescoes are finally restored, and in my opinion, as indicated in the text, there was, at least to a certain extent, from the outset an effect of aerial perspective.

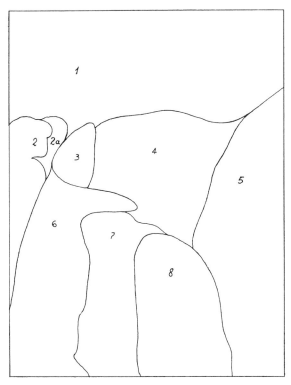

Diagram of the "day's work" segments of the *Baptism of the Neophytes*

247) The *Tribute Money*: 8′ 4⅜″ × 19′ 7⅝″. Allowing for foreshortening, the figures are therefore roughly life-size. SALMI (1948, pp. 188-90) points out traces of restoring in the garments, in some heads (for example, that of the tax-collector in the central group), and in the landscape; our text discusses the absence of haloes for four of the Apostles to the right and also the area with the steps at the far right which was repainted. RAGGHIANTI (1960, p. 54, n. 7) considers the two trees above the Christ "an alien and posthumous addition."
No one has taken seriously the strange idea of Lindberg that Andrea di Giusto collaborated on the admirable Saint Peter drawing out the fish. As for the head of Christ, it is difficult to decide: by Masolino as Longhi claims and as many of us are inclined to agree, or by Masaccio as Salmi still insists? This is aside from the technical fact that the head was painted after, and not before as Longhi believed, those in the same group (see our preceding chapter). If the head is really by Maso-

lino, it should be noted that the fresco would have to be dated either before September 1, 1425 or else after July 1427 and up to the beginning of 1428 when Masolino left for Rome.

248) See our second chapter.

249) Cf. ALBERTI, *Della Pittura*, ed. Mallé, p. 94.

250) See our first chapter.

251) ALBERTI, *Op. cit.*, pp. 91 ff.

252) 1959. Offner also proposed comparisons between Masaccio's figures and possible precedents in antique sculpture.

253) ALBERTI, *Op. cit.*, p. 99.

254) LONGHI, 1940, p. 166.

255) G. C. ARGAN, *Brunelleschi*, 1955, p. 111.

256) The episode of Ananias: 7′ 6½″ × 5′ 3¾″. Except for some repainting of the body of Ananias and a few abrasions at the left margin, the fresco is considered in excellent state. The "days' work" can be made out in it: (1) the vertical band, (2) all the background up to above the line of the heads, (3) the head of Saint Peter, (4) four heads to the right, (5) the mother with child from the right arm up, (6) the body and left forearm of the mother plus the right arm of Saint Peter and the kneeling figure to the rear, (7) the remainder of the body of Saint Peter, (8) the body of Saint John and the hands of Ananias, (9) the four figures to the left, (10) the figure of Ananias except for the hands.

257) The *Saint Peter healing with his Shadow*: 7′ 6½″ × 5′ 3¾″. On the small palace to the left, part of the projection above the door appears to be repainted and also the upper part of the palace, so that we do not know what its original height was. Salmi points out retouching in the lower part of the surface and damage to the head of the Saint John. The crutch held by the left hand of the half-nude man is difficult to make out. Nine "days' work" went into this fresco: (1) the left-hand vertical band, (2) the upper part of the small palace above its doors, and the flank of the first projecting storey, (3) the projecting storeys above the line of the supporting struts, (4) heads of the presumed Masolino and the standing supplicant, plus the area around them, (5) heads of Saint Peter, Saint John and the old man to the rear, (6) bodies of Saint Peter and Saint John, (7) the lower part of the small palace to the left exclusive of the figures, (8) the body of the standing supplicant, the entire figure of the kneeling man, and the head of the prostrate man, (9) the body of the latter and the remainder of the terrain.

258) See our first chapter.

259) The episode of Theophilus: 7′ 6½″ × 19′ 7⅜″. In addition to those areas painted by Filippino (for which see Note 260), SALMI, 1948, pp. 191-92 points out repainting in the figures on the left, and Procacci finds that the heads of the courtier standing to the left of Theophilus is in part repainted. In view of Trapesnikoff's opinion that the figure seated to the right of Theophilus represents Cosimo dei Medici (Meller believes it to be Salutati), Salmi considers it almost entirely redone by Filippino. Besides, the vases and trees in the background have been redone, the beard and head of the enthroned Saint Peter retouched, the head of the kneeling figure to the right of Saint Peter reworked, and the lower part of the three kneeling figures has new areas. BALDINI (1957) suspects that the figure on the far right, which Meller thinks is meant to be Brunelleschi, was actually entirely redone in the early nineteenth century.

The subject of the fresco derives, as is known, from the Golden Legend: Theophilus, the prefect of Antioch, who had imprisoned Saint Peter, liberated him at Paul's urging so that he might resuscitate the prefect's son who had died fourteen years before; Peter accomplished the miracle, and Theophilus and all the people of Antioch became converted and built a church in which they enthroned Saint Peter. MELLER (1961, p. 200), as explained in our first chapter, has convincingly identified Theophilus as a portrait of Gian Galeazzo Visconti and some other figures from the hand of Masaccio as contemporary personages: from left to right, the fourth head in the group by Filippino, this head being in fact by Masaccio, would be Cardinal Branda Castiglione; the figure seated to the right of Theophilus, Coluccio Salutati; whereas in the other part of the fresco beyond the enthroned Saint Peter is a self-portrait of Masaccio (according to Salmi) turned in three-quarter profile towards the viewer; and finally, following the next figure to the right (which I believe is not Alberti) the last figure to the right is Brunelleschi. But what is the significance of the identification of Theophilus with Gian Galeazzo? There would seem to be not only a generalized allusion to the tyrannical character of Visconti but also to the mediating efforts of Pope Martin V (Saint Peter) who converted the Viscontis to more peaceful ways. A chronological clue is furnished by the fact that the first son of Gian Galeazzo (Theophilus), Giovanni Maria, was assassinated in 1412: adding the fourteen years after which Theophilus' son was resuscitated, this proves to be 1426 or, in the Florentine calendar, 1427. Meller maintains that the fresco dates from precisely the beginning of 1427. However, the entire argument of Meller forms part of a subtly worked-out complex whose validity can be judged only by reading the complete study.

260) For Filippino's completion of Masaccio's fresco, cf. among recent studies R. HAMANN, "Masaccio und Filippino Lippi," in *Festschrift für W. Waetzoldt*, Berlin, 1941, pp. 81 ff.; L. BERTI and U. BALDINI, *Filippino Lippi*, Florence, 1957, pp. 23-24 and 76-77 (with dating as 1481-82 instead of 1484-88); and also G. FIOCCO, "Incontro tra Filippino e Masaccio," in *Saggi su Filippino Lippi*, Florence, 1957, pp. 89 ff.; F. GAMBA, *Filippino Lippi nella storia della critica*, Florence, 1958, pp. 30-31 and 86-87 (in which the trees in the background and retouching of the architecture on the left are attributed to Filippino); and MELLER, 1961. RAGGHIANTI in *Critica d'Arte*, 37, 1960, p. 34 and Fig. 24 dates Filippino's additions as 1484-85.
There are certain variants between the passages in Vasari's *Lives* of 1550 and 1568 concerning Filippino's work in the chapel. In the first edition he cited, besides the completion of the episode of Theophilus, two other frescoes, *Saint Paul visiting Saint Peter in Prison* (GAMBA, p. 32, is guilty of an oversight in claiming that Vasari never spoke of this) and the *Dispute of Simon Magus and the Crucifixion of Saint Peter*. In the second edition he still mentions at least indirectly the second of these ("and in the stories which follow") besides the completion of the Theophilus scene and moreover states that Filippino "brought the chapel to its ultimate perfection." However, there is no reason to suspect that the change between the two passages was due to Michelangelo's advice. Michelangelo would, if that were true, have erred also about what was authentically by Masaccio in the chapel, thus continuing the "pan-Masaccio" attitude for which he is responsible in Vasari's second edition (see our chapter III). Rather, I am inclined to think that the interpolation into the second edition of the names of the various personages portrayed led to a certain confusion and truncation of the text. Nevertheless, Vasari's reworking of the biography is responsible for the erroneous attribution to Masaccio of the entire chapel (except for the Theophilus episode) which was prolong-

ed by Patch (1770), Lastri (1791), D'Agincourt (1811), Lasinio (1812), and Rosini (1850) but denied by Rumohr (1827) and Gaye (1838) until at last Cavalcaselle (1864) succeeded in distinguishing correctly everything Filippino had done in the chapel.

261) Cavalcaselle's opinion has recently been taken up again by myself, Baldini and Meller. Further proof of it is the fact that while there are five heads in the group, Filippino painted only the four pairs of legs belonging to his figures.

262) This area of the paneled wall, examined by Baldini and myself together with the restorer Dino Dini, seemed to us executed last to connect up the line of the heads and that of the vases, trees, and sky of the garden behind it (cf. *Op. cit.*, 1957, p. 76). Yet it is clear that, even if we suppose a probable later reworking of it, this solution must go back to Masaccio himself, as is proved by the typical and fundamental importance this motif assumed in Florentine painting of the Renaissance. Cf. however the contrary thesis of Hamann which was opposed by Gamba (*Op. cit.*, 1958, pp. 86-87).
Finally, in my humble opinion there may be some doubt about the head of Saint Peter as well as that, already mentioned, of the first Carmelite in profile.

263) The case is obviously quite different from that in which part of a fresco cycle is not completed, as in the Brancacci chapel, and then completely painted anew by Filippino. Here it could have been taken care of by some provisional decoration.
It should be remarked that Felice Brancacci, confined for ten years at Capodistria in 1435, was again subjected to inquisition and declared a rebel in 1458 with the confiscation of his goods (C. CARNESECCHI, in *Miscellanea d'arte*, 1903, commemorative number on Masaccio, p. 192).

264) On the basis of a diagram by Tintori (Fig. 62) —which is no more than a rough sketch included here only as a handy reference—there can be made out the following twenty-nine "days' work" for Masaccio's share in the Theophilus fresco, not counting the border. Beginning at the right with Saint Peter enthroned: (1) the upper part of the building up to the line of the eaves in front; (2) the roof in perspective at the side and the sky up to the first vase and tree, and, below, down to the top of the garden wall plus the walls of the building (except for the figure of Saint Peter enthroned framed by the hanging and the four figures in front of the hanging at the far right; (3) the head of Saint Peter and the upper part of the hanging behind him; (4) the bust of Saint Peter plus the hanging behind it; (5) the last head in profile at the far right (the supposed Brunelleschi) with the area around it; (6) the other three heads in that group (with Masaccio's self-portrait); (7) the bodies of those four figures; (8) the lower part of the body of Saint Peter; (9) the heads and half-busts of the two Carmelites to the left; (10) the head in profile of the other Carmelite; (11) the bodies of these figures below their hoods; (12) the entire figure of the kneeling Carmelite except for his hands joined in prayer; (13) the entire figure of the kneeling prelate on the opposite side; (14) the kneeling figure seen from the rear in the center (however a broad zone below has been redone) and the hands of the kneeling Carmelite to his left already mentioned. Then, in the center: (15) the trees, vases and sky above the garden wall up to and including the last vase to the left; (16) the paneled wall; (17) the head of the personage with the green hood against the third panel of the wall; (18) six heads and busts to the left of that figure and the head of the kneeling Saint Paul; (19) the head of Saint Peter; (20) the body of Saint Peter except for the right forearm; (21) the group of four heads to the left of Saint Peter's; (22) the head of

the following figure, alongside Theophilus; (23) the head of the figure seated below and the busts of the five figures mentioned above; (24) the upper part of the buildings above the overhanging eaves; (25) the remainder of the building down to the heads; (26) the head of Theophilus; (27) the body of Theophilus and the bust of the figure seated on his right (which Meller identifies as Salutati); (28) the latter's body and the lower part of the figure seated on the left of Theophilus. In addition (29), the single head by Masaccio within the group by Filippino at the far left.

265) The war with the Viscontis, after the peace of April 1428, began again in 1430 and only ended with the victory of Anghiari in 1440. In 1436 Rinaldo degli Albizzi joined the Duke of Milan, and in 1436-37, inspired by the Florentine exiles, there was an attempt by the Milanese troops, captained by Piccinino, to push on from the Lucca region towards Florence. Once again instigated by the Florentine exiles, the most perilous Milanese attempt occurred in 1440.

266) Cf. SALMI, 1948, pp. 70-71 and pl. 215 with relevant commentary; also V. MARIANI, "L'arte di Filippino Lippi," in *Saggi su Filippino Lippi*, 1957, pp. 76-77: Mariani points out the affinity there must have been between the original figure by Masaccio and the Isaac in Brunelleschi's model for the door of the Baptistery, supposing that both nudes "go back to some classical sculpture or relief admired and studied in the early Quattrocento."

267) PROCACCI, 1951, p. 25; BRANDI, *Corso*, 1961-62; see also our chapter III, Note 178. SALMI (1948, p. 155) on the other hand maintains this chronology: 1426, the *Baptism of the Neophytes*; 1427, *Expulsion from Paradise*, the *Tribute Money*, the *Saint Peter Healing with his Shadow*; 1427-28, the episodes of Ananias and of Theophilus.

268) It will be recalled what was said in our third chapter with reference to the collaboration between Masaccio and Masolino in the chapel: whoever painted the box-like room of Tabitha must have, in the same "day's work," also painted the admirable stretch of street bathed by light (see Fig. 61).

269) Cf. R. OERTEL, "Wandmalerei und Zeichnung in Italien," in *Mitteilungen des Kunsthistorisches Institut in Florenz*, 1940, pp. 307-12; U. PROCACCI, *Sinopie e affreschi*, 1960, n. 8 on p. 46; E. BORSOOK, *The Mural Painters of Tuscany*, 1960, p. 144.

270) The *Trinity*: it was cited in the *Libro di A. Billi* with praise, in the Magliabecchiano manuscript, in Albertini and Vasari who, in the 1568 edition, discusses it in detail and praises it. The precise location, where it has now been re-installed, is on the wall of the third bay on the left in Santa Maria Novella, beneath but slightly to the left of the center of the window. Moreover (cf. Florence Soprintendenza photograph 69719) it was painted over two earlier frescoes, of which one according to Cavalcaselle depicted the Adoration of the Shepherds. At the top the window opening, originally much lower, was closed off by bricking over.
At the time Vasari prepared his second edition, in 1568, the figures of the two donors were already partly "covered by a gold ornamentation." It is therefore perplexing, as stated in our text, to know where on the altar was placed the wooden Crucifix of Maso di Bartolomeo which was removed in 1565 when remodernization of the basilica was begun. In 1568 the altar was dedicated by Cammilla Capponi to the Madonna of the Rosary. In 1570 Vasari painted an altarpiece for it and set up the new altar, covering up (not without complaints, as for example in the chronicler Biliotti) Masaccio's painting, although to spare it he consented to

displace his altar with respect to the window (cf. PROCACCI, 1956, pp. 212-13) as also he was so considerate as not to saw into the fresco to encase the supports of his panel. This however—relocation of the altar exactly in the middle and supports driven into the wall—was done after 1861 (see the photograph mentioned above), the year in which the fresco was rediscovered (on its condition at that time there is the fundamental testimony of CAVALCASELLE, in the Italian edition of 1883, vol. II, p. 316, n. 1). It was then detached and moved to the inner wall of the façade between the central door and the door to the right (as in Florence Soprintendenza photograph 66380).
Procacci deserves great credit for having looked for and found in 1951, behind the altar table, the admirable remains of the "Death" which had been mentioned in the earliest sources. In August 1952, the altar was removed, the "Death" together with the Trinity recomposed in their original location, on the basis of precise indications gleaned from vestiges on the wall as to the original height of the upper architrave and as to the breadth from the area of the previous fresco scraped off by Masaccio to provide an adherent surface for his new coat of plaster (cf. Fig. 67).
A problem which nevertheless remained in part unsolved, for lack of sufficient data, was that of the integration of the vestiges of the "Death" with the reconstruction of the original altar table (which was apparently painted in *trompe-l'oeil* like the rest of the fresco). It should be noted that the capitals of the two small double columns were re-invented (although it was necessary to decide arbitrarily on their height), using as model contemporary examples as well as the Ionian columns of the vault depicted in the fresco. It was also necessary to complete much of the sarcophagus and to re-do the two small columns on the left.
But how exactly was the painted altar table integrated into the fresco? In the reconstruction finally made (pl. 67), the two praying figures are on a second step which, obviously, broad as it must be (at least twenty inches must be calculated to provide a proper base for the kneeling figures), could not simply rest on the altar table but must have been completed by a solid foundation below—as in Sanpaolesi's diagram (p. 119). However, in the recomposition as we now have it, it must be longer than the table, considering the foreshortening necessary for the table, and weighing down on it. Besides, as shown by comparison with the altar in the Capponi chapel in Santa Felicita, if Masaccio had painted the surface of the table in *trompe-l'oeil* profile over the capitals of the slender columns, the table-top would probably have been much higher than the present reconstruction because of the several layers of moulding he would have painted, as in the throne of the London *Madonna*. Schlegel has proposed a different reconstruction (Fig. 72) which raises the capitals and lengthens the columns, makes the profile of the table more elaborate, and succeeds in eliminating the second step by having the two praying figures kneel directly on the table-top. However, does this not make the support of the altar-table, along with the rest of the lower portion of the fresco, too slight in relation to the architecture above? Moreover, were the small columns really originally coupled? Or, given the difference in their calibre in what remains of the original, may they not have been conceived with the outermost ones farther forward, the innermost ones farther back at the rear of the table and against the wall? Finally, the possibility has been considered that there may have been a real altar supported by pairs of slender columns in stone to the front (Fig. 68). Schlegel's reply to this is that an entirely illusionistic ensemble would have greater coherence, and she thinks also that there may have been a painted frame all around the fresco (Fig. 72) as later in the *Sir John*

Hawkwood of Paolo Uccello, but this, I find, would exceed the limits of the area scraped away underneath the fresco.

At the moment this is written, I find that Tintori, who had in the meantime detached the fragment with the skeleton, has now reintegrated it in the ensemble and provided a solution for the altar table which is more prudent although still debatable.

The two sources which speak of Cardoni are the *Cronica* by M. BILIOTTI (sixteenth century, roughly contemporary with Vasari according to Orlandi but actually a little later) and the *Cronaca* by U. BORGHIGIANI of the eighteenth century, both of them Dominicans whose manuscripts have been preserved in the archives of Santa Maria Novella. The earlier chronicle has this to say about the altar: "Fecerat illud fr. Laurentius Cardonius et sanctissime consecraverat Trinitati, quando cenobio presidebat. Santissime autem Trinitatis figuras, et beatissime Marie Virginis, et sancti Joannis apostoli et evangeliste effigies illi assistentes, una cum ornamentis quibusdam, mirabili depinxit gratia Thomas a S. Joanne, cognomento Massaccius, pictor etate (uti affirmant) insignis. Supra omnes illas figuras, magna illi crucifixi perstabat imago, quom hodie intra sacrarium supra cernimus, auratis columnis et arcu decenter ornatum, que in nova ecclesie accomodatione fuerat inde remota, insuper et figure multe delete non tamen sine multorum dolore, quippe que pulcre erant, et pulcherrime edi magnum decus afferrabant et ornamentum. Affirmant qui affuere, quasdam earum post altare rosarii tabulam in pariete consulte dimissas." This is interesting evidence, among other things, of the fame of the fresco and of the bitterness and well-advised precautions (*consulte*) with which it was covered up. Borghigiani, describing the interior of the church "as it was before Vasari restored it (1566)" states: "In the middle of the bay, now occupied by the Altar of the Rosary, there was the Altar of the Holy Trinity, quite well adorned, which was erected by the former Grand Prior Fra Lorenzo Cardoni, who later became Bishop, and above that altar was the Crucifix by Masaccio which, when the said altar was demolished, was placed inside the Sacristy above the door." Cardoni, master in theology, was prior of Santa Maria Novella from December 1422 to November 1425, but it should be noted that, to relieve his successor Alessio Strozzi, he continued to exercise his charge until June 1426 (cf. ORLANDI, *Op. cit.*, below, p. 194, but with the erroneous date of 1428, and pp. 189 and 565); in 1434 he was made Bishop of Sagona in Corsica by Eugene IV and died in 1438. As has been said, Borghigiani however wrote: "Fra Lorenzo Cardoni, later Bishop, erected in that year (1430) the Altar of the Holy Trinity... at his own expense." The Crucifix believed to be by Maso di Bartolomeo is however dated in the second quarter of the fifteenth century and would therefore be later than the date indicated.

Finally, as indicated in the text, I believe that the decisive role in obtaining the commission for Masaccio was played by the very learned and versatile Fra Alessio Strozzi the Younger whose succession was taken over by Cardoni and who is known to have been a good miniaturist and besides "Architethonica preterea fabrilique arte, ita habebatur ydoneus ut philippus ipse brunelleschus mire illius testudinis que ad sancte marie floris edem prominet, fabrefactor omnium ingeniosissimus, nil absque huius alexii sententia faciundum sibi ulla ratione proponerent" (for this Strozzi, cf. ORLANDI, *Op. cit.* below, II, pp. 188-90 amd 479-80).

Relevant bibliography (for complete listing up to 1941, see W. PAATZ, *Die Kirchen von Florenz*, III, 1952, pp. 783-85): J. WOOD BROWN, *The Dominican Church of Santa Maria Novella at Florence*, 1902, p. 118; PROCACCI, 1951; S. ORLANDI, *Necrologio di Santa Maria*

Novella, 1955, II, p. 193 and n. 15, pp. 401-2; BORSOOK, *Op. cit.*, 1960, pp. 143-44 (with the information about Lenzi found by Procacci); DE TOLNAY, 1958; U. SCHLEGEL, 1963 plus two emendations in *Art Bulletin*, June 1963, p. 177.

The *Trinity* reconstructed in its entirety measures 21' 10⅝" x 10' 4¾". The diagram by Tintori (Fig. 69) shows how much remains of the original as well as the perspective lines and the "days' work" required for its execution which total around twenty-five exclusive of the base (as can be seen, particular care was concentrated on the architectonic details, capitals, half-vaulting, etc.). Moreover, Procacci maintains that "while it was held that the work was in a miserable state of conservation [damaged when detached, according to Cavalcaselle] a recent restoration has shown on the contrary that, fortunately, the poor condition of the painted surface resulted especially from the substances which were spread over it during the work of moving it in the nineteenth century." This is the price that must perhaps be paid (reasonable as it is) for the measures taken in restoration.

271) Maintained in the past, variously, by Reymond (1905), Kern (1931), Frey (1924) and opposed by Mesnil (1913 and 1928), Oertel (1933), Pittaluga (1935) and Salmi (1948). Relative bibliography in GIGLIOLI, 1929, pp. 81-82 and SALMI, 1948, pp. 193-95, also for the sources indicated for the architecture in the *Trinity* (the Donatello tabernacle of Orsanmichele and the far end of the portico of the Hospital of the Innocents although both of these are later in date, and the Barbadori Chapel in Santa Felicita). It should be understood that the present writer has in mind an architectonic conception by Brunelleschi and perhaps a preliminary drawing by him on the wall but with the pictorial realization probably *carried out by Masaccio alone* under the guidance of Filippo.

272) P. SANPAOLESI, *Brunelleschi*, 1962, pp. 51-53. What is open to doubt in Sanpaolesi's reconstruction is the altar (see Note 270 above for the divergent thesis of Schlegel) and the excessive projection of the platform on which stands God the Father.

273) As also in the tabernacle of the Parte Guelfa or the Barbadori chapel. The fact is, the horizontal division of the lower third of the pilasters in the *Trinity* proves to be proportionately too high if it begins from the lower step.

274) See on the other hand U. SCHLEGEL, "La Cappella Barbadori et l'architettura fiorentina del primo Rinascimento," in *Rivista d'Arte*, 1957, pp. 77 ff. She maintains that the Barbadori Chapel should be dated not 1425 but instead around 1430 and that its author was Buggiano who would have taken his inspiration from Masaccio's *Trinity* and not vice versa.

275) SCHLEGEL, 1963, pp. 25 ff. and DE TOLNAY, 1958. The latter remarks on the progressively greater plastic modeling of the figures in the *Trinity* the deeper into the background they are; supposes that the niche may have been surmounted by a triangular pediment like that of Donatello in Orsanmichele (but this appears most improbable); claims that the framed rectangle behind God the Father (supposing that there is a niche as does Sanpaolesi) may represent the sarcophagus of Christ (but it would be very narrow); sees in the alternation of red and blue, as in the caissons of the vault and the mantle of God the Father, an allusion to the colors of the Empyrean and the Heavens and likewise, in the brick-red of the architectonic elements the purple-red colors symbolic of dominion over the heavens. As for the humanization of the entire representation, "Masaccio ne voulait pas seulement humaniser le divin, mais sanctifier notre monde. Le langage

dépouillé, monumental et plastique des formes devient ainsi l'expression d'un monde empli par la substance divine. A l'homme, guéri de la peur de la mort, des complexes d'infériorité et d'humilité, sont conférées la 'dignitas,' la 'fortitudo' et la 'majestas'."

276) Schlegel points out that the interior of the Cardini chapel in Pescia is similarly inaccessible because of the altar near its entrance. Furthermore, the tradition, followed in Santa Maria Novella as in Pescia, was that the Chapel of Golgotha should be placed on the left side of the church.

277) The back of the niche has a *memento mori* inscription: IO . FU . GIA' . QUEL . CHE . VOI . SETE: EQUEL CHI- SON VOI . ANCOR . SARETE. (I was what you are: and what I am you shall be). For the palaeographic aspect, see M. MEISS, "Toward a more comprehensive Renaissance Palaeography" in *Art Bulletin*, 1960, p. 101, and D. A. COVI, "Lettering in Fifteenth-Century Florentine Painting," in *Art Bulletin*, March 1963, p. 5.

278) Similarly the central, unifying, dominant position of the Christ in the *Trinity*, achieved without falsifying proportions, has its analogy in Cusanus who sees in Christ "the universal spiritual content of humanity," the true " *natura media* holding together in unity the infinite," the "keystone of the universe": "Et in hoc passu mediatio Christi intelligitur, quae est copula huius coincidentiae, ascensus hominis interioris in Deum, et Dei in hominum." Also by analogy the concept of man as microcosm, that is, of man as the measure of all things, was considered by the masters of the early Renaissance as well as by Cusanus an *antique* theme (CASSIRER, *Individuo e cosmo della filosofia del Rinascimento*, pp. 66-69).

279) Cf. BRANDI, "Filippino Lippi o l'ultimo quattrocentista," in *Saggi su Filippino Lippi*, 1957, p. 40, and his *Corso*, 1961-62, pp. 71-72.

280) See also in our Chapter II the article by BORSOOK, 1961.

281) This was intuited also by MALLE in his comment in his 1950 edition, p. 32: "Alberti interposes himself between Masaccio and Piero. One need only think of Masaccio's *Trinity* and how the principle of perspective, applied by him with unheard of rigor, led him to a development which does not deny previous expressions but is another kind of expression and equally legitimate, rich with new elements . . .What is involved is a new orientation toward uniting figures and their environment; and that solid construction—in which the forms are laid out amply and solemnly, renouncing a too peremptory plastic affirmation to extend themselves, instead, in flat geometrical zones of color— was a superb realization at which Alberti must have looked with special interest and enthusiasm."

282) The *Story of Saint Julian* (Horne Collection inventory no. 60; $9\frac{29}{64}$ x $16\frac{7}{8}$") was published for the first time by GAMBA (in *Dedalo*, 1920, p. 177) and hypothetically related to Masaccio to whom Horne himself had attributed it (cf. GAMBA, *Catalogo del Museo Horne*, 1961 ed., p. 43) and also to the predella of the triptych of Santa Maria Maggiore in Florence. It was not accepted by Somarè (1924), Giglioli (1929), Lindberg (1931), Pittaluga (1935) or Steinbart (1947). Stechow (1930) and Oertel (1933) ascribed it to the young Domenico Veneziano, Schmarsow (1930) to Pesello, Berenson (1932) returned it to Masaccio, and Longhi (1940) held it to be perhaps a first idea for the predella of the Pisa polyptych, a hypothesis rejected by Salmi (1948) who considered it to come from the workshop of Masaccio. Ragghianti (1949) agreed with Longhi, and Procacci (1951) returned to the original hypothesis

of Gamba. For the exhibition of "Quattro Maestri del Primo Rinascimento" it was placed among the attributed works (BALDINI, catalogue of the exhibition, pp. 16-17 with history and bibliography). BRANDI (1961-62, pp. 76-77) re-proposed the idea that it belonged to Masaccio and to the Carnesecchi triptych. The latter notion is not impossible in theory. Masolino's panel with Saint Julian is 20 ¾" wide, and there is no insurmountable obstacle in the objection that Vasari, in the second edition of the *Lives*, described the subject of the predella as "Saint Julian killing his father and mother," whereas here the actual parricide is not depicted, unlike the panel in Montauban. Indeed, in Masolino's painting in Montauban the light comes from the right, as Oertel noted, while here the illumination would agree with that of the two major panels of the triptych since, as in them, it comes from the left. Nevertheless, it seems still preferable to hold to the connection between the *Saint Juian* of Settimo and the Montauban panel which is most convincing on stylistic grounds also and which has been maintained also by Parronchi in his article of 1962 on the Carnesecchi triptych already cited. On the other hand equally convincing is Salmi's rejection of Longhi's idea that it might be a first version for the predella of the Pisan polyptych. The Horne panel is higher than the predella panels of the polyptych ($9\frac{29}{64}$" as against their $8\frac{17}{64}$"), and also, since each of the lateral stories (width c. 24") is exactly subdivided into two episodes, one for each saint in the polyptych above, the story of Saint Julian could not extend beyond $11\frac{19}{16}$" in width (but is in fact 16 ⅞" wide) to leave room for the story of Saint Nicholas. Perhaps it is best to fall back on the idea of a predella panel conceived before the exact plan of the polyptych was settled, or it might even have been a story of the saint whose name was borne by the man who commissioned the Pisa polyptych, ser Giuliano di Colino, which was intended as a separate picture and thus, for the occasion, narrated "elliptically" without actually depicting the homicide. Against this is the fact that there is no evidence of it in the documents concerning the relations between Masaccio and ser Giuliano.

283) The birth salver in Berlin: inventory no. 58 c; diameter 22" with frame. It does not really correspond to the work described by F. BOCCHI as being in the house of Baccio Valori (in *Le bellezze della città di Firenze*, Florence, 1591, p. 183; and BOCCHI-CINELLI, p. 366; and BALDINUCCI, ed. Batelli, 1845, I, p. 474): "the birth of a female saint from the hand of Masaccio of great beauty in its lifelikeness; in which, besides the childbearing woman rendered with supreme care, most beautiful also is a figure knocking at a door with a basket on her head in which is a capon; the latter figure is draped with such elegance that it appears entirely true to life" (the motif of the woman with a basket can be found in Lippi's tondo in the Pitti gallery). On the other hand, the birth salver is certainly (even its measurements agree: "the diameter of a cubit," that is, eighteen inches) the painting mentioned by F. GHERARDI-DRA-GOMANNI (*Memorie della Terra di San Giovanni nel Valdarno Superiore*, Florence, 1834, p. 45, n. 2) as being in the house of Prof. Cav. Sebastiano Ciampi; this is also the source of the allegorical interpretation given in our text (it can be added that the edifice represented may allude symbolically to Orsanmichele where on June 26th was celebrated the expulsion of the Duke of Athens).
The salver was acquired in Florence by the Berlin museum in 1883. Few have doubted the ascription to Masaccio except for Morelli (1893) who awarded it to the mediocre Andrea di Giusto; Brandi (1934) who suggested Domenico di Bartolo; Pittaluga (1935) who proposed the hypothesis of an anonymous Florentine

of around 1430; Procacci (1951) who held it to be from the fourth decade of the century; and RAGGHIANTI (in *Sele Arte*, 1952, 2, p. 65) who thought it might be by Domenico Veneziano. Bibliography up to 1948 in SALMI, 1948, pp. 192-93, who also recalls the examples on the same subject published by Schubring (the salver of 1428 is however Late Gothic, and the dates proposed for the Bardini and André salvers both seem too early). In his *Corso*, 1961-62, pp. 106-7, BRANDI once again denies that it can be by Masaccio because the construction of the perspective contains, he says, certain errors, the setting is out of harmony with the circular form, the hair styles come from later than 1428 (but is this true? To me they appear identical with those in the Berlin predella), the motifs of the marble intarsia derive already from Alberti rather than from Brunelleschi, and everything, according to Brandi, agrees with "a dating later than 1428 and with a painter not intimately linked with the beginning Renaissance."
For the reverse of the salver (Fig. 73), certainly from the workshop, and the copy of it in private hands in Florence, see our Chapter III, Note 200.

284) Cf. 1948, pp. 75-76 and 158. In the same inventory of Lorenzo the Magnificent (MUNTZ, p. 58) figure "two paintings on wood above the fireplace with a Saint Peter and a Saint Paul from the hand of Masaccio, f. 12" (the *Skirmish* however was valued at only two florins, an incredibly low estimate, although this is typical in general of this entire inventory). As for the Saints Peter and Paul, I should like to mention the two small panels (each $14\frac{1}{8} \times 3\frac{35}{64}''$) with the same saints in the Silesian Museum at Wroclaw, Poland, inv. VIII, 741-42, attributed to the Sienese School of the second half of the fourteenth century, although I think they are by Paolo Schiavo. However, I do not in any way wish to suggest that they derive from the missing panels by Masaccio but only that there is something of Masaccio in their style.

285) VASARI, *Lives*, 1568: "In the Badia at Florence he painted on a pillar, opposite one of those which bear the arch of the high altar, St. Ivo of Britanny, represented in a niche with his feet foreshortened, as seen from below. This brought him no small praise, because it had not been so well done by others before. Beneath the saint, and above another cornice, he represented the widows, children and poor assisted by him in their want." The fresco, whose location has been determined as the pilaster between the first and second bays of the left nave, was destroyed when Segaloni redecorated the church in 1627, and only the head of the Saint Ives, and not the entire picture, was sawed off the wall (UCCELLI, *Della Badia fiorentina*, 1858, p. 66; after Puccinelli) and set up in the abbot's room (BOCCHI-CINELLI, *Bellezze della città di Firenze*, Florence, 1677, p. 383) but unfortunately later disappeared. On the basis of the daring perspective, PITTALUGA (1935, p. 172) considered the Saint Ives to date from around the time of the Pisa polyptych. That, at the time he worked in Prato, Paolo Uccello (to whom I believe the Prato frescoes belong; cf. *art. cit.* in *Pantheon*, VI, 1961, pp. 302-3) may have been very much under the influence of Masaccio is proved in Prato not only by the figure of Saint Paul which is much related to that by Masaccio in the Pisa polyptych but also by the female saint with the two praying children in the Contini-Bonacossi Collection, Florence, which recalls the Virgin in the Crucifixion from Pisa and may, broadly speaking, echo the figures at the bottom of the Saint Ives fresco.

286) Mentioned already by MANETTI as a "marvellous figure" and then by Albertini and the other sources and praised by Vasari as early as the 1550 edition, the Saint Paul—which must have been a quite exceptional figure —was painted in the Carmine "between the chapel of the Serragli, where there is the Holy Cross, and the chapel decorated with the story of Saint Jerome," that is, I think, on the pilaster to the viewer's left of the chapel of Saint Andrea Corsini (formerly belonging to the Serraglis) facing the Brancacci chapel (the Corsini chapel was redone in Baroque style in 1675). PROCACCI, in *Rivista d'arte*, 1932, pp. 196-8, gives all the relative sources for the remodeling of the chapel which are rather confused; he tends to interpret them differently, locating the lost fresco on the pilaster which makes an angle to the nave. In 1675, as we know from Baldinucci, there disappeared both the Saint Paul by Masaccio and a Saint Peter by Masolino which was its companion-piece on the right-hand pilaster (cf. also PROCACCI, in *Bollettino d'Arte*, 1933-34, p. 332; today however, he tells me, he has some hope that the figure may have survived under the marble decoration of the pilaster in the Corsini chapel where it has not been looked for until now: let us hope!). Vasari says that the Saint Paul was frescoed "as a specimen of his skill" before he began the Brancacci chapel. While this may be no more than an embroidery on Vasari's part without factual basis, the execution of the two figures by Masaccio and Masolino still implies as date the first half of 1425 and so there must have been a similarity in style with the upper tier of the Brancacci frescoes. Nevertheless, it remains possible that the figures were painted in the second half of 1427 upon Masolino's return from Hungary. The Angiolini portrayed by Masaccio, having been born in 1373 (he died in 1432 after having held important public offices) would have then been over fifty.

287) See the paragraph there about Gentile. The *Annunciation*, mentioned by Vasari in 1568 as being on the rood screen of San Niccolò, is not discussed by later writers (Bocchi-Cinelli, Richa) because it must have been removed during the restoration of 1580-85. SALMI (1948, pp. 210-11) holds that this lost work may have been the prototype for the Annunciations by Fra Angelico. On that point, I. R. SPENCER, "Spatial Imagery of the Annunciation in Fifteenth-Century Florence," in *Art Bulletin*, 1955, pp. 273 ff., argues that the prototype by Masaccio must be reconstructed on the basis of the Annunciation by Domenico Veneziano in Cambridge, the one by Angelico which was on the sacristy cupboard doors of the Nunziata and is now in San Marco, one by a secondary master in the Ashmolean Museum, and Piero's in Perugia: in essence, then, clearly centralized perspective construction with two lateral wings of porticoes, a view of a garden path in the center, and the dialogue occurring directly between the two protagonists within a cloister. On the other hand, according to Spencer, the Virgin sheltered beneath the portico derives from the traditional Trecento motif of which Angelico's Annunciation in Cortona is no more than a development somewhat brought up to date. However, besides presuming a distinct influence from Alberti as well as perfect symmetry in the lost work by Masaccio, Spencer's thesis fails to take into account that the scheme he imagines would fit badly into a normal rectangular format. For my part, I believe that in the archetype by Masaccio there was, above all and perhaps for the first time, the new Renaissance manner of framing a picture: a rectangle with a frame based on pilasters to each side and a classical architrave (what Neri di Bicci, in his *Ricordanze*, calls "*tavola d'altare quadra a l'antica*"—an altarpiece framed in antique manner). Moreover, there must have been the new setting of the scene in a Renaissance portico with columns (still, however, of the same type as the court in the Berlin salver with several columns) while on the left perhaps there must have been a widening of space for a walled courtyard beyond which could be seen the green trees of a garden (as

in the Theophilus fresco). But the type made popular by Angelico had a single portico viewed frontally and in depth, not two symmetrical porticoes. I am presenting here an unpublished Annunciation by the Master of the Adimari Cassone (Fig. 74) as presumably yet another if vague derivation from the archetype by Masaccio. It is of interest both for the upper storey of the building—a solution typical of Masaccio—and for the perspective forshortening of the left hand of the Virgin.

288) For full information on the Santa Maria Maggiore triptych, cf. the Davies catalogue of 1961, pp. 352-61. It was originally located "in a small chapel near the sacristy" (Vasari) under the patronage of the Colonnas. Procacci has localized it as at the end of the left nave, between the nave and the choir (the old sacristy was where the Cappella Paolina is now). The triptych, painted on both front and back, was set up on an altar between columns. The surface facing the choir which was higher, showed the *Foundation of Santa Maria Maggiore*, whereas the *Assumption* faced the nave and was thus seen in perspective from below. The chapel was dedicated to Saint John the Baptist, and this is of importance in the reconstruction of the now dismembered double-faced triptych. The side toward the choir included: in the center, the *Foundation of Santa Maria Maggiore* (Naples, Museum of Capodimonte, panel, $56\frac{3}{4} \times 29\frac{7}{8}$", but slightly cut down in the pointed arch); to the left, *Saint Jerome and the Baptist* (London, National Gallery no. 5962, panel, $44\frac{7}{8} \times 21\frac{5}{8}$", the top cut down $1\frac{1}{2}$"); to the right, *Saint John the Evangelist and Saint Martin* (Philadelphia, Johnson Collection, panel, $42\frac{1}{8} \times 20\frac{1}{2}$"; the chasuble of Saint Martin with its decorative motif is clearly an allusion to Pope Martin V who was a Colonna). On the side toward the nave were: in the center, the *Assumption* (Naples, Museum of Capodimonte, panel, $55\frac{7}{8} \times 29\frac{7}{8}$"); on the left, *Saints Peter and Paul* (Philadelphia, Johnson Collection, panel, $42\frac{1}{8} \times 20\frac{1}{2}$"); on the right, *Saints Liberius and Matthew* (London, National Gallery no. 5963, panel, $44\frac{7}{8} \times 21\frac{5}{8}$", the top cut down $1\frac{1}{2}$"). It is considered also that the triptych may have had smaller pictures in the cusps as well as a predella, to which have been referred, but entirely hypothetically, two small predella scenes in Masolino's style: a *Betrothal of the Virgin* (Artaud de Montor Collection, but now lost) and a *Death of the Virgin* (Vatican no. 139, $19\frac{1}{4} \times 5\frac{7}{8}$"); a *Crucifixion* (Vatican no. 138, $20\frac{5}{8} \times 12\frac{7}{8}$") has been thought of as the apex of the triptych. There has been no further exploration of the idea of J. Pope-Hennessy ("The Santa Maria Maggiore Altarpiece," in *Burlington Magazine*, January 1952, pp. 31-32) that the double-faced triptych may have had the *Assumption* and the *Foundation of Santa Maria Maggiore* in the second tier flanked by side-wings, and in the first tier, between the pairs of saints, a *Madonna and Child* in front, and on the back another panel whose subject cannot be defined. Dismembered, its two faces separated by sawing through the thickness of the panel, already in 1653 the polyptych had entered the Palazzo Farnese. An inventory of that year lists the individual pieces clearly relating them to each other, followed by another in 1697 whose inventory numbers with the Farnese seal can still be read on the back of each of the panels except for the two in Philadelphia which have been planed down. In 1760 the panels now in Naples passed into the Bourbon collection. Of the other four, from 1815 to 1845 in the collection of Cardinal Fesch in Paris and Rome and finally dispersed, the two panels in America were published by L. Venturi in 1930 and the two in London acquired by the National Gallery in 1950.
There was prompt and general agreement with the attribution to Masaccio of the side-panel with Saint Jerome and the Baptist first proposed by Clark (1951, but dated as 1425-26), Longhi (1952, with the same dates), Salmi (1952, dated 1428), Meiss (1952, dated 1422-23), followed by Brandi (1957, dated 1428, but in his lecture course of 1961-62 he supposes that part of it was finished by some collaborator other than Masolino), Hartt (in *Art Bulletin*, 1959, 2-3, p. 163, with the date of 1423), and Berti (1961, dated 1428). Davies (1961) however remained reluctant to accept the attribution, while Procacci (1951, p. 38; 2nd ed. 1952, pp. 36-37, and oral communication to Davies) successively accepted that the overall design was Masaccio's as well as the execution of certain parts such as the foot, but claimed collaboration by Masolino or others in most of the execution, dating it 1428). Middeldorf (in an oral communication to Davies) held the work to be from around 1435 with traits from Angelico and Domenico Veneziano, but more recently (in *Scritti in onore di Mario Salmi*, II, 1962, p. 287) he has labeled it "Masaccio and assistants," still expressing some doubts. In the meantime, Gioseffi (1962) has proposed attributing it to Domenico Veneziano who would have executed this side panel in 1431-32 when Masolino would have repaired to Todi to avoid the reaction against the Colonna party after the death of Pope Martin.
It should be understood that here we do not exclude the possibility that the London panel may have been partially completed by another hand after the death of Masaccio, *but it remains substantially a work by Masaccio*. Also there may be something to the hypothesis (cf. Clark, Salmi) that the companion-piece with Saints John the Evangelist and Martin may be based on an idea of Masaccio, but this I would exclude for the central panel with the Foundation of Santa Maria Maggiore. Not acceptable is the proposal that there is some relation between the London panel and that by Sano di Pietro with the same two saints in the church of San Marcellino in Uopini (Monteriggioni) included in the exhibition of art of the Valdelsa, Certaldo, 1963 (P. Dal Poggetto, catalogue, no. 49 and pl. XL).

289) The Chapel of San Clemente and in particular the *Crucifixion*: the attribution of the cycle to Masaccio goes back to Vasari, but already in the last century it was questioned. Now it is definitively ascribed to Masolino, except by the usual "pan-Masaccio" enthusiasts, and as early as 1908 Toesca advanced the very likely date of sometime between 1428 and 1431 and the patronage of Cardinal Branda Castiglione. For the *Crucifixion*, however, some continued to insist on Masaccio: A. Venturi (1925); Toesca himself (1934) on the basis of the horsemen, the Good Centurion and the Magdalen and encouraged probably by the engravings of Seroux d'Agincourt; Lindberg (1931) for the landscape and the three crucified figures; Beenken (1932) who was reminded of the lost Book of Hours of Van Eyck by the amplitude of space in the fresco; and, after the restoration by Pelliccioli in 1939, Longhi (1940) who dated the *Crucifixion* at 1425 with Masaccio responsible for the horsemen on the mountain top and who thought the cycle may have been completed later by Masolino; likewise Lavagnigno (1943) who proposed 1423 for the date of both Masaccio's intervention and the entire cycle by Masolino. The bibliography is listed by Salmi (1948, pp. 203 ff.). For his part, Salmi rules out any direct collaboration by Masaccio on the fresco which, for him, is "a haphazard cultural figurative anthology" with elements derived from the North as well as from Masaccio and typical of Masolino, aided perhaps by a collaborator like Arcangelo di Cola (pp. 100 ff.). Procacci (1951, p. 37), on the basis of general historical circumstances, held that the chapel could not have been frescoed before 1428. He recognized in the horsemen of the *Crucifixion* the closest approach ever made by Masolino to Masaccio's style, but nevertheless thought of "a brief intervention by Masaccio" but only for the head

of the horseman in the far distance and to the right of the Magdalen (the head believed to be a self-portrait by Masaccio) (also reproduced by RAGGHIANTI in *Sele Arte*, 2, 1952, p. 65). To me that head seems to be due to a sixteenth-century restoration (Fig. 82). In 1952, however, the Instituto Generale del Restauro of Rome lifted off the *Crucifixion* and detached the under-drawing (cf. G. URBANI, in *Bollettino del Istituto Centrale del Restauro*, 21-22, 1955, pp. 11-35 with valuable information). According to Salmi, the fresco had undergone three previous restorations, in the sixteenth, eighteenth and nineteenth centuries in addition to the last one in 1939. Now it became clear that there were certain zones that had been redone (a very large one at the bottom done in the eighteenth century) and it was found that the much-discussed figures of the horsemen corresponded to a zone overlapped by preceding "days' work," although in my opinion it was not proved that the fresco and under-drawing were executed in two parts at two separate times. The under-drawing (I quote textually), "whose lacunae—except for those of the sky, the group of old Hebrews in the lower left and the last horseman on the right—correspond to the zones redone in the fresco," reveals also the particularity of "incompleteness in the drawing of the Longinus, interrupted abruptly and in rather mysterious manner at the confused sketch of the bust and half of the horse's head. A little higher, almost where the head of the figure should come, one finds instead an architectonic detail which seems to be the profile of a marble cornice which continues towards the left with a rather, unusual ornamental motif (?)." On the same occasion there were also restored the scenes already detached fifty years earlier, the *Saint Ambrose Leaving the House of the Rich Man*, the *Death of Saint Ambrose*, and the *Study of Saint Ambrose* (the latter supposed to be by Masaccio by PARRONCHI, "Postilla sul neo-gaddismo degli anni 1423-25," in *Paragone*, 137, 1961, pp. 19 ff.). The *Decapitation of Saint Catherine* was also detached and the under-drawing recovered. BRANDI

(1957) was therefore able to study the latter under-drawing in relation to that of the *Crucifixion* and declared that there had now been removed from that fresco "the astute integrations carried out in Masaccio's style as a kind of plastic surgery" (in 1939). He came to the conclusion that what did not belong to Masolino in the under-drawing of the *Crucifixion* (which, among other things, revealed that red ochre, charcoal and even watercolor had been used) could hypothetically be attributed to Domenico Veneziano, an opinion to which he returned in his lecture course, 1961-62, pp. 82 ff. On the other hand, GIOSEFFI (1962) does not find any autograph work of Masaccio in either the fresco or the under-drawing but claims that the characteristics of Masaccio one finds there must have come from a drawing by that artist and that, upon his death, the work was carried out by some assistant of Masolino but not Domenico Veneziano. Worthy of consideration is the hypothesis of Gioseffi (pp. 60 ff.) that the chapel in San Clemente, dedicated to Saint Ambrose and to Saint Catherine, the patroness of schools and philosophers, was intended by Branda Castiglione for the college for poor students he founded which was recognized by Martin V in a brief dated November 3, 1427; this date, he believes, provides a *terminus post quem* for the fresco cycle.
Cf. also M. MEISS, "Highlands in the Lowlands," in *Gazette des Beaux-Arts*, June 1961, p. 295.

P. S. In connection with the reference in Note 178 and elsewhere to the Della Foresta Chapel in Figline (cf. P. D. NERI, *La Chiesa di San Francesco in Figline, Notizie storiche e restauri*, Florence, 1931), it should be understood that even if the chapel was not constructed, as appears likely, because of the financial collapse of the Della Foresta family not much after 1427, in that year Masolino could very well have begun work in view of the undertaking, for example beginning the altarpiece.

COMPARATIVE PLATES

1

2

GIOTTO · · PAOLO · VCCELLO · · · DONATELLO · · ANTONIO · MANETTI · FLIPPO · BRVNELLE

3

Fig. 1) ANDREA DI GIUSTO - *Preaching and Baptism of Saint Andrew* - Church of Sant'Andrea, Ripalta (Note 191). –
Fig. 2) ANDREA DI GIUSTO - *Calling of Peter and Andrew* - Church of Sant'Andrea, Ripalta (Note 191). – Fig. 3) ATTRI-
BUTED TO PAOLO UCCELLO - *Portraits of Five Renewers of Art* - The LOUVRE, Paris (P. 47 and Note 134).

4

5

6

7

Fig. 4) Francesco d'Antonio - *Madonna and Child with Saints Michael and John the Baptist*, Oratory, Montemarciano (P. 41). – Fig. 5) Francesco d'Antonio - *Trinity with Madonna and Child between Saints Nicholas and Julian* - Collegial, Bibbiena (Note 116). – Fig. 6) Bachiacca - *City Scene* - Rijksmuseum, Amsterdam (P. 1). – Fig. 7) Giovanni Pisano - *Flight into Egypt* - Duomo, Pisa (Pp. 35, 93 and Note 88). – Fig. 8) Related to Early Masaccio - *A Sainted Bishop* -

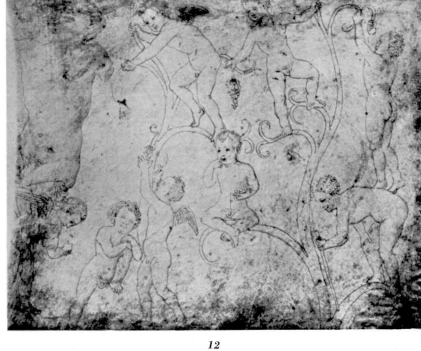

Church of San Lorenzo, San Giovanni Valdarno (P. 120). – Fig. 9) GIOTTO AND WORKSHOP - *Obedience* - Church of Santa Croce, Florence (P. 46). – Fig. 10) GIOTTO - *The Sultan* - Church of Santa Croce, Florence (P. 46). – Fig. 11) DONATELLO - *Prophet* - Duomo, Florence (P. 49 and Note 139). – Fig. 12) PISANELLO - *Putti Harvesting Grapes* - Musée Bonnat, Bayonne (Pp. 44, 63 and Note 163).

13

14

15   *16*   *17*

Fig. 13) Piero della Francesca - *Annunciation* - Gallery, Perugia (P. 64). – Fig. 14) Masolino - *Head* - Church
of Santo Stefano, Empoli (P. 68 and Notes 174-175). – Fig. 15) Gentile da Fabriano - *Madonna* - National Gallery,
London (P. 62). – Fig. 16) Gentile da Fabriano - *The Baptist* - Uffizi Galleries, Florence (P. 63. – Fig. 17) After
Masolino - *Photomontage of the Metterza Saint Anna and the Bremen Madonna* (Note 191). – Fig. 18) Bicci di Lorenzo -

18

19

20

21

Madonna - Museum, Empoli (Pp. 50, 51 and Note 144). – Fig. 19) MASACCIO - *Triptych of San Giovenale* (with perspective lines) (P. 48). – Fig. 20) BICCI DI LORENZO - *Two Saints* - Museum, Empoli (P. 50 and Note 144). – Fig. 21) BICCI DI LORENZO - *Triptych* - Vertine, Gaiole in Chianti (P. 51 and Note 146).

22   23   24

25   26   27

Fig. 22) MASOLINO - *Madonna* - Kunsthalle, Bremen (Pp. 51, 66 and Note 170). – Fig. 23) ARCANGELO DI COLA DA CA-MERINO - *Madonna* - Collegial, Bibbiena (Note 154). – Fig. 24) ANONYMOUS FLORENTINE AROUND 1515-1525 - *Madonna* - Museum, Warsaw (P. 52 and Note 146). – Fig. 25) BICCI DI LORENZO - *Head* - Church of Santo Stefano, Empoli (Note 144). – Fig. 26) MASOLINO - *Figure in the Resurrection of Tabitha* - Church of the Carmine, Florence (P. 51). – Fig. 27) BICCI DI LORENZO AND WORKSHOP - *Figure* - Church of Santo Stefano, Empoli (P. 51). – Fig. 28) - STARNINA - *Saint An-*

28

29

30

31

32

33

thony Abbot - Church of the Carmine, Florence (P. 56). – Fig. 29) D'Agincourt - *Engraving after the fresco by Starnina in the Carmine* (P. 55). – Fig. 30) Starnina - *Saint Benedict* - Church of the Carmine, Florence (P. 56). – Fig. 31) Starnina and workshop - *Under-drawing* - Museum, Empoli (P. 54 and Note 152). – Fig. 32) Starnina and Workshop - *Saints* - Museum, Empoli (P. 144 and Note 152). – Fig. 33) Master of the Bambino vispo - *Resurrection of Lazarus* - Museum of Santa Croce, Florence (P. 144 and Note 152).

Fig. 34) Paolo Uccello 1416? - *Prophet* - Tabernacle of Lippi and Macia, Novoli (P. 77 and Note 202). – Fig. 35)
Paolo Uccello 1416? - *Tabernacle of Lippi and Macia* - Church of Mater Dei, Novoli (P. 77 and Note 202). – Fig. 36)

39

40

41

42

Red ochre under-drawing of the preceding. – Figs. 37 and 38) ANONYMOUS FLORENTINE AROUND 1420? - *Cusps with Annunciation* - Formerly in Florence (Note 202). – Figs. 39-42) MASOLINO - *Stories of the Cross* (red ochre under-drawings and vestiges of fresco) - Church of Santo Stefano, Empoli (P. 55, 67 and Notes 172-3).

Fig. 43) ANONYMOUS FLORENTINE, EARLY CINQUECENTO - *Copy of the Consecration* - Private collection (P. 80 and Note 216). – Fig. 44) MICHELANGELO - *Copy of the Consecration* - Albertina, Vienna (Pp. 3, 80 and Note 9). – Fig. 45) ANONYMOUS FLORENTINE, LATE CINQUECENTO - *Copy of the Consecration and after Ghirlandaio* - Museum and Art Gallery,

49

50

51

52

Folkestone (Note 216). – Fig. 46) ANTONIO MINI? - *Copy of the Consecration* - Casa Buonarroti, Florence (Note 216). –
Fig. 47) ANONYMOUS FLORENTINE, SECOND HALF OF THE CINQUECENTO - *Copy of the Consecration* - Uffizi Galleries, Florence (Note 216). - Fig. 48) BICCI DI LORENZO - *Consecration of Saint Egidio* - Museum of Santa Maria Nuova, Florence
(P. 80). – Fig. 49) PAOLO UCCELLO? - *Portrait of a Youth* - Isabella Stewart Gardner Museum, Boston (P. 83 and Note
222). – Fig. 50) ATTRIBUTED TO MASACCIO - *Madonna of Humility* - National Gallery of Art, Washington (P. 94 and Note
243). – Fig. 51) X-ray photograph of Fig. 49. – Fig. 52) Fig. 50 before the most recent restoration.

53

54

55

Fig. 53) FLORENTINE SCHOOL, FIRST HALF OF QUATTROCENTO - *Portrait of a Youth* - National Gallery of Art (Mellon Collection), Washington (P. 83 and Note 221). – Fig. 54) ANONYMOUS FLORENTINE, FOURTEENTH CENTURY - *Madonna* - Campanile of the Duomo, Florence (Note 241) – Fig. 55) ANDREA DI GIUSTO? - *Christ Exorcising a Possessed Man* -

Johnson Collection, Philadelphia (P. 86 and Note 228). – Fig. 56) PIERO DELLA FRANCESCA - *Crucifixion* - Museum, Sansepolcro (P. 90). – Fig. 57) WORKSHOP OF MASACCIO *The Eternal Father Blessing* - National Gallery, London (Note 230). – Fig. 58) Original plan of the Pisa polyptych according to Salmi.

59

60

Figs. 59-60) The Brancacci Chapel (after Borsook) - Church of the Carmine, Florence (Note 224).

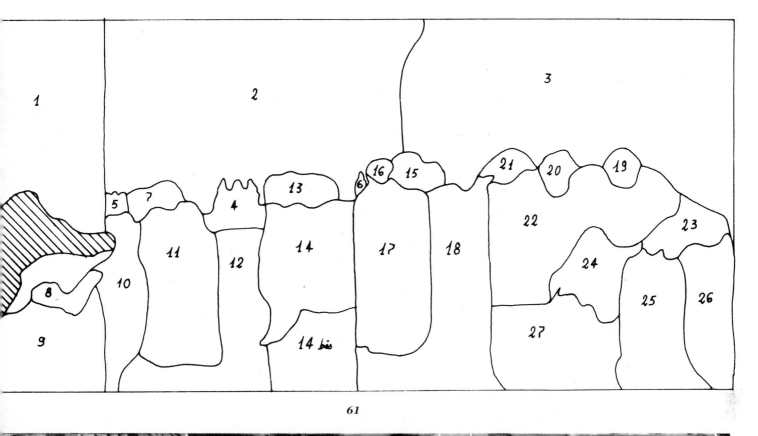

61

62

Fig. 61) Diagram of the days' work sections of the *Resurrection of Tabitha* by Masolino (P. 71). – Fig. 62) Diagram showing areas done by Masaccio and Filippino respectively in the *Story of Theophilus* (P. 109 and Notes 260-62 and 264).

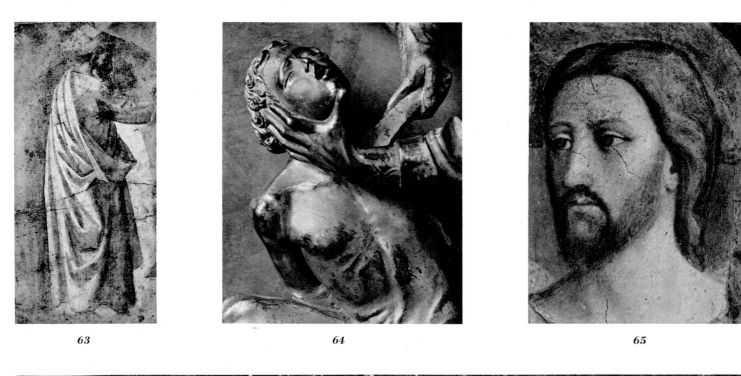

63   64   65

66

Fig. 63) LATE FIFTEENTH OR EARLY SIXTEENTH CENTURY - *Copy of the Saint Peter Baptizing* - Uffizi Galleries, Florence
(Note 246). – Fig. 64) BRUNELLESCHI - *Isaac* - Museo Nazionale, Florence (P. 97). – Fig. 65) MASOLINO? - *Head of Christ
from the Tribute Money* - Church of the Carmine, Florence (P. 71 and Note 183). – Fig. 66) MASACCIO - *Story of Saint*

67 68 69

70 71 72

Julian - Horne Museum, Florence (Pp. 111, 124 and Note 282). – Fig. 67) *Wall behind the Trinity* - Church of Santa Maria Novella, Florence (Note 270). – Fig. 68) Proposed reconstruction of the *Trinity* (Note 270). – Fig. 69) Diagram of the days' work sections of the *Trinity* (P. 117 and Note 270). – Fig. 70) MASACCIO - *The Madonna* - Church of Santa Maria Novella, Florence (P. 117). – Fig. 71) BRUNELLESCHI - *Crucifix* - Church of Santa Maria Novella, Florence (P. 118). – Fig. 72) Hypothetical reconstruction of the *Trinity* (after Schlegel) (Note 270).

73

74

75

76

77

78

Fig. 73) Workshop of Masaccio - Putto on the reverse of the birth salver - Museum, Berlin (Note 283). – Fig. 74) Master of the Adimari Cassone - *Annunciation* - Whereabouts unknown (Note 287). – Figs. 75-78) Nineteenth-Century Copyist - Copies of the Berlin birth salver and of another - Private collection, Florence (Note 200).

79

Fig. 79) D'Agincourt - Engraving of the Chapel decorated by Masolino in San Clemente, Rome (Note 289).

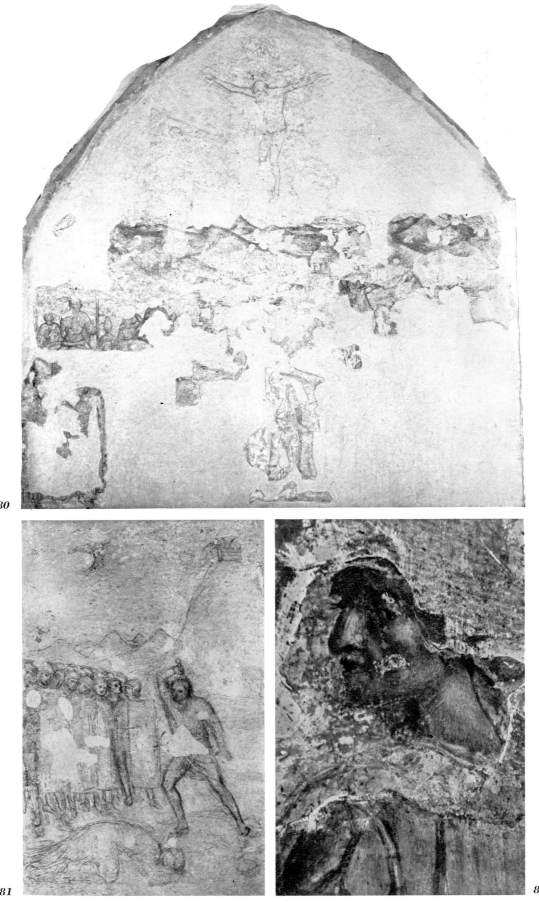

80

81

82

Fig. 80) MASOLINO AND MASACCIO - Under-drawing of the *Crucifixion* - Church of San Clemente, Rome (P. 130 and Note 289). – Fig. 81) MASOLINO - Under-drawing of the *Martyrdom of Saint Catherine* - Church of San Clemente, Rome (P. 130 and Note 289). – Fig. 82) ANONYMOUS PAINTER OF THE SIXTEENTH CENTURY - Restored head in the *Crucifixion* - Church of San Clemente, Rome (Note 289).

CATALOGUE OF THE WORKS

(For more detailed information, refer to the index)

Triptych of San Giovenale
[Plates 1-6]
Church of San Giovenale in Cascia (Reggello)
Panels: side wings $34\frac{5}{8} \times 17\frac{3}{8}$ in.; central panel $42\frac{1}{2} \times 26$ in.
In restoration.

The recent discovery and attribution by L. BERTI (1961) has had almost general approval, although there have been some reservations and a few sporadic negative insinuations. Dated 1422.

The Metterza Saint Anne
[Plates 7-10]
Florence, Uffizi Galleries
Panel, $68\frac{7}{8} \times 40\frac{1}{2}$ in.

Cited by VASARI in the *Lives* of 1568 as being in the church of Sant'Ambrogio in Florence. LONGHI was the first to distinguish those parts done by Masaccio: the Madonna, the Child, the angel holding the curtain on the right, the base of the throne. The rest is by Masolino. Although some scholars date it around 1420, in my opinion it belongs to 1424-25 and perhaps more precisely to the first half of 1425.

Madonna and Child with Angels
[Plates 13-15]
London, National Gallery
Panel: $53\frac{3}{8} \times 28\frac{3}{4}$ in.

Originally the central panel of the polyptych for the Carmine in Pisa (1426) which was described by Vasari and was dismembered in the eighteenth century. Rediscovered by BERENSON in 1907.

Saint Paul
[Plate 16]
Pisa, Museo Nazionale
Panel: $20\frac{1}{8} \times 11\frac{3}{4}$ in.

Originally part of the second tier of the polyptych of the Carmine in Pisa (1426).

Saint Andrew
[Plate 17]
Vienna, Collection Lanckoronski
Panel: $20\frac{1}{8} \times 11\frac{3}{4}$ in.

Originally part of the second tier of the polyptych of the Carmine in Pisa (1426). Identified by SCHMARSOW as early as 1896.

Crucifixion
[Plates 18-23]
Naples: Museo di Capodimonte
Panel: $32\frac{5}{8} \times 25$ in.

Originally at the apex of the polyptych of the Carmine in Pisa (1426). Acquired in 1901 by the Naples museum, it was identified by A. VENTURI and SUIDA.

Adoration of the Magi
[Plates 24-26]
Berlin, Museum
Panel: $8\frac{1}{4} \times 24$ in.

Originally the central part of the predella of the polyptych of the Carmine in Pisa (1426). Acquired by the Berlin museum in Florence in 1880 and identified by CAVALCASELLE in 1883.

Martyrdoms of Saint Peter and of Saint John the Baptist
[Plates 27-32]
Berlin, Museum
Panel: $8\frac{1}{4} \times 24$ in.

Originally in the predella of the polyptych of the Carmine in Pisa (1426), Acquired in Florence by the Berlin museum in 1880 and identified by CAVALCASELLE in 1883.

Stories of Saint Julian and of Saint Nicholas
[Plates 33-34]
Berlin, Museum
Panel: $8\frac{3}{4} \times 24\frac{3}{8}$ in.

Originally in the predella of the polyptych of the Carmine in Pisa (1426). Acquired in 1908 by the museum. Generally presumed to have been done in collaboration with Andrea di Giusto.

Saint Augustine and Jerome - Two Carmelite Saints
[Plates 11-12]
Berlin, Museum
Panels: 15 × 5 in. each

Originally on the small pilasters of the polyptych of the Carmine in Pisa (1426). Acquired by the Berlin museum in 1905.

Madonna and Child
[Plate 38]
Florence, Palazzo Vecchio (Collection of works recovered from Germany)
Panel: $9\frac{5}{8} \times 7\frac{1}{8}$ in.

Published by LONGHI in 1950. The attribution, which until now has encountered some opposition, is accepted here along with the date of around 1426.

Prayer in the Garden—Saint Jerome Penitent
[Plates 35-37]
Altenburg, Lindenau Museum
Panels: respectively $11\frac{3}{4} \times 13\frac{5}{8}$ and $7\frac{7}{8} \times 13\frac{5}{8}$ in.

Acquired in Rome during the last century. Although some scholars held them to be by the "School of Masaccio," OERTEL (1961) claimed them for the master, with possible collaboration. That attribution is accepted here with the supposition that the collaborator from the workshop was Andrea di Giusto and that the date is around 1426-27.

Frescoes in the Brancacci Chapel
[Plates 39-65]
Florence, Church of the Carmine
Expulsion from Paradise, $81\frac{7}{8} \times 34\frac{5}{8}$ in.
Baptism of the Neophytes, $100\frac{3}{8} \times 63\frac{3}{4}$ in.
The Tribute Money, $100\frac{3}{8} \times 235\frac{3}{8}$ in.
Story of Ananias, $90\frac{1}{2} \times 63\frac{3}{4}$ in.
Saint Peter Healing the Sick by his Shadow, $90\frac{1}{2} \times 63\frac{3}{4}$ in.
Story of Theophilus, $90\frac{1}{2} \times 235\frac{3}{8}$ in.
Background of the Resurrection of Tabitha, $235\frac{3}{8}$ in. in width
The frescoes were damaged when the church burned in 1771.

As is well known, the rest of the cycle in the chapel is the work of Masolino and Filippino Lippi, the latter of whom also completed the Story of Theophilus. The long history of the question of attributions is gone into fully in our text along with certain recent more detailed distinctions. As for the chronology, it is maintained here that Masaccio's share was done between the end of 1424 and the beginning of 1428.

The Trinity
[Plates 66-72]
Florence, Church of Santa Maria Novella
Detached fresco, total dimensions $262\frac{5}{8} \times 124\frac{3}{4}$ in.

This famous fresco was covered over in 1565-70 when the basilica was modernized. In 1861 it was re-exposed and its principal section detached and relocated on the interior wall of the façade. In 1951 PROCACCI discovered what remained of the lower part with the figure of the dead man, and the entire fresco was re-assembled in its original location. Here we accept fully the hypothesis that Brunelleschi collaborated in the perfect construction of the perspective as well as the dating of 1427 or early 1428. We also propose that among the donors, besides Fra Lorenzo Cardoni and the Lenzi family, was also Fra Alessio Strozzi who was known to be a man of great culture especially interested in the arts and was a close friend of Brunelleschi and Ghiberti.

Story of Saint Julian
[Plate 73 and Figure 66]
Florence, Horne Museum
Panel, $9\frac{29}{64} \times 16\frac{7}{8}$ in.

Attributed to Masaccio by HORNE himself, it was published by GAMBA in 1920. It is not accepted by some scholars, and it is certainly difficult to evaluate because of the deplorable condition in which it has come down to us. Here it is accepted as Masaccio's but not as part of either the polyptych of Pisa or of the Carnesecchi triptych in Santa Maria Maggiore, Florence.
Supposed date, early 1427.

Birth salver with scene of birth
[Plates 74-76 and Figure 73].
Berlin, Museum
Panel: diameter 22 in.; on the reverse, a putto with a marten.

The salver, which came from San Giovanni Valdarno, was acquired by the Berlin museum in 1883. The attribution to Masaccio has been doubted by a few critics, among them MORELLI (1893) who assigned it to Andrea di Giusto, BRANDI (1934) who proposed Domenico di Bartolo, PITTALUGA and PROCACCI who make a more general attribution to Florentine School of the fourth decade of the 1400's, and RAGGHIANTI (1952) who supposes it to be by Domenico Veneziano. Here it is accepted as an autograph work dating from late 1427 or early 1428.

Saints Jerome and John the Baptist
[Plates 77-79].
London, National Gallery
Panel: 44$\frac{7}{8}$ × 21$\frac{5}{8}$ in.

Side wing of the triptych formerly in Santa Maria Maggiore, Rome, the rest of which is by Masolino. The first attribution was made by CLARK (1951) but with a date pushed forward to 1425-26. Accepted by most critics but still with some exceptions.

Insert (soldiers on horseback and landscape) in the under-drawing of the Crucifixion by Masolino
[Plate 80 and Figure 80].
Rome, Church of San Clemente
Sinopia (it is difficult to judge if the insert is carried over into the fresco).

While the attribution to Masaccio of the entire cycle in San Clemente, which goes back to Vasari, has generally been transferred to Masolino, many scholars continue to predicate an intervention by Masaccio, and his contributions have been analyzed in particular by LONGHI (1940). The attribution is accepted here, along with the date of the very end of Masaccio's life, 1428.

LOST WORKS

Christ exorcising a Possessed Man
Florence, in the home of Ridolfo del Ghirlandaio

A panel with small figures cited by VASARI. The painting in the Johnson Collection, Philadelphia attributed to Andrea di Giusto is probably a copy of this (Fig. 55).

The Consecration
Florence, Cloister of the Carmine

Fresco in chiaroscuro mentioned as early as MANETTI. Destroyed apparently around 1600.

Portraits of Eminent Florentines
Florence, in the home of Simone Corsi

Cited by Vasari in the second edition of the *Lives*.

Saint Paul
Florence, Church of the Carmine

Fresco, on the side of the transept opposite the Brancacci Chapel. Mentioned as far back as MANETTI. Destroyed, it is believed, in 1675.

A fresco
Cloister of the Monastery of the Angels

Mentioned by ALBERTINI (1510) as being in the second cloister of that monastery, and supposedly depicting a Last Judgment.

Saint Peter resuscitating the Dead
Florence, Church of the Carmine

Fresco perhaps painted in the third tier of the Brancacci Chapel alongside the window and above the Baptism of the Neophytes. It is mentioned by VASARI, but PROCACCI believes it was confused with the Story of Ananias.
(SALMI, 1948, pp. 157-8, and here, notes 9 and 178).

Saints Peter and John the Baptist; Saint Julian and Nicholas; also at least two Saints in half-length and some smaller Saints
Pisa, Church of the Carmine

Portions of the Pisa polyptych, 1426, which were detached and lost in the eighteenth century.
(Notes 230-231).

Saint Ives and his Wards
Florence, Church of the Badia

Fresco destroyed in 1627 except for the head of the Saint which was detached from the wall for safe-keeping but later lost.

Annunciation
Florence, Church of San Niccolò

Panel. Mentioned by VASARI in his second edition, lost probably around 1580-85.

A Male and a Female Nude
Florence, in the home of the Rucellai

Panel with life-size figures mentioned by VASARI.

Saints Peter and Paul (on panel)
Birth Salver with a "Skirmish"
Florence, once in possession of Lorenzo il Magnifico

Appear in the inventory of 1492.
(Note 284).

ATTRIBUTED WORKS

(This list is limited to those works still seriously discussed and, except for the first item, generally accepted up to now)

Sainted Bishop
(Figure 8).
San Giovanni Valdarno, Church of San Lorenzo

Mutilated and ruined fresco attributed to Masaccio by the present writer but only as a hypothesis because of its affinity with the Saint Bartholomew and Blaise of the San Giovenale triptych.
(Note 115).

Madonna and Child with Saints John the Baptist and Michael
(Figure 4).
Montemarciano, Oratory of the Madonna delle Grazie

Fresco attributed to Masaccio for the first time by MACHERINI-GRAZIANI followed by many scholars even as recently as the BERENSON lists of 1963. Should be given to Francesco d'Antonio as LINDBERG was first to propose.
(Note 116).

Portrait of a Youth
(Figure 53).
Washington, National Gallery, Mellon Collection

Formerly in the Artaud de Montor collection in Paris and catalogued there (1843) as Masaccio.

Accepted by SALMI (1948). Should be considered Florentine School around Paolo Uccello.
(Note 221).

Portrait of a Youth
(Figures 49, 51).
Boston, Isabella Stewart Gardner Museum

BERENSON's attribution to Masaccio has been more or less generally accepted. For RAGGHIANTI, it is by the young Piero della Francesca. More likely it should be assigned to Paolo Uccello, as E. SINDONA has proposed.
(Note 222).

Madonna of Humility
(Figures 50, 52).
Washington, National Gallery

Panel, formerly in the reserves of the Vienna museum (?), then in a Hungarian collection. Attributed to Masaccio by BERENSON (1929) and dated around 1425. This is generally accepted, but not by PROCACCI and BRANDI. It is a work which still requires an objective and thorough analysis and scrupulous research on its documentation.
(Note 243).

BIBLIOGRAPHY

1436. L. B. ALBERTI, *Della Pittura* (ed. Mallè, Florence, 1950).

14??. A. MANETTI, *Vite di XIV uomini singhulary in Firenze dal MCCCC innanzi* (ed. G. Milanesi, Florence, 1887).

1481. C. LANDINO, *Commento a Dante*, ed. princeps, Florence, c. 5.

1510. F. ALBERTINI, *Memoriale di molte statue e pitture... di Florentia*, Florence (ed. 1863).

1516-30 c. A. BILLI, *Il libro* (ed. C. Frey, 1892).

1537-42 c. ANONIMO GADDIANO O CODICE MAGLIABECHIANO (ed. C. Frey, 1892).

1550. G. VASARI, *Le Vite*, 1st ed., Florence.

1568. G. VASARI, *Le Vite*, 2nd ed., Florence.

1584. R. BORGHINI, *Il Riposo*, Florence.

1591. F. BOCCHI, *Bellezze della città di Fiorenza*, Florence (new ed. with additions by Cinelli, 1677).

1662. F. MONTI and G. TANCREDI, *Masaccio*, Rome.

1675. P. COCCAPANI, *Descrizione delle feste... per la solenne traslazione de corpo di Sant'Andrea Corsini*, Rome.

1681-1728. F. BALDINUCCI, *Notizie de' professori del disegno*, II (1728), Florence.

1699. F. DE SEINE, *Nouveau voyage en Italie*, Lyons, II.

1754-62. G. RICHA, *Notizie istoriche delle chiese Fiorentine*, 10 vols., Florence.

1769-91. J. REYNOLDS, *Discourses delivered at the Royal Academy* (ed. Fry, London, 1905, p. 337).

1770. T. PATCH, *The Life of Masaccio*, Florence.

1782. G. PELLI, "Elogio di Tommaso, o Maso detto Masaccio," in *Elogi degli uomini illustri toscani*, Lucca, II.

1789. L. LANZI, *Storia pittorica dell'Italia*, Bassano.

1790. V. FINESCHI, *Il Forestiere istruito in Santa Maria Novella*, Florence.

1809. G. DALL'ARMI, *Le pitture di Masaccio esistenti in Roma nella Basilica di San Clemente*, Rome.

1823. J. B. SÉROUX D'AGINCOURT, *Histoire de l'Art par les monuments*, Paris, III.

1827. C. F. RUMOHR, *Italienische Forschungen*, Berlin-Stettin, 2nd ed., pp. 243-51 (ed. Schlosser, Frankfurt, 1920, pp. 376-81).

1830. A. NIBBY, *Itinerario di Roma*, Rome, I.

1832. M. VALÉRY, *Voyages historiques et littéraires en Italie*, Paris, III, p. 127.

1832-38. G. MASSELLI, Notes for *Opere di Giorgio Vasari*, Florence, I, pp. 249-53.

1834. F. GHERARDI-DRAGOMANNI, *Memorie della Terra di San Giovanni nel Valdarno superiore*, Florence.

1839. G. GAYE, *Carteggio inedito d'artisti*, Florence, I, pp. 115-17.

1840. G. GAYE, *Carteggio*, Florence, II, pp. 469-73.

1840. G. Rosini, *Storia della pittura italiana*, Pisa, II, pp. 263-86.

1845. A. M. Jameson, *Memoirs of the Early Italian Painters*, London.

1846. M. Missirini, *Masaccio* (oration), Florence.

1847. F. D. Kugler, *Handbuch der Geschichte der Malerei*, Berlin, pp. 304-98.

1848. G. Rosini, *Sulle pitture di Masaccio nella Cappella Brancacci*, Pisa.

1848. A. Reumont, "Kapelle Brancacci, Masaccio und Filippino," in *Das Kunstblatt*, Stuttgart-Tubingen, p. 117.

1848. C. Milanesi, G. Milanesi, C. Pini, P. V. Marchese, "Sulle pitture della Cappella Brancacci," in *Le Vite* of Vasari, III, Florence, pp. 165-91.

1850. E. Breton, *Notice sur Tommaso Guidi dit Masaccio*, Saint-Germain-en-Laye.

1855. J. Burckhardt, *Der Cicerone*, Basel, pp. 798-99 (and subsequent editions and translations).

1855. A. H. Springer, *Handbuch der Kunstgeschichte*, Stuttgart (Vol. III, Leipzig, 1897; Italian ed., ed. C. Ricci, Bergamo, 1913, III, pp. 105-14).

1856. P. Selvatico, *Storia estetico-critica delle arti del disegno*, Venice, pp. 333-38.

1856. F. Fantozzi, *Nuova guida di Firenze*, Florence.

1860. G. Milanesi, "Le vite di alcuni artefici fiorentini scritte da Giorgio Vasari," in *Giornale storico degli Archivi toscani*, IV, Florence, pp. 194-96 (republication, Siena, 1873).

1861. A. F. Rio, *De l'Art chrétien*, Paris, I, pp. 344-49, II, p. 13.

1861. *Intorno ai lavori di Santa Maria Novella di Firenze*, Florence, p. 2.

1861. *Interno della Chiesa di Santa Maria Novella dopo i restauri fatti nell 1861*, Florence, p. 14.

1863. M. Amari, *I diplomi arabi del Reale Archivio fiorentino*, Florence.

1864. J. A. Crowe and G. B. Cavalcaselle, *A New History of Painting in Italy*, London, I, pp. 519-50 (ed. E. Hutton, London, 1909, II, pp. 233-58; ed. Langton Douglas-De Nicola, London, 1911, IV, pp. 34-65).

1868. A. H. Layard, *The Brancacci Chapel*, London.

1869. P. Santi Mattei, *Ragionamento intorno all'antica chiesa del Carmine di Firenze*, Florence, pp. 40-60.

1869. A. Zahn, "Masolino und Masaccio," in *Jahrbücher für Kunstwissenschaft*, pp. 155-71.

1870. W. Lübke, "Masolino und Masaccio," in *Jahrbücher für Kunstwissenschaft*, pp. 280-86.

1870. A. Reumont, "Die Kapelle der heilige Katharina in San Clemente zu Rom," in *Jahrbücher für Kunstwissenschaft*, pp. 75-79.

1876. H. Delaborde, "Des oeuvres et de la manière de Masaccio," in *Gazette des Beaux-Arts*, pp. 369-84.

1876. M. Thaussing, "Masaccio und Masolino in der Brancacci-Kapelle," in *Zeitschrift für bildende Kunst*, pp. 225-38.

1877. J. A. Symonds, *Renaissance in Italy*, London, pp. 229-31.

1877. C. Pini and G. Milanesi, *La scrittura di artisti italiani*, s.l., I, n. 14.

1878. G. Milanesi, in Giorgio Vasari, *Vite*, Florence, II, pp. 287-326.

1880. K. Woermann, "Masaccio und Masolino," in *Grenzboten*, XXXIX, p. 324.

1881. D. Catellacci, "Diario di Felice Brancacci ambasciatore con Carlo Federighi al Cairo," in *Archivio Storico Italiano*, pp. 157-88.

1882. A. Woltmann and K. Woermann, *Geschichte der Malerei*, Leipzig, II, pp. 138-51.

1885. J. P. Richter, *Notes on Vasari*, London.

1887. W. Lübke, *Essai d'histoire de l'Art*, Paris, II, pp. 158-60.

1887. L. Tanfani-Centofanti, *Donatello in Pisa*, Pisa.

1888. E. Müntz, *Les Collections des Médicis au XVe siècle*, Paris, pp. 58, 62, 86.

1889. F. Wickhoff, "Die Fresken der Katharinen Kapelle in San Clemente zu Rom," in *Zeitschritft für bildende Kunst*, pp. 301-10 (reviewed by C. De Fabriczy in *Archivo Storico dell'Arte*, 1889, pp. 381-83).

1889. W. J. Stillman, "Masaccio," in *The Century Magazine*, September, pp. 653-59.

1889. T. Cole, "Masaccio," in *The Century Magazine*, September, p. 659.

1889. E. Müntz, *Histoire de l'Art pendant la Renaissance*, Paris, I, pp. 336, 612-19 (reviewed by O. Maruti in *Archivio Storico dell'Arte*, 1890, p. 147).

1893. I. Lermolieff (G. Morelli), *Kunstkritische Studien über italienische Malerei*, Leipzig, p. 17.

1893-94. *Catalogue of the Exhibition of Early Italian Art in the New Gallery*, London.

1894. E. Müntz, "Les Plateaux d'accouchées," in *Fondation Eugène Piot*, Paris, pp. 203-32.

1894. A. Cocchi, *Notizie storiche intorno antiche immagini di nostra Donna*, Florence, pp. 57-60.

1895-99. A. Schmarsow, *Masaccio-Studien*, Cassel.

1896. B. Berenson, *Florentine Painters of the Renaissance*, New York-London, 1st ed. (2nd ed., 1900).

n.d. L. Justi, *Die italienische Malerei des 15. Jahrhunderts*, Berlin, pp. 13-23.

1897. A. Philippi, *Die Kunst der Renaissance in Italian*, Leipzig, I, 187-205.

1898. L. Tanfani-Centofanti, *Notizie di artisti tratte da documenti pisani*, Pisa, pp. 176, 178-80.

1901. M. Creutz, *Masaccio*, Berlin.

1901. A. Filangeri di Candida, "La Pinacoteca Nazionale di Napoli," in *Napoli nobilissima*, March, p. 34.

1901. A. Filangeri di Candida, "Un quadro acquistato dalla Galleria del Museo Nazionale di Napoli," in *L'Arte*, p. 74.

1901. W. Bode, "Donatello als Architekt und Decorator," in *Jahrbuch der Königlichen Preussischen Kunstsammlungen*, p. 28.

1901. W. Weisbach, "Der Meister des Carrandschen Triptychous," in *Jahrbuch der Königlichen Preussischen Kunstsammlungen*, p. 37.

1901. B. Marrai, "Il tabernacolo col gruppo del Verrocchio in Orsanmichele," in *L'Arte*, pp. 346-52.

1902. J. B. Stupino and B. Marrai, "Ancora del tabernacolo col gruppo del Verrocchio in Orsanmichele." in *L'Arte*, pp. 185-89.

1902. J. Wood Brown, *The Dominican Church of Santa Maria Novella*, Edinburgh.

1902. A. Bayersdorfer, "Masaccio und Filippino, Fresken in der Brancacci Kapelle," in *Leben und Schriften aus seinem Nachlass*, Munich, pp. 56-58.

1902. B. Berenson, *The Study and Criticism of Italian Art*. London, pp. 77-89.

1902. A. H. Layard, *The Italian Schools of Painting*, London, 1902, I, pp. 140-46.

1903. B. Marrai, "Il tabernacolo col gruppo del Verrocchio in Orsanmichele," in *Rivista d'Arte*, pp. 36-38.

1903. J. Del Badia, "Tommaso... detto Masaccio e Giovanni suo fratello," in *Rassegna Nazionale*, Florence.

1903. C. Carnesecchi, "Messer Felice Brancacci," in *Miscellanea d'Arte*, Florence, pp. 38-40.

1903. P. D'Ancona, "La tavola di Masaccio ora nella R. Galleria di Belle Arti," in *Miscellanea d'Arte*, Florence, pp. 174-77.

1904. G. Magherini-Graziani, *Masaccio, Ricordo delle onoranze rese in San Giovanni Valdarno nel di 25 ottobre 1903*, Florence.

1904. M. Marasse, "Masaccio und San Clemente in Roma," in *Die Kunst-Halle*, pp. 257, 273, 290.

1904. R. Pantini, "La cappella della Passione in San Clemente a Roma," in *Emporium*, pp. 31-52.

1905. V. Leonardi, "Affreschi dimenticati del tempo di Martino V," in *Atti del Congresso internazionale di Scienze Storiche*, Rome, pp. 286-308.

1905. M. Reymond, "L'Architecture des peintres aux premières années de la Renaissance," in *Revue de l'Art ancien et moderne*, pp. 41-2, 48-50.

1905. G. Sortais, "Masaccio et la chapelle Brancacci," in *Etudes*, pp. 343-71.

1905. A. Chiappelli, *Pagine d'antica arte fiorentina*, Florence, pp. 97-105.

1906. W. Suida, "L'altare di Masaccio, già nel Carmine a Pisa," in *L'Arte*, pp. 125-27.

1906. P. Schubring, "Notizie di Berlino," in *L'Arte*, p. 384.

1907. B. Berenson, "La scoperta di un dipinto di Masaccio," in *Rassegna d'arte*, p. 139.

1908. A. Peraté, in *Histoire de l'art*, Paris, III, 2, pp. 597-600.

1908. F. X. Kraus, *Geschichte der christlichen Kunst*, Freiburg, II, 2, pp. 180-84.

1908. P. Toesca, *Masolino da Panicale*, Bergamo.

1908. B. Berenson, "La Madonna pisana di Masaccio," in *Rassegna d'Arte*, VIII, pp. 81-85.

1908. D. F. Von Hadeln, "Andrea di Giusto und das dritte Predellenstück von pisanischen Altarwerk des Masaccio," in *Monatshefte für Kunstwissenschaft*, pp. 785-89.

1908. R. Pantini, "Masaccio," in *The Connoisseur*, pp. 25-28, 87-90.

1909. B. Berenson, *The Florentine Painters of the Renaissance with an Index to their Works*, New York-London, 3rd ed.

1909. R. Muther, *Geschichte der Malerei*, Leipzig, I, pp. 92-98.

1909. A. Venturi, *Storia dell'Arte italiana*, Milan, VIII, 1, pp. 86, 113-126.

1911. R. Fry, "Exhibition of Old Masters at the Grafton Galleries," in *Burlington Magazine*, November, p. 71.

1911. A. De Rinaldis, *Pinacoteca del Museo Nazionale di Napoli*, Naples, pp. 14-19.

1912. J. Mesnil, "Per la storia della cappella Brancacci," in *Rivista d'Arte*, pp. 34-40.

1912. K. Woermann, *Von Apelles zu Böcklin und weiter*, Esslingen, pp. 41-48.

1913. G. J. Kern, "Das Dreifaltigkeits Fresko von Santa Maria Novella," in *Jahrbuch der Königlichen Preussichen Kunstsammlungen*, pp. 36-58.

1913. J. Mesnil, "La fresque de la Trinité," in *Bulletin de l'Art ancien et moderne*, pp. 223-24.

1914. J. Mesnil, "Masaccio et la Théorie de la perspective," in *Revue de l'Art ancien et moderne*, pp. 145-46.

1920. C. Gamba, "Il Palazzo e la raccolta Horne a Firenze," in *Dedalo*, I, p. 177.

1920. H. Wieleitner, "Zur Erfindung der verschiedenen Distanzkonstruktionen in der malerischen Perspektive," in *Reportorium für Kunstwissenschaft*, p. 253.

1921. W. Bode, *Beschreibendes Verzeichnis der Gemälde im Kaiser-Friedrich Museum*, Berlin-Leipzig, p. 272.

1921. O. H. Giglioli, *Masaccio*, Florence.

1922. K. Escher, *Malerei der Renaissance in Italian*, Berlin, I, pp. 35-46.

1923. P. Schubring, *Cassoni*, Leipzig, pp. 84, 104, 238.

1923. W. Bode, *Die Kunst der Frührenaissance in Italien*, Berlin, pp. 34-35.

1923-24. A. SCHMARSOW, "Masolino oder Masaccio in Neapel?," in *Repertorium für Kunstwissenschaft*, pp. 289-93.

1924. E. SOMARÉ, *Masaccio*, Milan.

1924. S. POPOVITCH, "Conception of Space in Old Masters," in *Burlington Magazine*, p. 227.

1925. A. SCHMARSOW, "Neue Beiträge zu Masolino und Masaccio," in *Belvedere*, pp. 145-57.

1926. A. CHIAPPELLI, "Un capolavoro antico sotto nuova luce," in *Il Marzocco*, June 20.

1926. H. BEENKEN, "Masaccio," in *Belvedere*, pp. 167-78.

1926. J. MESNIL, "Masaccio and the Antique," in *Burlington Magazine*, XLVIII, pp. 91-98.

1927. M. DVORAK, *Geschichte der italienischen Kunst im Zeitalter der Renaissance*, Munich, 1, pp. 47-62.

1927. R. LONGHI, *Piero della Francesca*, Rome, pp. 15-18, 21-22, 75.

1927. J. MESNIL, *Masaccio et les débuts de la Renaissance*, The Hague.

1928. J. MESNIL, "Die Kunstlehre der Frührenaissance in Werke Masaccios," in *Vorträge 1925-26, Bibliothek Warburg*, Leipzig, pp. 122-46.

1928. C. GAMBA, "L'influsso di Masaccio nel Quattrocento," in *Il Marzocco*, April 8.

1928. N. TARCHIANI, "La fortuna di Masaccio," in *Il Marzocco*, April 22.

1928. A. SCHMARSOW, *Masolino und Masaccio*, Leipzig.

1928. R. VAN MARLE, *The Development of the Italian Schools of Painting*, The Hague, X, pp. 251-307.

1929. O. H. GIGLIOLI, *Masaccio*, Bergamo.

1929. G. BACCHI, P. CAIOLI, G. FIOCCO, O. H. GIGLIOLI, M. PITTALUGA and M. SALMI, "Contributi" in *Rivista Storica Carmelitana* (on the occasion of the 5th centenary of the death of Masaccio).

1929. O. H. GIGLIOLI, "Masaccio" (bibliography), in *Bollettino del Reale Istituto di Architettura e Storia dell'Arte*, III, pp. 55-101.

1929. J. MESNIL, "Masolino ou Masaccio?" in *Gazette des Beaux-Arts*, pp. 206-9.

1929. B. BERENSON, "Un nuovo Masaccio," in *Dedalo*, pp. 331-36.

1929. M. PITTALUGA, "Masaccio e L. B. Alberti," in *Rassegna italiana*, pp. 779-90.

1929. M. PITTALUGA, "Rinascimento italiano," in *L'Arte*, pp. 90-93.

1929. M. PITTALUGA, Review of J. Mesnil, *Masaccio et les débuts de la Renaissance*, in *Belvedere*, pp. 240 ff.

1929-30. H. BEENKEN, " Zum Werke des Masaccio, II, Die Altarbilder für Santa Maria Maggiore in Florenz," in *Zeitschrift für bildende Kunst*, pp. 156-65, 112-19.

1929-30. W. STECHOW, "Zum Masaccio-Masolino Problem," in *Zeitschrift für bildende Kunst*, LXIII, pp. 125-27.

1930. H. BROCKHAUS, " Die Brancacci-Kapelle in Florenz," in *Mitteilungen des Kunsthistorisches Instituts in Florenz*, III, pp. 160-182.

1930. B. KLEINSCHMIDT, *Die Heilige Anna*, Düsseldorf, p. 226.

1930. B. BERENSON, "A New Masaccio," in *Art in America*, pp. 45-53.

1930. L. VENTURI, "A Madonna by Masaccio," in *Burlington Magazine*, LVII, pp. 21-27.

1930. O. H. GIGLIOLI, "Masaccio," in Thieme-Becker, *Allgemeines Lexikon der bildenden Künstler*, Leipzig, XXIV, pp. 193-95.

1930. L. VENTURI, "Contributi a Masolino, Lorenzo Salimbeni e Jacopo Bellini," in *L'Arte*, p. 165.

1930. M. PITTALUGA, "La Critica e i valori romantici di Masaccio," in *L'Arte*, pp. 139-64.

1930. A. Schmarsow, "Zur Masolino-Masaccio Forschung," in *Zeitschrift für bildende Kunst*, LXIV, April, pp. 1-3.

1931. L. Venturi, *Pitture italiane in America*, Milan.

1931. H. Lindberg, *To the Problem of Masolino and Masaccio*, Stockholm.

1932. M. Salmi, *Masaccio*, Rome.

1932. A. Colasanti, "Masaccio," in *Leonardo*, pp. 436 ff.

1932. J. Mesnil, "Vues nouvelles sur l'art de Masaccio," in *Revue de l'art ancien et moderne*, LXII, pp. 145-62.

1932. H. Beenken, "Masaccios und Masolinos Fresken von San Clemente in Rom," in *Belvedere*, p. 7-13.

1932. E. Trenkler, "Beiträge zur Masaccio-Forschung," in *Wiener Jahrbuch für Kunstgeschichte*, pp. 7-16.

1932. U. Procacci, "L'incendio della chiesa del Carmine," in *Rivista d'arte*, pp. 141-232.

1932. U. Procacci, "Documenti e ricerche sopra Masaccio e la sua famiglia," in *Rivista d'Arte*, pp. 489-503.

1932. B. Berenson, *Italian Pictures of the Renaissance*, Oxford.

1933. R. Oertel, *Die Frühwerke des Masaccio*, Marburg am Lahn (*Marburger Jahrbuch für Kunstwissenschaft*, VII, pp. 191-289).

1933. A. M. Brizio, reviews of studies by Salmi, Mesnil, Lindberg and Beenken, in *L'Arte*, pp. 147-49.

1934. M. Salmi, *Masaccio*, Paris.

1934. R. Wedgwood Kennedy, review of the study by Salmi, in *Art Bulletin*, pp. 396-97.

1934. P. Toesca, "Masaccio," in *Enciclopedia italiana*, XXII.

1934. T. Oertel, "Masaccio und die Geschichte der Freskotechnik," in *Jahrbuch der Preussischen Kunstsammlungen*, LV, pp. 229-40.

1934. C. Gamba, review of study by Salmi, in *Pan*, II, November, pp. 470-72.

1935. G. Wassermann, *Masaccio und Masolino*, Strassburg.

1935. M. Pittaluga, *Masaccio*, Florence.

1935. U. Procacci, "Documenti e ricerche sopra Masaccio e la sua famiglia," in *Rivista d'Arte*, pp. 91 ff.

1936. M. Meiss, "The Madonna of Humility," in *Art Bulletin*, XVIII, p. 435.

1939. P. Bargellini, *Città di pittori*, Florence.

1939. G. Fiocco, "Masaccio e la conquista dello spazio," in *Domus*, February.

1939. C. Gamba, " Masaccio," in *Emporium*, April, pp. 173-88.

1940. R. Longhi, " Fatti di Masolino e di Masaccio," in *Critica d'Arte*, pp. 145-91.

1940. R. Oertel, "Wandmalerei und Zeichnung in Italian," in *Mitteilungen des Kunsthistorisches Instituts in Florenz*, pp. 217 ff.

1943. M. Salmi, *Civiltà fiorentina del primo Rinascimento*, Florence.

1943. E. Lavagnino, "Masaccio: 'Dicesi è morto a Roma'," in *Emporium*, pp. 97 ff.

1944. M. L. Gengaro, *Umanesimo e Rinascimento*, Turin.

1945. G. Fiocco, *Pittura toscana del Quattrocento*, Novara, pp. xii-xv.

1945. E. Berti Toesca, "Per la Sagra di Masaccio," in *Arti Figurative*, pp. 148-50.

1946. U. Procacci, in catalogue, *Mostra d'opere d'arte restaurate*, Florence, pp. 45-46.

1947. M. Pittaluga, comment on the monograph by Mesnil, in *Dizionario Letterario Bompiani*, IV, Milan, pp. 571-72.

1948. M. Salmi, *Masaccio*, 2nd ed., Milan.

1948. K. Steinbart, *Masaccio*, Vienna.

1949. C. L. Ragghianti, notes for G. Vasari, *Vite*, Milan, pp. 325-27.

1950. R. Longhi, "Recupero di un Masaccio," in *Paragone*, 5, pp. 3-5.

1950. R. Longhi, "Gli affreschi del Carmine, Masaccio e Dante," in *Paragone*, 9, pp. 3-7.

1950. M. Pittaluga, review of the 2nd ed. of M. Salmi, *Masaccio*, in *Rivista d'Arte*, XXVI, pp. 229 ff.

1951. U. Galetti and E. Camesca, "Masaccio" in *Enciclopedia della Pittura italiana*, Cernusco.

1951. U. Procacci, *Masaccio*, 2nd ed., Milan.

1951. M. Davies, *The Earlier Italian Schools* (National Gallery Catalogues), London.

1951. K. Clark, "An early Quattrocento Triptych from Santa Maria Maggiore, Rome," in *Burlington Magazine*, pp. 339-47.

1952. M. Salmi, "Masaccio" in *Enciclopedia Cattolica*, Vatican City, VIII, pp. 266-71.

1952. R. Longhi, "Presenza di Masaccio nel trittico della Neve," in *Paragone*, 25, pp. 8-16.

1952. M. Salmi, "Gli scomparti della pala di Santa Maria Maggiore acquistati dalla National Gallery," in *Commentarii*, pp. 14-21.

1952. J. Pope Hennessy, "The Santa Maria Maggiore Altarpiece," in *Burlington Magazine*, p. 31.

1952. M. Meiss, "London's New Masaccio," in *Art News*, LI, pp. 24-25.

1952. R. Salvini, *Catalogo della Galleria degli Uffizi*, Florence.

1952. C. L. Ragghianti, review of U. Procacci, *Masaccio*, in *Sele-Arte*, 2.

1953. U. Procacci, "Sulla cronologia delle opere di Masaccio e di Masolino tra il 1425 e il 1428," in *Rivista d'Arte*, pp. 3-55.

1954. U. Baldini, "Masaccio," in catalogue *Mostra di 4 Maestri del Primo Rinascimento*, Florence (1st and 2nd eds.), pp. 11-17.

1954. U. Baldini, "Restauri dei dipinti fiorentini in occasione della Mostra di quattro maestri del Rinascimento," in *Bollettino d'Arte*, pp. 221-40.

1940-54. W. and E. Paatz, *Die Kirchen von Florenz*, Frankfurt.

1955. G. C. Argan, "La Peinture en Italie centrale: Masaccio," in J. Lassaigne and G. C. Argan, *De Van Eyck à Botticelli*, Geneva, pp. 83-97.

1955. C. Carrà, "Masaccio," in *Il Cinquecento* (Libera Cattedra di Storia della Civiltà fiorentina), Florence, pp. 209-16.

1956. A. Hauser, *Storia sociale dell'arte*, II, Turin [*The Social History of Art*, London, 1951].

1956. U. Procacci, "Il Vasari e la conservazione degli affreschi della Cappella Brancacci al Carmine e della Trinità in Santa Maria Novella," in *Scritti in onore di L. Venturi*, Rome, pp. 211-22.

1957. A. Chastel, *L'Arte italiana*, Florence, pp. 273-76 [*L'Art italien*, Paris, 1956, I, pp. 208 ff.].

1957. C. Brandi, "I cinque anni cruciali per la pittura fiorentina del '400," in *Studi in onore di Marangoni*, Pisa, pp. 167-75.

1958. C. De Tolnay, " Renaissance d'une fresque," in *L'Oeil*, January, pp. 37-41.

1959. E. Micheletti, *Masolino da Panicale*, Milan.

1959. R. Salvini, *Pittura italiana, il Quattrocento*, Milan, pp. 8-17.

1959. R. Offner, "Light on Masaccio's Classicism," in *Studies in the History of Art dedicated to W. Suida*, London, pp. 66-73.

173

1959. L. Gori-Montanelli, *Architettura e Paesaggio nella pittura toscana*, Florence.

1960. P. Francastel, *Lo spazio figurativo dal Rinascimento al Cubismo*, Turin, pp. 32-37, 89-90 [Peinture et Société, Lyon, 1954].

1960. F. Antal, *La pittura fiorentina e il suo ambiente sociale nel Trecento e nel primo Quattrocento*, Turin [*Florentine Painting and its Social Background*, London, 1947].

1960. E. Borsook, *The Mural Painters of Tuscany*, London.

1960. C. L. Ragghianti, in *Critica d'arte*, 37, pp. 28 ff.

1961. B. Berenson, *I disegni dei pittori fiorentini*, Milan (esp. I, p. 272, n. 1) [*Drawings of the Florentine Painters*, Chicago, 1938, 3 vols.].

1961. M. Davies, *The Earlier Italian School*, 2nd ed. (National Gallery Catalogues), London.

1961. E. Borsook, "A Note on Masaccio in Pisa," in *Burlington Magazine*, pp. 212-15.

1961. L. Berti, "Masaccio 1422," in *Commentari*, pp. 84-107.

1961. P. Meller, "La Cappella Brancacci, Problemi ritrattistici e iconografici," in *Acropoli*, III, pp. 186 ff., IV, pp. 273 ff.

1961-62. C. Brandi, *Masaccio* (Lecture notes, University of Palermo).

1962. E. Carli, *L'arte nel Rinascimento* (ed. Touring Club Italiano), Milan, pp. 119-21.

1962. L. Berti, "Masaccio a San Giovenale di Cascia," in *Acropoli*, II, pp. 149-65.

1962. D. Gioseffi, "Domenico Veneziano, l'esordio masaccesco e la tavola con i S.S. Gerolamo e Giovanni Battista della National Gallery di Londra," in *Emporium*, February, pp. 51-72.

1962. M. Chiarini, "Una citazione della 'Sagra' di Masaccio nel Ghirlandaio," in *Paragone*, 149, pp. 53-55 and figs. 54-56.

*1962. V. Lajos, *Masolino és Róma*, Budapest.

*1962. G. Vasari, *Le Vite*, ed. Club del Libro, with notes by G. Previtali and P. Ceschi, II.

1962 (1958). U. Baldini, "Masaccio," in *Enciclopedia Universale dell'Arte*, Rome, VIII, pp. 866-77.

1963. U. Schlegel, "Observations on Masaccio's Trinity Fresco in Santa Maria Novella," in *Art Bulletin*, March, pp. 19-33.

*1963. E. Carli, *Rinascimento fiorentino*, Novara, pp. 9-15.

*1963. M. Meiss, "Masaccio and the Early Renaissance: the Circular Plan," in *Studies in Western Art* (Acts of the 20th International Congress of History of Art). Princeton, II pp. 123-45.

*1963. F. Oertel, "Perspective and Imagination," in *Studies in Western Art*, Princeton, II, pp. 146-59.

1963. B. Berenson, *Italian Pictures of the Renaissance: Florentine School*, London.

*1964. D. Gioseffi, "Prospettiva," in *Enciclopedia Universale dell'Arte*, Rome, XI, p. 142 and Plate 120.

1964. *Verzeichnis der Gemälde in Museum Dahlem*, Berlin, p. 72.

*1964. G. Previtali, *La fortuna dei Primitivi*, Turin.

1964. P. Barocchi, Catalogue, *Mostra dei disegni, manoscritti e documenti di Michelangelo*, Florence, nos. 2-3.

* The author has not been able to take into account these recent publications in preparing his text which was for the most part written in 1963.

INDEX

Numbers in heavy type refer to plates; italic numbers refer to comparative illustrations.

175

ACKNOWLEDGMENTS

ALBERTINA, Vienna: *Fig. 44.*

ALINARI, Florence: *Plates 27-28; Figs. 7, 48.*

BEVILACQUA, Milan: *Plates 16.*

PHOTOTEQUE, Dresden: *Plates 35, 36, 37.*

FREEMAN, London: *Plates 13, 78.*

GIRAUDON, Paris: *Fig. 3.*

ISTITUTO CENTRALE DEL RESTAURO, Rome: *Plates 80; Figs. 80, 81.*

JOHNSON COLLECTION, Philadelphia: *Fig. 55.*

MUSÉE, Geneva: *Fig. 74.*

ISABELLA STEWART GARDNER MUSEUM, Boston: *Figs. 49, 51.*

NATIONAL GALLERY, London: *Plates 14, 15, 77, 79.*

NATIONAL GALLERY OF ART, Washington: *Figs. 52, 53.*

RIJKSMUSEUM, Amsterdam: *Fig. 6.*

SOCIETA SCILLA, Florence: *Plates 38, 39, 44, 45, 48, 49, 52, 57, 62, 65, 66.*

SOPRINTENDENZA ALLE GALLERIE, Florence: *Plates 1, 2, 3, 4, 5, 6, 7, 8, 9, 10, 17, 40, 41, 42, 43, 46, 47, 50, 51, 53, 54, 55, 56, 58, 59, 60, 61, 63, 64, 67, 68, 69, 70, 71, 72, 73; Figs. 1, 2, 4, 5, 8, 9, 10, 11, 12, 13, 14, 15, 16, 17, 18, 19, 20, 21, 23, 24, 25, 26, 27, 28, 29, 30, 31, 32, 33, 34, 35, 36, 37, 38, 39, 40, 41, 42, 43, 45, 46, 47, 50, 54, 56, 57, 58, 59, 60, 62, 63, 64, 65, 66, 67, 68, 69, 70, 71, 72, 73, 75, 76, 77, 78, 79, 82.*

SOPRINTENDENZA ALLE GALLERIE, Naples: *Plates 18, 19, 20, 21, 22, 23.*

STICKELMANN, Bremen: *Fig. 22.*

STEINKOPF, Berlin: *Plates 11, 12, 24-25, 26, 29, 30, 31, 32, 33, 34, 74, 75, 76.*